The Christi

When I was a publisher I had the privilege of publishing the I Believe Series and the Jesus Library, working with Michael Green who was the series editor. It is now a still greater privilege to be writing this foreword as the series editor for the new Christian Ministry Series, designed to equip individual Christians and the local church for effective ministry into the new millennium. The Christian Ministry Series will explore a wide range of vital issues for individual Christians and for the Church. The series is committed to excellence, with each book produced by a prominent leader in their field. Every author will be asked to provide a bedrock of stimulating biblical reflection, combined with a practical approach designed to ensure that the particular dimension of Christian ministry they are exploring has every opportunity to take off both for individuals and within the local church.

While some will come to the series as a result of a book that deals with their specialist ministries, we believe that many will decide that the growing series is a resource that they cannot afford to be without. The Christian Ministry Series will help readers to develop and improve their present ministry but will also enable many to branch out into areas they have never explored before. We believe that many individual leaders and many local churches will recognise the value of collecting the entire series, whether to add to an existing range of resources or to begin such an investment in resources for effective ministry. In a world of constant and rapid change, both in society and in the Church, the Christian Ministry Series will take us back to the unchanging foundations of Scripture and enable us to move forward with confidence and effectiveness. My prayer is that these books will release *maximum ministry* in many churches, not only in Britain but around the world.

In recent years, the Christian debate about women and leadership has often generated more heat than light. Out-and-out feminists have been ready to ditch the Bible, writing it off as a mere offscouring of patriarchal religion. Out-and-out chauvinists within the Church have presumed to claim the Bible as their ally, without recognising how often their prejudices and assumptions have more to do with rigid sexual stereotypes that were already dying back in the 1950s than with the searching radicalism and sexual equality found in the actual biblical texts.

Rosie Nixson's invigorating book is far more than another rehearsal of well-worn arguments. She does argue persuasively for an alternative middle path, biblical and radical, in which women and men explore the liberation of the gospel in partnership together. But the most striking contribution of her book is to demonstrate a simple truth: despite often being patronised, dismissed and opposed, women have made a startlingly rich contribution to evangelism and preaching throughout the history of the Church. *Liberating Women for the Gospel* is nothing less than a recovery and a thrilling exploration of her-story, the remarkable contribution of women to the evangelistic mission of the Church, across the centuries and across the denominations and streams.

Those who have suffered under the delusion that women's ministry and leadership are novelties in the Church, newly minted in the last quarter-century, will be made to think again by the witness of what has often remained a hidden history. Women who know they are called to evangelism, preaching and leadership will be able to draw from this book a great sense of encouragement in ministry, discovering many inspiring examples from previous generations. I trust the same will be true for many men. I know that Rosie's timely and refreshing book has both inspired me in my own ministry and stirred me afresh to continue to work for the liberation of women in the service of Christ. I warmly commend this book.

Rob Warner
Queen's Road Church
Wimbledon
April 1997

Liberating Women for the Gospel

Women in Evangelism

Rosie Nixson

Hodder & Stoughton
LONDON   SYDNEY   AUCKLAND

British Library Cataloguing in Publication Data
A record for this book is available from the British Library

ISBN 0 340 67890 9

Typeset by Avon Dataset Ltd, Bidford-on-Avon, Warks
Printed and bound in Great Britain by
Clays Ltd, St Ives plc

Hodder and Stoughton
A division of Hodder Headline PLC
338 Euston Road, London NW1 3BH

Liberating Women for the Gospel
Women in evangelism

Contents

Acknowledgments

I would like to thank Marion Mort, whose article on evangelism for the Bulletin of Men Women and God, Summer 1992, first set me thinking about the question of women evangelists, and I am also indebted to the ideas of several people, including Robert Warren and Colin Greene, who subsequently considered the issue.

I would like to express my gratitude to the large number of people who gave me their time and help, including those who told me about their experiences as women evangelists, their understanding of women in evangelism, and many who answered questions about their involvement in church planting. I have changed the names of most of these people, in order to protect their privacy.

I would especially like to thank Elizabeth Harper, Howard Peskett and Simon Ponsonby who read the manuscript and made many very valuable comments and suggestions, and Jocelyn Murray who cast an expert eye over the historical sections. I am particularly grateful to Trisha Dale, who read an early draft, allowed me to trawl her book and journal collection and gave me help and encouragement at each stage of the writing.

I

Women and evangelism

> I am impressed in being with Miss Gregg again during these
> days with the fact that in the diversities of gifts bestowed
> by the Spirit, she has manifestly been given that of the
> *evangelist*.
>
> (Mildred Cable of Jessie Gregg)[1]

Who was the evangelist who in one year preached 400 sermons
and saw 1,700 people brought into church membership? Who
were the team of Christians with a vision to enter a closed
country, who after waiting fifteen years entered and founded the
church? Who was the seventeen-year-old sent to South Wales,
who saw a powerful religious revival among miners and their
families, and hundreds of men converted in the Rhondda Valley?
Who was the Anglican revivalist preacher who preached over
four thousand times, to audiences of up to five thousand in the
south, east and west of England, before her death at the age of
thirty-one? Who was the Filipina sent to the city of Baguio, who
three days later saw four people converted, within a few months
had built up a self-supporting congregation, and two years later
had seen over two hundred conversions to Christ and had planted
four churches?

Striking stories, yet their names barely appear in the histories
of mission and evangelism. Why? They are women: Margaret
Van Cott;[2] Lily O'Hanlon, Hilda Steele and others;[3] an unnamed
Salvation Army officer;[4] Geraldine Hooper;[5] Evelyn Quema.[6]

And there are more: Sarah Crosby, Mary Fletcher, Margaret

Fell, Mary Barritt, Phoebe Palmer, Catherine Booth, Mary Porteous, Amanda Smith, Jessie Gregg, Geraldine Hooper, Jean Darnell . . . all of them evangelists. At most you may have heard of two or three of them.

And if you try asking a question about women evangelists today, you are likely to get the reply: 'Women evangelists? Are there any?'

'Why are there so few women evangelists?' asked the Archbishop of Canterbury, George Carey, in 1994. A good question. After all, for many churches the 1990s have been a 'Decade of Evangelism', so one might expect that all the resources of the Church would be used to the full to see people brought to faith in Christ.

There are several ways of answering the Archbishop's question. Is it true that there are not many women evangelists? It is certainly true that there are not many women who have a ministry of preaching evangelism, and this book asks why that is.

But is that the only form evangelism takes? A survey, published in 1992, *Finding Faith Today*, showed that the main route to faith for men was through their wives or partners, and for women was their friends.[7] So where are the women evangelists? Busy getting on with the job at the grass roots level. And doing very well at it.

And to some extent that is recognised. At a conference for women in mission in 1995, Clive Calver, Director of the Evangelical Alliance UK, challenged the Church to learn from women: 'It's time you ladies got back to showing us how to evangelise.'

That is not what happens at the moment. I think I have only once attended a workshop or talk on evangelism by a woman. Most books on evangelism are written by men. The people who teach and model evangelism are mostly men. Most of the biblical and contemporary examples of evangelists used in books and sermons on evangelism are men. Women are not, on the whole, given the opportunity to contribute.

The UK Christian Handbook lists evangelists and evangelistic agencies. There are two women evangelists out of twenty-eight listed. There are nineteen women's names given as contact people in evangelistic agencies, out of a total of 172. But those nineteen include secretaries, co-ordinators, administrators and a handful of women-only organisations. That leaves only two or three evangelistic organisations which appear to be led by women.

Women make up half the human race, and half the people who need the gospel. One might think, then, that when churches are considering how to reach women, women would share the decision-making. Or are churches only interested in reaching more men, and believe that only men could know how to do it? Women are 50 per cent of the human resource to carry out the task of evangelism, but for some reason their voice is seldom heard at the planning and equipping stages. At a conference on evangelism in New Zealand in 1993 there were 27 women out of 270 participants.[8] And that picture would not be untypical. Is the growth of the kingdom of God hindered by limitations on half its potential work force? Do we need to ask some hard questions about our strategy?

In the past ten or twenty years there has been an explosion of books by and about women. Go into a general bookshop, and you will find a section on 'gender' or 'women's studies', with books about every aspect of women's lives. Go into a Christian bookshop, and you will find books on women here, too – on how to be a good wife and mother, on the question of women in church leadership, on how biblical women can inspire you, perhaps the biographies of a few women missionaries. You might also find more radical books written by women who have parted company with historic biblical faith. Look for something on 'women and evangelism', and you will find books on working with under-fives and their families, books on children's evangelism through after-school or holiday clubs, but not much else.

You will also find plenty of books on evangelism. But there seems to have been little consideration of women in relation to evangelism. Male authors may assume they are writing for men and women, but their examples of evangelists are generally men, and women are ignored. The books which come nearest to considering women specifically are a handful which concern women in the history of mission – overseas mission. When it comes to home mission there are a few academic pieces of writing, and an occasional page or two in general books. The subject of women's

involvement in evangelism has hardly been touched. So this book
is a start.

Does God expect less of women?

When Jesus was teaching his followers, equipping them to carry
on the task he had begun, he never implied that the job was
confined to one sex. Though the twelve disciples were all men,
women were part of the apostolic band, and had a prominence
most unusual for women at that time. In Luke's Gospel women
are shown as better disciples than men, last at the cross and first
witnesses of the resurrection. Sadly, the men did not believe the
women's story (Luke 24:11) probably because they had always
been taught that women were unreliable witnesses.

Mary Magdalene (falsely associated in popular understanding
with prostitution) was also given a message, according to John's
account. Called the 'apostle to the apostles' by Bernard of
Clairvaux, Mary was commissioned by the risen Jesus himself.
She saw Jesus at the tomb, and was instructed by him, 'Go to my
brothers and tell them . . .' (John 20:17). Mary is named in Luke
8:2 as one of Jesus' travelling party, and so would have heard
much of his teaching, including his teaching about his coming
death (as implied in Luke 24:6–8). As the evangelists' choice as
pre-eminent woman disciple, and Jesus' choice as first Easter
witness, she is testimony to the fitness of women to spread the
good news.[9] Women were the first to do so. And they have done
so ever since.

But women's role in evangelism has been barely visible in
much church history. More liberal-minded Christians have tended
to follow the trends of society, and have seen no reason why
women should not take an equal place alongside men in ministry.
But evangelicals, those usually more concerned with evangelism,
have generally taken the line that the Bible defines the roles of
men and women. Thus women's ministry has often been restricted by interpretations of specific biblical passages in Paul
which appear to forbid the public ministry of women, as well as
by teaching which assumes that by creation women are destined
to be subject to men and to use their gifts in the private rather

than public sphere. And when in past centuries women stepped beyond the roles assigned to them by men, their contribution was often undervalued and unrecorded.

Now, thanks to recent retellings of 'herstory', it is clear that through the centuries women have shared in God's mission to the world. Some have done so while remaining in the conventional roles of wives and mothers – and nuns – while others have been called to more unconventional roles, often challenging the status quo.

For some Christians, particularly some evangelicals, the idea that women and men are called to different roles in the Church is deeply held. Women are called to the private sphere of home and family, men to the public sphere of work and witness. But when Jesus gave his followers the task of going into the world and taking the good news to all nations, did he really intend this apartheid system? Did he give only men the gifts of leadership and decision-making, preaching and teaching, and only women the gifts of getting alongside people, listening and talking?

If so, what do we make of the exceptions, the women I've already mentioned, women like Phoebe Palmer and Catherine Booth, Mary Slessor and Jessie Gregg, and the thousands like them? What do we make of women like them today? There are women who preach and see people come to faith. There are women who teach about evangelism. There are women who have written books, who have planted churches, whose voices are heard round tables where decisions are made. Are they just that, exceptions? Are they, as some have said, really 'men'? And what of those who feel called to evangelism, but who feel thwarted because they do not fit the stereotypes of what women are expected to do and be?

Many women on the mission field did the same things as men; but some were not even allowed to speak in public when they returned on furlough. More exceptions? Did these women miraculously acquire new gifts and skills as soon as they got on the boat to Africa or China, and lose them on their return? Did the supposedly biblical restrictions on their ministry not apply overseas? Or could it be that God does not gift men and women in stereotypical ways, and that the Bible does not restrict women's ministry in the way it has sometimes been held to do?

I am the Lord's servant

Given the negative views of rabbis concerning women and their role in religious life, it is amazing that God should have chosen a woman for such an important role in the new religious movement which became Christianity. There was nothing special about Mary, except that she had 'found favour with God' (Luke 1:30), and she believed that God could use her to fulfil his purpose: 'May it be to me as you have said' (Luke 1:38).

Part of my aim in this book is to suggest that as God used a woman who was willing to be the servant of the Lord for the greatest missionary initiative of all, so women have continued to be at the forefront of those taking his message of salvation to the ends of the earth. In doing so I hope to show that, as I have already hinted, there have been far more women involved in evangelism (or mission – the distinction between 'evangelism' at home and 'mission' overseas soon breaks down) of every kind, than most Christians realise.[10]

Second, I want to provide women with role models and examples, from history and today. Today's women need to know that God has always called women to use their gifts to the full, and that in the past many women have laboured in very challenging situations because they believed they could do no other.

Women need the confidence to know that God may indeed be calling them to 'do the work of an evangelist'. Evangelism is a crucial aspect of the Church's life, the essence of its existence. Yet many women struggle to find the part God wants them to play in it, as they see some forms of service hedged about with restrictions.

So, third, I want to challenge the assumptions behind restrictions on the ministry of women by looking at the passages which are most commonly used to do this. I also want to look at the related assumptions about 'difference' between men and women. Much ink has been spilt on these two issues, and they are complex. The appendix attempts to summarise the main arguments and suggest conclusions about current scholarly thinking on the so-called 'difficult passages' of Paul in 1 Corinthians 14 and 1 Timothy 2. While attempts to arrive at an agreed interpretation of these passages still prove fruitless, I take the view that the apparent prohibitions are intended to be temporary, and that they should be read in the light of the whole sweep of Scripture which sees women and men as equally gifted and called to ministry in the new order of things inaugurated by Christ.

Chapter 6 explores the issue of gender difference, where some have claimed that science bears out Scripture on the subject of clearly defined differences between men and women, suiting them for different roles and responsibilities. But I believe that argument to be flawed, since the Bible has nothing to say about specific gender roles, and it is not borne out by experience. Throughout the book there are examples of women who have thought they can do all the same things as men can, as well as women who have felt that women have particular gifts and qualities to contribute to the task of evangelism. Again it is impossible to reach agreement. Faced with competing claims that men and women are fundamentally different and that they are really very similar, my own conclusion is that the truth lies somewhere in between the two views – or beyond either of them.

For such a time as this

Christians who see women as possessing certain stereotypical characteristics which predispose them towards certain roles have problems even with the Bible. Deborah emerged as a judge. Jesus seemed to treat people as people, and not to worry too much about their gender. When he called people to follow him, he did not ask any less of women than of men. The book of Acts has its women evangelists, and Paul had women as well as men working with him as he established churches throughout the known world: Priscilla, Junia, Phoebe, Lydia, among others.

Is it time to say of women, as of Esther, 'Who knows but that you have come to royal position for such a time as this?' (Esther 4:14)? We are drawing to the end of the Decade of Evangelism. For the Church to announce a Decade of Evangelism is, as someone has suggested, rather like the Ford Motor Company announcing a decade of making cars. Nevertheless, if it has helped us to focus our priorities, it can only be a good thing.

Many churches have put evangelism on the agenda, even if they have not got much further. Traditional methods such as preaching have been supplemented by seeker services, and more process-oriented approaches such as Alpha and Emmaus. Churches have begun to work together in town-wide or city-wide missions, using a variety of events from concerts to coffee parties. There have been a variety of national initiatives, using gospel distribution and advertising. On an international level, initiatives such as DAWN 2000 have started to work towards seeing the Great Commission fulfilled by the millennium by helping denominations and countries to set targets in church planting.

All these things have their place. But one of the most obvious resources has remained overlooked: women. Some women are happy in what one might call traditional 'women's roles'. Others are not, and feel that God has called them to different things. But often their churches have seemed more anxious to clarify and enforce what Paul restricts them from doing rather than to encourage them to find out what God has gifted them to do. As Miriam Adeney, a researcher and teacher of mission, put it,

> Today bright women in our churches pour their lives into trivia, partly because they are uneasy about getting involved in significant big issues, lest they usurp the prerogatives of men. Waiting for clarification on what Paul 'gives permission' to do ... instead of 'attempting great things for God, and expecting great things from God' ... they tiptoe around stirring messes of potage.[11]

For many women it is a terrible dilemma. If God seems to have gifted and called me in a way which is seen as the prerogative of men, do I go ahead and risk all the opposition and rejection that entails? Or do I conform to the teaching of my church, but risk being disobedient to what may be the call of God on my life? And how can I be sure?

I know a little about that dilemma, since I have been there too. It took me a long time to decide whether God could be calling me to public ministry when I found such mixed messages in the Church.

Let not a fish try to live on land

I became a Christian at the age of eighteen, and I was keen to find out what God wanted me to do with my life. Some Christians experience dramatic calls at an early age, but not being one of those I tried to work out what sorts of things I should be doing. Finding out what gifts God had given me seemed a good place to start. One book which I can remember finding very helpful was *Discover Your Spiritual Gift and Use It*, by Rick Yohn. It helped me to understand different gifts, and the ways in which God uses people in his Church. But I wonder what any aspiring women evangelists made of it? I want to give a few examples from the book as typical of the kind of teaching which many women have encountered.

Yohn talks about the importance of evangelism, and then draws out examples from the life of Philip, the only person in the NT to be specifically described as an evangelist. The Bible tells us little about the evangelist but much about evangelism, he suggests, and clearly some, such as Peter and Paul, who were apostles, were involved in evangelism. Philip was a 'layman', he notes. An evangelist does not have to be an ordained minister.

Then he asks a question: 'Is it possible for a woman to possess the gift of evangelism?' Given that all his examples so far have been men, it is a fair question. But I found it hard to believe that the answer might be no. As one brought up to see David, Moses, Abraham and all the great heroes of faith as models of the Christian life in one way or another, that seemed a little strange to me. Were women not meant to find in Philip a model for them? That implies that the Bible is addressed to only half the human race.

In answer, Yohn gives some examples. One is of a young woman who was available to speak at evangelistic teas. Another woman invited a crowd of female friends to tea, and six of them responded to an invitation at the end of the address. Women evangelising women. But the policy of the student organisation involved was that they should *only* evangelise women. Why should that be? On the basis, so far as I can see, of an analogy with teaching. But if a woman is a gifted enough speaker to 'preach' at a tea and invite women to respond, why should she not do the same to a mixed group?

Elsewhere in the book Yohn deals with the gift of teaching. After discussing the interesting observation that God seems to give women this gift but also seems to place restrictions on women, he concludes that women can teach other women and children. He cites the theologian William Hendricksen: 'Let a woman not enter a sphere of activity for which by dint of her creation she is not suited. Let not a bird try to dwell under water. Let not a fish try to live on land. Let not a woman yearn to exercise authority over a man by lecturing in public worship.'[12] That strikes me as very beautiful poetry, but very poor biblical interpretation. Women are neither birds nor fish, but human beings made in the image of God.

Like all writers who take 1 Timothy 2 at face value, rather than interpret it in its context, Yohn has to deal with one or two apparent exceptions. Priscilla teaching Apollos (Acts 18:26) is one. But this was all right. Priscilla was not usurping her husband's authority. She was a teaching helpmate.

Rather more tricky is the question of missionaries. The task of evangelism is important, but sometimes there do not seem to be enough men. Will a woman do? This time he quotes another theologian, Charles Ryrie. It must be better to get the job done than not to do it. So, if there are no men, a woman is not ideal but will do. But once a trained man comes along, the woman must hand over the work to him. I have heard stories of where that has been implemented, causing incredible pain to the women involved. Why should it be right to do something if no man is available, but wrong to do it when there is?

When a man hears a sermon or reads a book, he knows he is included. But women have heard or read the same thing and wondered: 'Am I included? Is he talking about all Christians, or just men?' No wonder we see few women evangelists, when the task of fulfilling the Great Commission has for women been hedged around with qualifications and the threat of spiritual disobedience.

Stick to gossiping the gospel, talking to women at the school gate, evangelistic lunches and coffee parties for women, and you are all right. Try anything else and likely as not you will be unrecognised by your church, you will certainly not be authorised or commissioned, you will not have your experience written up in your denominational newspaper or your wisdom consulted. But how many women have said, with Florence Nightingale, 'I offered myself to the Church, but she did not want me. I would have given her my head, my hand, my heart. She told me to go back and to crochet in my mother's drawing-room.'?[13] And how many of those have then given up, not just on the path of evangelism, but on the Church?

Gossip – reclaim it or reject it?

One of the ways in which women's role in evangelism has been sidelined has been by promoting their effectiveness in 'gossiping the gospel'. Why aspire to speak or preach? Women can make their contribution to fulfilling the Great Commission by doing what they are best at, personal evangelism, 'gossiping the gospel'. Surely that is more than enough to do?

'Gossiping the gospel' has become a catch-phrase. It sums up the sphere of evangelism in which many women do feel most comfortable, being around with friends and neighbours, passing on the gospel in conversation. Just as women talk about children and food and families and illness and fashion and hairdos and TV programmes, so they talk about Jesus. 'Gossiping' has been reclaimed from its pejorative meaning of talking idly and too much, of telling stories and malicious tales.

Or has it? The word 'gossip' is not one women use of themselves, but is always used of others. Its negative connotations are firmly entrenched. Women's talk is characterised by men as 'gossiping', an activity with low value, while men's talk is conversation or discussion, task-oriented rather than people-oriented, an activity with a higher value.

A group of women in New Zealand attempted to reclaim the negative attitudes to women by calling a book of women's reflections on evangelism *Gossiping the Gospel*. But the result locks women into stereotypes, and cannot break the implications society puts on the activity. The danger is that by reclaiming 'gossip', the women are actually imprisoning women into one particular form of conversing, and by implication shutting themselves out of others.

If personal evangelism is indeed the sphere of women, then we have the answer to questions about the lack of women evangelists and why we cannot expect to see women teaching evangelism. The strengths of women in informal conversation are also weaknesses which make it hard for them to preach or to teach others. Observations of these differences in ways of talking are now commonplace. Deborah Tannen, in her book *You Just Don't Understand*, suggests that men and women often fail to understand each other because they talk in different ways. She maintains that women talk to make connections and relationships, while men talk to create status and compete with each other.

But suppose that instead we see 'gossiping the gospel' as a stereotype imposed on women by men. Then we can ask a different set of questions. Is it really true – that women find it easy to 'gossip the gospel'? Are they 'naturally' good at it? Can men not converse with other men? If men don't 'gossip', does that mean they are incapable of personal evangelism? Men, though, retain the right to tell women how to do personal evangelism, often in highly inappropriate terms, such as how to 'close the deal' (a phrase which it is hard to imagine on the lips of Jesus), or by suggesting that a good way to learn your memory verses is to stick them up by your shaving mirror! But if gossiping the gospel is so important, should men not be learning how to do it better, too, even if it does not come naturally?

I do not want to imply that personal evangelism is not important, or that men leave that form of evangelism to women. Many men take personal evangelism very seriously. But I want to stress the result of assuming that we can allot certain roles in a stereotyped way: it has enabled the Church to avoid concerning itself with women evangelists or decision-makers or trainers. The Church thinks it has legitimately excluded women from 'male' spheres of service and left them to do what comes naturally. Such are the outworkings of the idea of 'difference'.

This book is a challenge to the Church, to reassess the areas of evangelism in which men and women are involved. Often we have slipped into traditional patterns which have been rarely questioned. I want to recover 'herstory' in the world of mission and evangelism. By doing this I hope to show what roadblocks have sometimes prevented women from fulfilling their God-given callings, and to provide inspiration and encouragement to women, and a challenge to men.

Jerusalem . . . to the ends of the earth

The most common conception of an evangelist is that of the preacher. So I begin with that, seeking to show how many women have been active in that kind of ministry, despite the obstacles. Next I move on to personal evangelism, the kind of role with which women are more often associated, and after that to the role of women in evangelising their families – husbands and children, sisters, brothers and parents. In practice these areas often overlap.

I might just as easily have started with a woman's 'Jerusalem', her family, and moved outwards, which is indeed how women's public ministry has often arisen, spilling over from the home to friends, neighbours, and more widely. For a married woman with children her role in evangelising her children is perhaps the most obvious one of all. But there are important questions to be asked about the role of both parents in evangelising children, and about how the task may be done in an age when many parents are either reluctant to pass on their faith or do not know how to do so.

Then, after the chapter on difference, I move on to look at church planting. Church planting has been hailed as a 'new thing', the key to evangelism as we approach a new millennium. Of course it is as old as the apostle Paul, and most mission through the ages has proceeded by the planting of churches. But as a 'new thing' the role of women is particularly instructive. Finally, I look at the area of training and strategy – those aspects of the evangelistic task which are least visible but which are essential if evangelism is to happen at all. Women have contributed in this area as in all the others, but often their work has been underestimated or neglected, and who knows what the Church has missed through excluding women from much of the thinking on evangelism, even in recent years?

As I have already mentioned, the Appendix deals with the 'difficult passages'.

Of course I bring my own story, and my own bias to the book. But I have tried to indicate where there are strongly held views which differ from my own. I write as a British evangelical Anglican but draw on stories from the Church worldwide, and from many denominations. I cannot hope to be comprehensive. But if I can challenge men and women to see what women have already achieved, and to be inspired to work towards a Church where women and men are able to use all their gifts for the extension of the kingdom of God and for his glory, I shall be more than satisfied.

For me, that is the heart of the issue. How may we best fulfil our Lord's command to make disciples of all nations? I would echo the words of mission historian Ruth Tucker:

> When the church is outwardly focused, energy is expended on mission and evangelism and there is little time to fight battles to keep women out of ministry. With the realisation that there is far more work to be done than workers to do it, the issue of gender becomes inconsequential ... If our theologians and biblical scholars remain confined to their ivory towers the future looks bleak, but if they come out and confront the needs of the world they will quickly realise that men and women must work in true partnership to get the job done.[14]

To explore how that may be done is the task of this book.

Women preachers: deterred but determined

I have been wanting to convert half the world, forgetting it's none of my work at all. Then came the chance question, 'should a woman speak publicly in face of 1 Timothy 2:12 and 1 Corinthians 14:34?' Of course we may deliver a message, but it seems to touch some of my doings a little closely. I feel inclined to say, 'Oh, that I were a man' for the minute.[1]

Newcastle upon Tyne, England, 1820. Thirty-seven-year-old Mary Porteous was listening to a Methodist woman preaching. She had left school at seven, started work in a factory at eleven. She began to learn about God, and propped her religious reading material up in front of her spinning wheel as she worked. She only learned to write after she was finally converted at the age of eighteen, and her new skill enabled her to open a school to supplement the irregular income of her seaman husband.

Mary was already involved in visiting the sick, hosting weekly prayer meetings and organising a class of young women, as well as looking after her five children. Suddenly, as she listened to the preacher, she became aware of the spiritual needs of all the people around her. 'Instantly it was as powerfully impressed on my mind as if the words had been pronounced audibly, "Why liest thou there as if prayer were in itself sufficient to snatch souls from woe? Go forth, and preach the Gospel." '[2]

Like many women, before and since, she felt inadequate to the task, and reluctant to take on a role which for a woman was controversial. After several exchanges she replied: ' "I am a woman; and I never could see it right for a woman to preach." Again, with power, it was answered, "Woman was the first that brought sin into the world – woman ought not to be the last to proclaim the remedy." '[3]

For her, as for the many other women called to preach the gospel around this time (by 1823 there were a hundred women preachers active in the Bible Christian group of Methodists alone), a key verse was Acts 2:18, where Peter quotes the prophet Joel: the Spirit will be poured out on both men and women.

It was two years before Mary Porteous felt the time had come. The Wesleyan Methodists, with whom she was associated, did not permit women to preach. But she was invited by a member of the Primitive Methodists, another group, to preach in a nearby village, and soon she started to travel short distances to preach at weekends, still keeping her school, doing needlework and caring for her family during the week.

Preaching was an extension of being a mother. Among people of that society conversion to Christ and turning away from sin meant becoming better husbands, wives, parents and neighbours: 'converted drunkards shunning the public house, women dashing their straw bonnets [symbols of vanity] to pieces', people giving away clothes and food.[4] Mary saw many people converted. But her ministry was still limited.

In 1825 she resolved to become a travelling preacher. Encouraged by her husband, she agreed to travel round the area of North Yorkshire. Her youngest child was only eight, but she was now a grandmother, and there were older children to look after the younger ones. She visited her family frequently. In her first six months she travelled 260 miles on foot and spoke sixty times on each trip round the circuit, and she continued her preaching for the next fourteen years.

Cumbria, England, 1977. Another woman, Elizabeth Brazell, experienced a calling from God to be an evangelist and to be ordained. Like Mary, she was hesitant. She was not sure if she believed women could be priests. She was not sure about being an evangelist, but if this was God, she would let God work it out.

Her husband was called to ordained ministry at the same time.

The church welcomed his calling, and suggested to her that she became a pastoral worker. But her sense of calling was strong. Her college expected mothers to be at home, not taking an equal part in college life with their husbands. The church gave her the same training as the men, but expected her to be used in pastoral work; yet her gifts did not fit the 'normal' pattern. 'If only you were a man . . .' people said.

In the parish, she, like Mary, arranged a pattern of work around her children, who were then aged seven to thirteen. Her children and her husband knew that if God had called her to be an evangelist she must do it. She went on seventeen missions in three years in the UK and overseas, but was never away for too long at a time. When her children grew up and left home, she was able to be involved in missions for longer periods. Now she works full time as an itinerant evangelist and teacher at home and overseas. She also directs Arts in Mission, an organisation which aims to enable Christian artists, and to use arts to assist the whole Church in mission.

Unlike Mary, who ministered among those sympathetic to women's ministry, Elizabeth had to operate in a climate where many people did not accept a woman as a priest or evangelist. She used to find the hostility shown towards women very hard. Now that she is more experienced, she finds it easier to cope with.

Elizabeth is still rarity, a woman evangelist. She is more of a rarity than Mary was in her day. 'Woman evangelist'. That in itself is a clumsy term. We do not talk about 'women typists' or 'women teachers' or 'women accountants'. But 'evangelists' are different. Most people today expect evangelists to be men. Most of them are. In 1997, the membership of the Fellowship of Parish Evangelists (a network of parish-based Anglicans whose central focus of ministry is evangelism) was 208, of whom only 24 were women. Most Christians would find it hard to think of a woman whose main work is as an evangelist. There are a handful working with children, but few who work with all ages and with both men and women.

How shall they hear without a preacher?

So if there are few women evangelists, why should that be? How do we answer the Archbishop of Canterbury's question?

Say the word 'evangelist', and what do most people think of? Many people probably think of Billy Graham. Or some other evangelist they know, in a suit and tie, preaching to a packed stadium or hall or church. Others think of someone with a microphone in a shopping centre, preaching to passers by, or on a soap box at a street corner. Chances are, those are men too. When John Drane asked the question of some students, one drew a full-colour Rambo. That was his experience of an evangelist: someone with a rapid-fire religious gun, loaded with slick questions and answers with which to shoot down the opposition.

No one thinks of women in those pictures. Yet I have already argued that there are *more* women evangelists than men – but not of this sort. When we ask the question, 'Why are there so few women evangelists?' we probably mean the kind of evangelists I have just described: Christians called to stand up in front of groups of people, preach the gospel, and challenge them to come to faith in Christ.

The 'preaching evangelist' model was revived by John Wesley in the 1740s. He saw the need to take the gospel message to where people were. In his view many of the churches had been ineffective in bringing people to a saving faith in Christ, so using churches was not his way. Instead he encouraged the use of homes, or places where people gathered, the streets and market-places and open ground. His method of open-air preaching to large crowds seems to have worked, and has become part of our way of doing evangelism.

That model seems to have served quite well for 250 years. We have a legacy of crusade evangelism, meetings with preachers, in stadiums, halls and churches. But it may have outlasted its useful-ness. Is it becoming more difficult to bring people together to hear a preacher? Will it become even harder, as technology enables us, in the West at least, to shop, to bank, to go to the library, to engage in 'conversation' . . . all without leaving our computer screen? On the other hand, we have not yet discovered any one method which is to be the twenty-first-century equivalent of outdoor preaching.

There seems to be something about preaching that is foundational. Whatever new means we use to spread the gospel, I believe there will always be room for the good preacher, someone who stands up to proclaim in a new and challenging way what God has done in Jesus, and invites people to respond (Rom. 10:13–15). Even if we see the journey to faith as a process, there is still room for decision points along the way, for someone to say, 'Now is the day of salvation.'[5]

So this is a good place to start a consideration of women in evangelism. There have certainly been women evangelists like that in history, but there do not seem to be many today. A number of reasons for this lack have been suggested, which this chapter explores. Women have had the Bible quoted at them, they have been told to devote their energies to motherhood, they have been thought too weak, too ineffective as communicators. But in every case there have been women who preached the gospel despite the obstacles.

I permit not a woman . . .

One possible reason there are few women evangelists is because Scripture has been understood to forbid it. Evangelism and preaching are closely related. Women, it is alleged, cannot be preachers because of 1 Timothy 2:12: 'I do not permit a woman to teach or to have authority over a man; she must be silent.' So women cannot be evangelists. The passage has been read literally and given priority over other texts, and thus women evangelists, and their supporters, have been suppressed. The following examples show how often this argument has been used.

At every stage of history when women preachers have emerged, they have had to face criticism. Sometimes this has been about the novelty of it, such as the remark by the writer Samuel Johnson. Commenting on hearing a woman preach at a meeting of the Society of Friends (popularly known as the Quakers), Johnson wrote in 1763 that 'a woman's preaching is like a dog's walking on his hinder legs. It is not well done; but you are surprised to find it done at all.'6

Sometimes even men who have supported the cause of women have been opposed. At the time of the Reformation, the doctrine of the priesthood of all believers, which was rediscovered, was held by some to imply that women could participate in the Church as equals with men. English and French reformers John Lambert and Etienne Le Court were burnt at the stake for teaching that women would proclaim the gospel.7

In the seventeenth century, early Baptist women would be found preaching the gospel all over the south of England. But Mrs Attaway, who used to draw crowds of several hundred seekers at a church in London, was challenged by one man who argued that her conduct was 'most directly contrary to the Apostle's inhibitions'.8

John Wesley was confronted with the issue early in the eighteenth-century revival. He was anxious to maintain respectability, and not to arouse any unnecessary criticism. His brother Charles silenced a woman in Evesham on scriptural grounds: 'The Society walk as becometh the Gospel. One person I reproved; not suffering her any longer, notwithstanding her great gifts, to speak in the church; or usurp authority over the men.'9

Gradually John found that, as he saw God using the preaching of women, his initial prejudice melted away. The important thing was that the gospel was being preached. But at his death the issue of women preaching caused bitter controversy in Methodism and soon it was either restricted or forbidden. A conference for Irish Methodism held in 1802 ruled that 'It is the judgment of the Conference, that it is contrary both to Scripture and prudence that women should preach, or exhort in public';10 and at a conference at Manchester in 1803 a resolution was passed restricting the preaching of women. This led to the gradual silencing of women in Wesleyan Methodism. Some women moved to other groups such as the Bible Christians and Primitive Methodists.

Throughout the nineteenth century, as women felt called to preach, they were rebuked on biblical grounds. Many responded, or justified their ministries, by arguing their own position from

Scripture. Phoebe Palmer (1807–1874), a notable evangelist, wrote a book after hearing 'the anguished testimony of a woman who felt compelled to speak and yet was rebuked by the elders of her church'.[11]

Amanda Smith (1837–1915), a black American evangelist in the Holiness movement, began her preaching ministry in 1869. Born a slave, she had to overcome her fear of white people. Having done that, coping with prejudice against women was just another battle. She evangelised all over the United States at the time of the Civil War. In 1878 she went on a missionary tour of England, India and Monrovia. She was verbally attacked by Plymouth Brethren, and bombarded with biblical texts about women preaching, but like others, the fruitfulness of her ministry was unmistakable. Bishop Thoburn said of her time in India, 'She possessed a clearness of vision which I have seldom found equalled . . . During the seventeen years that I lived in Calcutta, I have known many famous strangers to visit the city, but I have never known anyone who could draw and hold so large an audience as Mrs. Smith.'[12]

In 1916 the Archbishop of Canterbury, Randall Davidson, launched his National Mission of Hope and Repentance. The mission, planned to foster a revival in the climate produced by wartime, relied on using a large number of 'archbishop's messengers', and it was intended that some of these should be women. But the plan drew a storm of opposition, on the grounds that this would be contrary to Scripture and to the order of the Church.

Some clergy refused to take part in the mission if women were to be allowed to speak in churches. The Archbishop's plans were withdrawn. It is interesting to consider what might have happened if the Archbishop's plan had been carried out and an army of women evangelists recruited. As it was, when some women took matters into their own hands by trying to preach in Anglican churches, they were seen as trouble-makers rather than pace-setters.

One of the most extreme opponents of women preachers was evangelist John Rice, who wrote in 1941, 'I have no doubt that millions will go to Hell because of the unscriptural practices of women preachers.'[13] A few missionary organisations, in asserting that Scripture forbids women to preach, have at least attempted to be consistent, and have attempted to restrict women serving overseas to non-preaching roles. Most, however, have turned a blind eye to missionary work, but kept women evangelists out of the pulpit at home.

If the Bible does forbid the preaching of women, then clearly that would cover evangelistic as well as other preaching. The arguments are complex, and interested readers are referred to the Appendix. On the other hand, if the Bible does permit preaching by women, as many evangelical scholars now believe, then those with the gift should surely be helped to develop it, and encouraged to explore how they might use it in evangelism. However, despite the scholars, in many churches only the negative arguments are expounded. So, anxious to be faithful to God (as they think) and to their churches, women have let their gifts lie fallow or have used them in some other direction.

Different words, different worlds

Another reason suggested for the lack of women evangelists is the force of stereotypes about women. Women have been represented as unreliable gossips and muddled thinkers. Men and women are thought to function differently – including in evangelism. In the minds of many people the typical evangelist is a male extrovert with an assertive presentation which sometimes spills over into 'hard sell' manipulative techniques. Women, on the other hand, are associated with caring, empathising and establishing relationships. The 'nurturing woman' model does not fit with the idea of a confident up-front preaching evangelist.

Some of the ways of communicating the faith are also those which are often understood as typically male: complex apologetic arguments and rational linear structures. Women are thought to be more personal and anecdotal, a style considered less authoritative, too subjective, and without value.[14] Being an evangelist seems to require authoritative speaking, and women do not speak with authority. This is not surprising, as many women have not had the practice and experience which would enable them to obtain it.[15]

It is also argued that the most successful evangelists, at least in terms of seeking decisions for Christ, are quite black-and-white people. The pastoral bent of many women makes them more able to see the grey areas, more sensitive. So how can women confront people with the gospel in a more direct way?

While it may be that we have seen few women evangelists because of stereotypes of women, it could also be that we see few women evangelists because they are unhappy with the stereotypes of evangelism. Some of the language associated with evangelism, such as 'crusade' and 'campaign', is male and military language, with which many women would feel uncomfortable. Other commonly used images are of 'thrust' and 'penetrating' an area, which are equally inappropriate. Such approaches, using military or sexual language, suggest someone with power seeking to impose it on others, an alien concept to many women, whose style tends to be more co-operative.[16]

Furthermore, certain male evangelists use a style of humour or a tone of voice, shouting (and banging the pulpit) or using other effects. Rebecca, a young woman in the process of establishing herself as an evangelist, felt that 'men can get away with a lot more in terms of humour and tone of voice: shrieking, or funny voices and accents which are often used to great effect. I simply could not get away with shouting or shrieking – thank goodness.' While some rhetoric is effective, carried to excess it can also be destructive, but these techniques are often perceived as part of the evangelist's toolkit.

But people are people, and it seems many of the women evangelists whom God has raised up have confounded the stereotypes of femininity. Women evangelists have been strong-willed and determined. (They had to be.) Many have been rational, clear, logical and convincing. They have not always been naturally pastoral people, at least not in the sense we understand it today. (More pastoral sensitive people would never have withstood the opposition!)

The stereotypes persist, despite all that is wrong with them, as chapter 6 explores. And some of our churches continue to perpetrate the idea of difference, and to 'teach' women that God is masculine and that leadership in the Church is largely masculine. Despite recent advances, women are still swimming against the tide if they feel called to any kind of ministry, such as that of evangelist, which is perceived as male.

Some women have also challenged the stereotypes of the evangelist. They have rejected aggressive rhetoric and the language of power – as many men have also done. Some began to show that one could combine aspects of mothering and home-making with a public speaking role, as we have already seen in the example of Mary Porteous. In the last few years I think we have begun to see changes in the model of what an evangelist is. As we see more women released into a speaking ministry, and also both men and women working as evangelists in ways other than up-front speaking, that will continue.

One example of a woman who seems to have combined pastoral sensitivity with determination and pioneering zeal is Brigid (455–523). She founded and led a monastic community at Kildare, and she also travelled widely, calling people from druidism to Christianity. She is respected with Patrick as one of Ireland's two greatest evangelists, and is also remembered in the tradition for her 'motherliness'. In her the Celtic Church appeared to find a model of one who could be both motherly and managerial. Our culture has tended to make these traits mutually exclusive, but there is no reason why they should be, as several examples in this book demonstrate.

More often, women's supposed feminine qualities were used to keep them in their place. A papal bull of 1631 suppressed the work of the Institute of the Blessed Virgin Mary because the members had been engaged in evangelism: 'Under the guise of promoting the salvation of souls, [they] have been accustomed to attempt and to employ themselves at many other works which are most unsuited to their weak sex and character, to female modesty and particularly to maidenly reserve.'[17]

Unfeminine boldness

The eighteenth-century revival saw an increase in evangelistic activity, and among it at least two hundred women known as cottage preachers. Their experiences as working women, wives and mothers informed their role as preachers. They challenge

our stereotypes of womanhood, but we need to remember that
the notion that the ideal woman is gentle, nice, the 'angel of the
house', reached its peak with the Victorians, and even then may
have related to middle-class women but was certainly not true of
working-class women; it had as much to do with culture as with
gender.

In many ways the women preachers of cottage religion in early
Methodism were much like their male counterparts: strong-
willed, vociferous and persistent. They were similar to many
working-class women today: it's a tough world, you have to fight,
stick up for your family, speak out to get things changed.

Ann Cutler (1759–1795), is one example of a woman with a
combination of stereotypically 'female' and 'male' characteristics,
if one has to put it like that. She was one of many women of the
eighteenth century skilled in the art of prayer (a skill at which
women have always been allowed to excel, except in public),
and was known as 'Praying Nanny' because of her exceptional
devotion to prayer:

> I cannot be happy unless I cry for sinners. I do not want any
> praise: I want nothing but souls to be brought to God. I am
> reproached by most. I cannot do it to be seen or heard of
> men. I see the world going to destruction, and I am burdened
> till I pour out my soul to God for them.[18]

Her times of private meditation, prayer and thanksgiving were
part of the secret of her public ministry. Her preaching sprang
from a life of prayer. She felt called to evangelism, and started to
do house-to-house visiting, and then to preach. Fervent praying
led to fervent preaching. And her preaching was powerful
precisely because she rejected propriety and delicacy. She used
directness, not tact – and people were converted. She was instru-
mental in a great revival that broke out in the West Riding of
Yorkshire in 1793.

Ann Carr (1783–1841) began her ministry within the Wesleyan
tradition and later worked independently, making her head-
quarters in a chapel in the Leeds slums. For her and others like
her, it was the conversion of sinners that was important;
respectability was irrelevant. She was a preacher for thirty-four

years, and when she died thousands followed her coffin. Apparently she was a robust-looking woman, bold and courageous. She had a 'spirit of singular energy', a 'powerful voice', a 'commanding manner' and an 'unfeminine degree of boldness' – in other words she was loud and aggressive! She apparently liked to point a finger at each sinner, one by one – hardly a sensitive pastoral approach! She was obviously seen even by her contemporaries as an unusual woman, but God seems to have used her very directness.[19]

Catherine Booth (1829–1890), co-founder of the Salvation Army, had a similar directness in her evangelism:

> 'Oh! people say, you must be very careful, very judicious. You must not thrust religion down people's throats.' To that opinion she responded vehemently: 'Then I say, you will never get it down. What! am I to wait till an unconverted Godless man *wants* to be saved before I try to save him?'[20]

An international survey carried out in 1995 by the Gallup Organisation on the roles of men and women in society shows that in some cultures aggression and ambition are recognised as suitable traits for women. Much depends on a variety of cultural factors.

From a theological point of view, surely women can have as much zeal for God, as much passion to see men and women come to faith, as men have? Then why should not this be translated into powerful evangelistic preaching?

'I shoot from the hip, just like a man would. I'm a very direct person,' Jenny told me – immediately challenging all I wrote earlier about military language being 'masculine'. Jenny is the kind of person who is called on if there is something difficult to be said. She won't hesitate to call a spade a spade. But she is nothing like Rambo.

As an evangelist she is happy preaching to mixed groups, or speaking one to one. She reckons that more men than women have come to know the Lord through her ministry. Yet there is an assumption that women cannot evangelise men, although the Church has seldom assumed that men cannot evangelise women. Many men – businessmen, for example – relate to her straight talking. But she also brings to any situation her experience of work and marriage and children. It would probably be true to say that women who have experience of both the world of work and the world of the home are better equipped to address a mixed audience and understand their concerns than would be most men.

In a nearby area of the city where I live there is a group of women who have banded together to tackle the problem of drugs and to support the parents of young drug users. Having heard their verbal attacks on the police or on agencies who seem to be failing to tackle the problem, no one could call them 'feminine' in their manner! But from time to time I dream about them, or women like them, as evangelists. If only they would look to God, and then be so certain that only he can help them that they would be on the street corners, or addressing meetings in each other's homes, and shouting, challenging and convincing their friends and neighbours into the kingdom. God makes women with many different personalities. Let's not fall into stereotypes of what women (and men) are like.

You are the devil's gateway

Another reason we have seen few women evangelists has been the persistence of one particular stereotype of women, that of their sexuality. Women have been seen as sexual temptresses. This is related to the allegation, attributed to Paul, that Eve was more guilty of the fall than Adam, and has existed in various forms throughout church history.

'You are the devil's gateway,' railed Tertullian, one of the church fathers of the second century. 'You are the unsealer of that tree: you are the first deserter of the divine law: you are she who persuaded him whom the devil was not so valiant enough to attack. You destroyed so easily God's image, man.' Billy Sunday, a nineteenth-century evangelist, began a sermon: 'Will all the women present please cross their legs and close the gates of hell.' A bishop, in relation to the debate about the ordination of women to the priesthood in the Anglican Church, argued that 'women, unlike men, radiate sex, and their temperament is inappropriate in church . . . Their ordination would introduce distractions and earthiness into worship' – and presumably also into evangelistic preaching.

'Do you use your sex?' a young female evangelist was asked. Did the questioner assume she was really a temptress in disguise, like her foremother Eve? Did he wonder how a young woman evangelist could be so effective, think that she must have some 'secret'?

Such a question says more about the questioner than about the recipient. But it is also a despicable question, another of the many barriers women evangelists have had to face. Who would ask that of a man?

You are a pretty-looking thing

Women have also been challenged on the basis of their appearance. Mary Cole, who received a call to dedicate her life to serving God in the 1880s in Missouri, at first, like most women (and men) before and since, felt inadequate to the task. But alongside the self-doubt from within came opposition from others. Her Methodist class leader told her, 'You are a pretty-looking thing to be called to preach.'[21] There seems to be a strange assumption by men that prettiness is a disqualification to ministry. On the other hand, looking unfeminine is also a disqualification. Some women, not surprisingly, feel they cannot win!

This male preoccupation with women's appearance goes back at least as far as some of the more misogynist writings of the early Church. St Bernard of Clairvaux called his sister a filthy whore and a clod of dung for coming to visit him wearing a new dress. In the late fourteenth century an English Dominican, quoting St Bernard as his authority, wrote, 'A beautiful woman is a temple built over a sewer.'[22] One might argue that some male evangelists are quite good-looking. But that never seems to have disqualified them.

Mary Cole met with considerable opposition to her preaching because she was a woman, but was sustained by the strength of her call. It is fascinating that some people thought she must really be a man: 'Falsehoods were told about me that should have shamed the devil himself. One rumor was that I was one of the famous outlaws, known as the "James boys", disguised as a woman.'[23]

Only a few years ago, when Helen was interviewed by an evangelistic organisation the first question she was asked was, 'Why do you want to be a man?' She was accepted, she says, because 'the interviewers thought I was sweet'. When the time came for her to leave, the principal suggested that she could aspire to be a secretary at a Bible college, or to marry an evangelist. But the calling she felt as a child sustained her through such insults and difficulties. The first woman at a previously all-male college, and later a woman out doing evangelism, she found herself blazing a trail. Some of her fellow- evangelists encouraged her, but at an evangelists' conference the men assumed she must be a secretary.

Somehow it seems that women can never get it right. Some are dismissed because it is assumed that someone attractive cannot be taken seriously as an evangelist. Helen wonders, on the other hand, whether women who are *not* attractive and lively get the breaks as easily as those who are. But as a woman evangelist who has been given good opportunities to speak at big events, she has evoked a lot of resentment and envy from men. She has been put down: 'I suppose all your converts are women.' In fact, like Jenny, she has seen more men than women come to faith through her ministry.

Motherhood and mission?

Married women have sometimes been discouraged from considering evangelistic ministry because of their calling to be mothers. 'A woman's place is in the home' – or more correctly, a mother's place is in the home. Some Christians might allow single women to take on such roles, but would disallow married women with children. Then there are the practical problems for women with children: how does one fit in the training which is necessary to be recognised and accredited? Is it right to leave one's children in the care of someone else, even if one has the energy? Can a woman pay someone to do the cleaning and the ironing, in order to make more time for study or ministry, and still be a 'real' woman?

The same arguments about women's calling to be mothers were used about women on the mission field. But while some missionary wives who felt an equal calling with their husbands found that in practice it was impossible, others took nannies with them or used house boys from the local population to help with child-care and housework, thus freeing them for ministry.

Women have shown that, with God, nothing is impossible. When Catherine Booth began to preach she already had four children, the eldest aged four. She frequently preached to large audiences and afterwards counselled those who came forward, unlike today's evangelists who can leave that to the back-up team. 'Catherine continued preaching right through eight children. When she travelled as an evangelist, they often travelled with her. The guest speaker would arrive, complete with children, nursery furniture, and also a big rug – so that her offspring would not ruin the carpets in the homes where she stayed!'[24] No disposable nappies or automatic washing machines in those days, and with the help of one assistant she made all the children's clothes until they were twelve years old. At the same time she wrote eight books.

So combining the work of mother and evangelist is not impossible. But those who aspire to follow her might note that Catherine had read the entire Bible through eight times before she was twelve, which was the best part of her theological education, and that she did not always find it easy:

> While I was nursing my baby [at the breast], many a time I was thinking of what I was going to say next Sunday; and between times noted down with a pencil the thoughts as they struck me . . . If I had only time to study and write I should not fear now, but I must be content to do what I can consistently with my home duties and leave the future to the Lord.[25]

With the modern advantages of electric lights, teaching tapes and videos, dictating machines and word processors, it ought to be no more difficult for women to combine their spheres of activity than it was for Catherine Booth. Each woman needs to work out for herself what is possible, and to change and adapt according to circumstances.

I have known husbands look after the children so that their wives could study, and then work half time so that they can continue to exercise their ministry. If women can leave children with grandparents while they go to work, could they not use family members or friends to free up some hours for evangelism? I used to babysit for a single mum in my home group, so that she could join in the church's evangelistic visiting. Some women are able to afford paid child-care. Jane, a woman with a heart for evangelism whose husband was less supportive, used sometimes to put her youngest child in a nursery during school hours so that she could do the door-to-door visiting which she felt called to do.

These days, women manage to combine every possible career with motherhood, with some degree of success. Many adapt to the changing needs of their children, recognising like Mary Porteous and Elizabeth Brazell that it is difficult to be itinerant when children are young, but it may well be possible as they grow older. On the other hand, it ought to be easier to adopt something like Catherine Booth's practice, since most families these days are nothing like so large. Who knows what women could do, given the right support and encouragement? When we look at Proverbs 31 we see a woman involved in business, as well as in her home. And she is supposed to be the model of an ideal woman!

Mary Slessor (1848–1915), who spent thirty-eight years as a missionary in what is now Nigeria and was made the first Vice-Consul in recognition of her service to the country, had some interesting ways of combining looking after children with the rest of her ministry. The children were not her own, but those she rescued from the bush where they had been thrown out. Often she had a dozen such children living with her in her makeshift house:

> Each infant was suspended in a cradle hammock made from a wooden crate. Tying a string to each crate, Mary would lie in bed at night and pull strings as each baby needed soothing. To bathe her babies, Mary would put four big

milk cans on the stove to warm the water, plop in four
babies, pull them out and dry them, plop in four more – all
the time discussing points of African law with those who
sought an audience with her.[26]

There is nothing like imagination and determination!

If such women as Catherine Booth and Mary Slessor could
combine motherhood and evangelism, then today's women, with
all the advantages we have, can surely do the same, if God calls
us to do it.

'The satisfaction of a single life'[27]

If marriage and children are a barrier to doing the work of an
evangelist in Britain, so, it has been argued, is the decline in
status of single women. Where married women may be constrained by the demands of husband and children, single women
have no such responsibilities. But it is now much harder than it
used to be for single women to feel valued in our partner-oriented
society. Women experience opposition, so many very capable
single women have opted to go overseas where somehow their
singleness does not seem so much of a handicap.[28]

It is certainly true that in the past many single women went to
the mission field when they realised there was more scope for
their gifts there than there was at home. For women in the late
nineteenth century it was a much more exciting prospect than
being a governess.

The first women to go overseas as missionaries went as wives
and sisters of male missionaries. William Carey took Mrs Carey;
Robert Moffett took Mrs Moffett. Sometimes if a missionary
died, his widow would continue the work, and sometimes was
officially adopted by the missionary society. But once it was seen
that women could be useful in their own right, single women
began to go too.

Some single women went overseas on their own. One notable
independent single woman was Mary Ann Aldersley (1797–
1868), who was already forty when she went to Batavia (now
Malaysia), started a school for girls, and continued it in Ningpo,

inland China, until her retirement in 1861. Other single women started independent societies: Amy Carmichael and Lilias Trotter.

The name Amy Carmichael (1867–1951) is one of the better-known missionary names, through books such as *Edges of His Ways* and many others which she wrote before and after she was confined to her room after an accident in 1931. Turned down on medical grounds by the China Inland Mission, she went briefly to Japan, and then in 1895 to South India with the Church of England Zenana Missionary Society. While doing itinerant evangelistic work she became aware that little girls were taken and trained as dancing girls for Hindu temples. She began working to save children from temple prostitution, and the work developed into a mission, the Dohnavur Fellowship, providing a safe house and school for girls. A house for boys was added in 1918, and five years later there were thirty nurseries in operation.

Lilias Trotter (1853–1928) was challenged at a missionary meeting to go to evangelise in the difficult area of North Africa, and with two other women she founded the Algiers Mission Band. They travelled around desert villages and addressed meetings, and distributed tracts.

The first party of missionaries that James Hudson Taylor took to China in 1866 included seven single women out of the fifteen new recruits, and women soon proved themselves as evangelists and pioneers. His wife Maria was the daughter of Samuel Dyer, a missionary in Penang. She was fluent in the vernacular, and was already teaching Chinese girls – thus a missionary in her own right – when she married him, and she became a role model for the single women Hudson Taylor recruited for the new China Inland Mission (now OMF).

When Hudson Taylor was ill in 1878 and could not travel, his second wife Jennie left her seven children in the care of her sister and went from Shanghai into the interior Shansi province to lead the mission's relief programme. Her success helped to convince her husband that women could go into the interior, and from then on single women were often stationed there, responsible for evangelism and church planting in large regions. In the 1880s Hudson Taylor justified the use of single women in provinces where there were no male missionaries, and emphasised the value of women in converting men because they were less threatening.[29]

In his missionary society at least, women were valued and given scope to use their talents to the full. Slowly, Hudson Taylor's lead was followed by others, and the main denominational missionary societies began to recruit single women from the 1870s and 1880s.

Two single women, Mildred Cable and Francesca French, began their work in China in the 1890s. After twenty-one years, during which time they were joined by Francesca's sister Evangeline, they felt that God was calling them to the un-evangelised areas of north-west China. Arriving at a town near the border, they began a ministry to traders and merchants. Such a strategic place was a good base for evangelism, so that 'men on the market places should hear, not only the political happenings of Europe or Afghanistan, but also that "Christ Jesus came into the world to save sinners" '.[30]

Single women were also very important in the early years of the Heart of Africa Mission (now WEC), founded by the cricketer-turned-missionary C.T. Studd. Two of the most thriving mission stations were 'manned' by single women, and single women conducted 'long evangelizing treks among the villages, where there is a shortage of men; in one district, the worst cannibal in the region, who was reputed to have "a hundred black men inside him", was led to Christ by a single woman missionary who visited his village'.[31]

In past years there were more single women working full time as evangelists than there are today. In the 1950s, for example, when there were around six hundred Church Army evangelists in England, two-thirds were women. These women worked in teams, often leading a team; some were itinerant evangelists, others worked as evangelists in parishes or in social work projects. Some of these women were part of a generation of 'surplus women', left unmarried after the First World War which had seen the loss of so many young men. Single women had entered the professions, and were similarly recognised when they entered church work as Church Army sisters or deaconesses.

Today the proportion of women in the Church Army is much smaller. While in the nineteenth century single women went overseas as one of very few options, and later found a similar outlet in the Church Army, today there are many more possibilities. Gifted women can channel their energies into many different fulfilling careers. The lack of women evangelists today is more likely attributable to the decrease of comparable opportunities for such women in the Church, and the opposition that women so often find, than to a supposed decline in status of single women; in fact, with more single people in society, and some women delaying childbearing until later or not having children at all, singleness and childlessness are now more, rather than less, acceptable.

Do you mind having a woman?

Another possible reason for the dearth of women evangelists is that women suffer from lack of expectation, support and encouragement. Men need, and usually find, encouragement. Women need it too. But perhaps surprisingly, Helen still feels that it is not for women to wait for men to open doors for them. If a woman is called to preach, she believes, she will find a way and do it. Some women have given up too easily.

But it is not easy to persist when your call is challenged, you are given no opportunities or encouragement, and you are insulted and put down. When you are invited to speak it is unpleasant to know that your audience may be asked, 'Do you mind having a woman?' Christians are usually taught that an inner sense of calling and a discernment of one's gifts is confirmed by the Church and by circumstances working out. I wonder how many women evangelists have been lost to the Church because the opposition they have faced has made them doubt the call of God, and they have given up.

One woman who nearly did not make it was the American revival preacher Margaret Van Cott. When she started to move from charity work and tract distribution to preaching, as a result of her growing reputation as a spell-binding speaker, she was spurned by a man in her audience. She already had reservations about entering a 'male' profession. But she continued to receive invitations, and in 1869 she became the first woman to be licensed to preach by the Methodist Episcopal Church. She spent thirty years as a preacher, seeing many hundreds of people brought to faith, and her ministry was compared to that of one of her contemporaries, D.L. Moody.

Even today it seems that for some men their position and status in the Church matter too much to allow them to stand out and support women in ministries which are controversial. Yet when men hold the power, often it is only men who can open doors for women and help them fulfil their calling.

All my role models are men

A further reason why there are few women evangelists is the lack of role models, and lack of information about historical role models. Women are deprived of some of the usual ways of gaining information about vocation and must search it out in more difficult and time-consuming ways. Male evangelists testify to the need for role models, so how much greater is the need for women, when they cannot immediately see women evangelists in the Church around them.

In an article on Pentecostal women preachers in Indiana and Missouri, Elaine Lawless notes the scarcity of role models for young women in their own churches. Visiting women preachers were important, acting as examples of women who had broken out of the normal prescribed role for women. The evangelists who she interviewed almost all remembered a significant revival when a woman came to preach, and it was in the context of a tent revival or religious camp meeting that they heard other women recount their stories:

> In many cases ... the pivotal point of their decision to undertake the ministry revolves around an important encounter with a woman preacher. Over and over, the turning point in the story is a reference to how a woman preacher helped her to make the decision to follow God's call. By this female association and perhaps even more importantly through the story of other women's lives, the call to preach was received in a context of possibility, if not probability, that what they sought to do was not queer or absurd, for other women had done it.[32]

*

For women in many churches, however, there is still a scarcity of women role models – more so perhaps than at times in the eighteenth or nineteenth centuries. In some churches women in an authorised pastoral role have become more familiar, but women evangelists are a rarity.

'All my role models are men, because I don't know any women,' Jenny told me. Another evangelist wrote:

> All the evangelists I work with are men, and I am stuck for finding role models for myself. I have worked with some excellent men, but would dearly love to spend some time with an experienced lady evangelist to watch, listen, and learn. It's finding one that's the problem! Young men coming through these days have a multitude of people that they can learn from and be mentored by, but for young women it's a nightmare!

That was Rebecca, the young woman beginning to work as an evangelist. She is already a role model to girls and younger women, just because there is no one else.

As I hope is becoming clear, there is no shortage of role models in history, but their stories are not well known. In the course of writing this book I have found out about far more women evangelists than I ever dreamed existed. And since history is selective, some stories have been lost for ever; other women have been self-effacing, so their stories have died with them, and no one has told their story for them. Before too long, though, I hope the stories which we can uncover can be told and re-told, and also that churches will see the need to help aspiring women find role models, and help those women already in ministry to encourage the next generation.

Little scope in their own land

It has also been suggested that a reason why the Church, in Britain at least, lacks women evangelists is because they have all gone to the mission field. In the past 150 years, women have been denied an outlet for their pioneering, leadership, preaching and teaching gifts at home, and so went overseas. Young women in turn have seen older women missionaries as role models, and have followed them. The option of being an evangelist at home has seemed much less obvious.

Now there are more women than men on the mission field (in 1991, 56 per cent of UK Protestant missionaries and 52 per cent of UK Roman Catholics), but at first many men were reluctant to let women go. In the mid-nineteenth century women missionaries were virtually unheard of. Women were considered not suited to the rigours of missionary life. Arguments from Scripture were used. But the decisive reasons for women to be sent to the mission field were the urgency of the task and the need for women to reach women (who were inaccessible to male missionaries). In certain areas, India for example, women were crucial, since only women could reach Indian women and girls. Why hold up the fulfilment of the Great Commission when there were many women willing to help fulfil it?

Thus the need outweighed biblical scruples, and out of sight was out of mind. So many capable women, denied opportunities in their home country, found more scope for their gifts in overseas mission.

Sometimes the motives for sending women overseas were not the best. The Revd H.R. Quinn wrote home to the Mashonaland Association in 1908: 'I was never very good with girls . . . I have tried to teach them sewing, but I am no good at it. I think I was teaching them to sew backwards.'[33] So women were needed on the mission field! But once women were there, even if they started off by teaching sewing to groups of women, they soon began to move into other roles, so great was the need.

As we have already seen, one of the greatest advocates of women missionaries was Hudson Taylor. He was aware of the women evangelists used in Mrs Ranyard's mission in London (see chapter 8), and soon discovered that on the mission field women were the equal of, and sometimes better than, men. He wrote rather mischievously: 'The women at Shansi are incomparably superior to the men as evangelists. Cannot you get possession of that useful [Buddhist] machine that grinds men into women and vice versa?'[34] To be valued so highly was clearly an encouragement to women.

Mary Slessor was determined to go overseas, though she found that opposition to women in mission started young. As a child she heard about the lands beyond the seas where millions of people had never heard of Jesus. Everyone in Scotland was talking about a new mission that had been started in a wild country called Calabar in West Africa. She used to hear stories of their customs, and how they killed twin babies. She dreamed of going to that land and saving the lives of the 'twinnies'. Sometimes she would look up and say:

> 'Mother, I want to be a missionary and go out and teach the black boys and girls – real ways.'
> Then Robert would retort in the tone that boys often use with their sisters: 'But you're only a girl, and girls can't be missionaries. *I'm* going to be one and you can come out with me, and if you're good I may let you up into my pulpit beside me.'[35]

At the age of twenty-seven she went, in the steps of her hero David Livingstone. In the Calabar Mary Slessor preached and taught, built churches and schools. Her pioneering independent spirit was well used overseas. She was convinced that in some situations women had advantages over men; that 'pioneer work was best accomplished by women, who, she believed, were less threatening to unreached tribes than men'.[36] Men had tried and failed to establish a mission base, overcome by tropical diseases. Where they failed, a woman succeeded and laid the foundations for those who followed.

Ten or twenty years ago, many woman who felt called to evangelism would first have assumed God was calling them to overseas mission. Helen, who had a call to be an evangelist at the age of eight, at first thought she had to go abroad, but eventually realised that she was called to this country, even though that may have been a more difficult path for her. She is one of the few women working full time as an evangelist in Britain today. But many others like her may have gone overseas, to the benefit of the Church overseas, no doubt, but also to the loss of the Church at home.

In more recent years, the needs of the mission field have

changed. There is less obvious scope for pioneering women, and many missionary societies are looking for Bible teachers, or people for various kinds of development work. So while many mission speakers are women, the kind of 'missionary heroines', women who have pioneered and preached overseas, female role models who inspired others in the past, are today in short supply.

Yet pioneering is needed as much as ever. Perhaps yesterday's overseas women missionaries are today's church planters, and there are certainly some parallels, as we shall see later in this book. Some women have gone into difficult situations. Some have been seen as less threatening than men. Some have succeeded where men have failed.

Where are the women?

So, women have been faced with opposition from the Bible, challenged with stereotypes about their sex, put down with sexist attitudes; they have struggled to cope with the callings of mother-hood and mission and they have lacked encouragement and role models. Given limited scope for evangelistic ministry in their own country, many women have gone overseas.

It is not surprising, then, that when women have had to endure such opposition to their ministries from their fellow-Christians only the toughest have survived. That is one answer to the question posed at the beginning of this book. There are indeed few women preaching evangelists today.

But history shows us that, in the past couple of hundred years particularly, there have been more than is commonly assumed. Women have heard their Lord's command. They have seen the needs around them and across the world. Their sense of faithful-ness to Scripture, the strength of their calling and the encourage-ment of other women, and of men, ensured that we have seen women preach the good news. We can ask why there are so few women evangelists. But we can also ask why, with all the obstacles they have had to face, there have been so many. That is the subject of the next chapter.

For reflection/action

1. In your church, are all the tasks related to evangelism open to men and women equally? If not, why is this?
2. How can we move beyond associating women with sin and sexuality to seeing them as people and co-heirs of grace?
3. Is bringing up children a barrier to evangelistic ministry, either for women or for men?
4. Why do the majority of missionary societies send an average of two women overseas for each man, yet there are not two women for every man in full-time evangelistic work in this country?

3

Women preachers: commissioned and called

By sweet experience now I know
  That those who knock shall enter in;
God doth his gifts and grace bestow,
  On women too, as well as men.

The sacred fire doth burn within
  The breasts of either sex the same;
The holy soul that's freed from sin,
  Desires that all may catch the flame.

This only is the moving cause,
  Induc'd us women to proclaim,
'The Lamb of God'. For whose applause
  We bear contempt – and suffer pain.[1]

'The sacred fire doth burn within . . .' Very often, it was the
strong sense of calling which prompted women to preach. But
calling in itself was not enough. An article by historian Olive
Anderson on women preachers of the nineteenth century considers the question of why biblical arguments did not decisively
silence women. It concludes that more important than the notion
of calling, or *exceptional* calling, was the fact that many women
and men who took Scripture seriously 'showed female preaching
to be both in accordance with God's will and with the practice of
the Church in apostolic times'.[2] They also argued that the Bible
(the King James Version) mistranslated certain Greek words, and

that the two passages most often used should be regarded as of only local application.

So while the previous chapter considered how biblical arguments were used against women, this one begins with some examples of the scriptural defence of women's ministry. If female preaching was scriptural, then the issue of sex was much less relevant. Armed with Scripture, women could feel confident that they were obeying, rather than disobeying, the will of God.

Your sons and your daughters will prophesy

I have already referred to Catherine Booth. Before she began to preach herself, she wrote a defence of women's ministry, *Female Ministry: or, Women's Right to Preach the Gospel*, which was first published at the end of 1859. Olive Anderson notes that numerous pamphlets on female preaching appeared between 1864 and 1866, the period of most controversy, when there were at least forty women preaching as part of the mid-century revival. In the USA there was a similar pattern. A number of defences of women's ministry were published, some by women preachers themselves, which gave scriptural evidence.[3]

Typical of the arguments used would be those of Phoebe Palmer, an outstanding preacher, who is said to have seen 25,000 converts through her ministry. She ministered in Canada, the United States and England, where she and her husband spent four years from 1859. Despite having a traditional stance and claiming that her preaching was an exception (in a period of revival), she encountered considerable opposition, and this drove her to write a 421-page book, *The Promise of the Father*, which was published in 1859.

One of her key arguments, used by many others also, was that the prophecy of Joel 2:28 had been fulfilled at Pentecost, and the Spirit was poured out on daughters as well as sons, compelling them to pray, prophesy and preach.

In her first chapter she discussed what she saw as the main objection to women's preaching: 'let your women keep silence in the churches' (1 Cor. 14:34). She pointed out the inconsistency of those who apply this, and noted that it related to disorder during times of prophesying at Corinth: 'Surely it is evident that the irregularities here complained of were peculiar to the church of Corinth, and in fact, may we presume, were not even applicable to other Christian churches of Paul's day, much less Christian churches of the present day, as no such disorders exist.'[4]

The passage in 1 Timothy 2 she regarded as concerning the usurping of authority, which is wrong for both men and women, rather than preaching. She discussed women in the New Testament such as Phoebe, and women in history. Mrs Palmer's contemporary, Frances Willard, suggested that Scripture should be harmonised with Scripture. She had found 'forty passages which support the public ministry of women, and only two against it, and these not really so when rightly understood'.[5]

Similar debate went on regarding women's involvement in overseas mission. Hudson Taylor argued that Paul was merely bringing order to the Church. The important thing was that in Christ 'there is no male or female'.[6] At the Mildmay Conference in 1886, C. H. Judd made the case for the ministry of women, including reference to Joel 2, and noting that at Pentecost the Spirit did not arrange a special 'women's meeting'.[7]

A.J. Gordon, in an article written in 1894, mentions two passages consistently used by women missionaries and evangelists, Isaiah 40:9 and Psalm 68:11. He discusses women of the New Testament: Phoebe, Priscilla, Tryphaena and Tryphosa, Persis and Junia. Others point to Jesus' attitude towards women.

The new humanity

Those upholding the scriptural responsibility of women to preach the gospel argue it from the whole of the Bible. In Genesis we see that man and woman were equally blessed and called to the care of creation. In the rest of the Old Testament, despite the relatively minor role of women in a patriarchal culture, we find an astonishing amount of value placed on women. Women such as Miriam, Deborah and Ruth play an important part in salvation history.

Jesus came to reverse the effects of the fall, including the domination of men by women. The Gospels show how he treated women in the same way as he treated men, as individuals. A number of women travelled with Jesus (Luke 8:1–3), something which would have been unheard of for a Jewish rabbi. He taught them. They were preparing for the day when they would preach his message. Jesus engaged in theological dialogue with women. He encouraged them in their faith. All four Gospels mention women as witnesses to the resurrection. Nothing in Jesus' teaching implies a low view of women; there are many places where there are pairings of men and women, suggesting a deliberate attempt to stress their equality. A man plants a mustard seed and a woman uses leaven in Jesus' parables of the kingdom (Matt. 13:31–5). A man loses a sheep and a woman loses a coin (Luke 15). When it comes to discipleship, women are often shown as better and more faithful followers of Jesus than men.

At Pentecost Peter explains what is happening with a text from Joel which emphasises the equal roles of men and women in establishing the new community. Paul's epistles are addressed to men and women in the churches: there is no 'senior pastor'. The authority they are given to pass on does not lie in clergy, but in the Word. 'For Protestants especially, the locus of authority is the Word of God, as given to both men and women.'[8] So why do we argue about the 'authority' of women?

When Paul was persecuting the Christians he 'dragged off both men and women and put them in prison' (Acts 8:3). His early experiences of Christians thus involved seeing women working alongside men to spread the good news. As he later travelled to plant churches, he found both men and women open to the message. Lydia was the first convert in Europe, and her home the base for the first church (Acts 16:14–15, 40). Women took part in worship alongside men, praying and prophesying (1 Cor. 11:4–5). Paul refers to women as his co-labourers, working side by side with him. He commends the work of Phoebe, and Junia he refers to as an apostle. Some of these women are discussed in more detail in chapter 7.

When Paul had women working alongside him it is not surprising that he saw men and women as equal in the new scheme of things inaugurated by Christ. Many Christians look to one particular verse as summing up this theology.

Galatians 3:28

There is neither Jew nor Greek, slave nor free, male nor female, for you are all one in Christ Jesus.

Some commentators cite Galatians 3:28 as the central point of Paul's theology of women, the interpretive key to all the other passages by Paul concerning women. It has been hailed as the 'Magna Carta of Humanity' and the 'Emancipation Proclamation for Women',[9] though others argue that it 'refers to equality as children of God (v. 26) not to equality in society',[10] and it therefore has no relevance for social relations in the body of Christ, and thus for the role of women.

The NIV translation above obscures the fact that, in the Greek, two pairings joined by 'nor' are followed by a third joined by 'and': there is 'no male and female'. This is generally taken to refer back to the creation of human beings as 'male and female' in Genesis 1:27. In God's future the tension between human opposites will disappear. But the question is, when? In the heavenly realm of relationships, or now, as God's kingdom on earth begins to be established? Commentators also disagree on how the third pairing is related to the first two. It seems certain that Paul meant the Church to show equality between Jew and Greek from its earliest days. But did he envisage the abolition of slavery, or not? Was the attitude he encouraged Philemon to take towards the runaway slave Onesimus an anticipation of the nineteenth century?

The theologian F.F. Bruce points out that the three-fold affirmation corresponds to other formulae around at the time Paul was writing, and may either express an insight of his own, or be a fragment of a baptismal formula.[11] The distinction between men and women which is abolished does not make for androgyny, but ends the inequality of religious role which men and women had under Judaism. 'The denial of discrimination which is sacramentally affirmed in baptism holds good for the new existence "in Christ" in its entirety. If a Gentile may exercise spiritual leadership in church as freely as a Jew, or a slave as freely as a citizen, why not a woman as freely as a man?'[12]

The context of these verses is the issue of law and circumcision and how these relate to the Christian community. Circumcision, argues Paul, should not be a bar to the Christian community. He points to baptism as the universal and inclusive Christian sign. Gentiles do not need to become Jews, nor females to become males before becoming part of the body of Christ. It is possible that the Judaizers were arguing that women had to marry in order for them to be full members of the community, and this would account for the reference back to Genesis in verse 29. Paul asserts that females can be part of the body of Christ as they are, not necessarily as 'male and female' in marriage. So perhaps for single women this verse was the proclamation of their emancipation, and new options were opened to them. Distinctions of various sorts (social, racial, sexual) exist, but they are secondary to the unity which Christians have in the new covenant. At times cultural expectations would have to be adhered to for practical reasons, but as the cultural situation changed, these would no longer apply.

According to F.F. Bruce, 'Paul states the basic principle here; if restrictions on it are found elsewhere in the Pauline corpus, as in 1 Cor. 14:34f. . . . or 1 Tim. 2:11f., they are to be understood in relation to Gal. 3:28 and not *vice versa*.'[13]

For all these reasons many women see the preaching of the gospel by women as well as men to be not only in harmony with Scripture but commanded by it. Catherine Booth clearly thought she had had the last word on the subject:

Whether the Church will allow women to speak in *her* assemblies can only be a matter of time; common sense, public opinion, and the blessed results of female agency will force her to give us an honest and impartial rendering of the solitary text on which she grounds her prohibitions. Then, when the true light shines and God's works take the place of man's traditions, the doctor of divinity who shall teach that Paul commands women to be silent when God's Spirit urges her to speak, will be regarded much the same as we should regard an astronomer who should teach that the sun is the earth's satellite.[14]

Not disobedient to the heavenly vision

Where women have moved into a ministry of evangelism, it has nearly always been in response to a clear and direct call from God, which could not be disobeyed. This helped to defeat a woman's own doubts as well as giving her confidence in facing her critics.

Some examples have already been given. In her book *Women in the Maze*, Ruth Tucker points out how the concept of call has varied in importance. It has been seen as more important in the foundational stages of religious movements and less important later, as official authorisation has been emphasised.[15] Some women (and men) have argued that since in the New Testament there were no such things as selection panels, examinations and ordination, only calling by God, then that is what matters. One missionary to China, Adele Fielde, was challenged because of reports that she had preached. 'And have you ever been ordained to preach?' she was asked. 'No, but I believe I have been foreordained.'[16]

Jarena Lee (b. 1783), an evangelist in the African Methodist Episcopal Church, heard the voice of God telling her, 'Go preach the gospel.' 'No one will believe me,' she immediately replied. 'Again I listened, and again the same voice seemed to say, "Preach the gospel; I will put words in your mouth . . ." '[17]

Jessie Gregg, a missionary in China in the early years of this century, looked back over her work in China and wrote, 'Praise God, I was not disobedient to the heavenly vision.'[18] She calculated that in fifteen years she had travelled 20,000 miles, visited fifteen provinces, held 183 missions, and seen 5,342 women and girls profess faith in Jesus Christ.

Another woman working in that huge country, rather more well known, might never have got there but for her sense of calling. Asked to leave the CIM training college because she was struggling with her study, Gladys Aylward kept her eyes on her goal set in motion when 'the urge to go to China had eased itself into her mind'.[19] Determined to be an evangelist, she studied her Bible, and learned to preach by standing on street corners, urging people to turn to God. The story of her journey to China is well known, and how from her base in Shansi province she saw many people converted and small churches founded before she had to make her escape from the Japanese over the mountains with a hundred refugee children. If she had regarded CIM's rejection as the will of God, she might have remained a parlourmaid in Belgrave Square.

The right hand of fellowship

Women evangelists have often suffered from lack of expectation, support and encouragement. But there have been notable individuals who have spoken out in support of the evangelistic ministry of women.

As we have already seen, women became involved early in the Methodist revival. Once Wesley was convinced of the value of the work which women were doing, he supported them in it, even if he still to some extent felt that each of them was an 'exception'! Extraordinary circumstances demanded unusual responses. In a growing movement of God, unordained preachers were a pastoral necessity, and so, if God appeared to bless it, were women.[20]

The first woman to receive Wesley's authorisation was Sarah Crosby (1729–1804). She was converted in 1749 and was immediately gripped with a burning desire to tell others: 'I laboured to persuade all with whom I conversed to come to Christ, telling them that there was love, joy, peace, etc. for all that come to him.'[21] She soon assumed the responsibilities of a class leader; one day, when she expected thirty people, around two hundred turned up. She was not sure whether it was right to speak publicly to them, but there were too many to speak to individually. She shared with them some of what God had done for her, 'persuading them to flee from all sin'.[22] Then she wrote urgently to John Wesley to ask his advice.

While she waited for the reply, people continued to come in equally large numbers. Her own doubts began to be allayed; 'Surely, Lord, thou hast much people in this place! My soul was much comforted in speaking to the people, as my Lord has removed all my scruples respecting the propriety of my acting thus publickly.'[23]

Then the letter arrived. What he seems to have told her was that it was all right to preach as long as she did not call her activities preaching:

> All you can do more is, when you meet again, to tell them simply, 'You lay me under a great difficulty. The Methodists do not allow of women preachers; neither do I take upon me any such character. But I will just nakedly tell you what is in my heart.' . . . I do not see that you have broken any law. Go on calmly and steadily. If you have time, you may read to them the *Notes* on any chapter before you speak a few words, or one of the most awakening sermons, as other women have done long ago.[24]

While Wesley does not use the word 'preaching', what he allows comes so close to it that this can be regarded as the beginning of his acceptance of women preachers. A few years later Sarah Crosby was exercising an itinerant ministry which lasted twenty years, sometimes holding as many as four meetings a day and addressing as many as 500 people at a time, and she often accompanied Wesley on his journeys.

Another Methodist, one of the most celebrated women preachers of the day, Sarah Mallet, had a similar resistance herself to God's call, when she first felt it. But she began speaking, and she wrote of following Wesley's advice to let the voice of the people be the voice of God – to speak where she was called. She received more definite confirmation in the form of a note from the Conference of 1787, which read: 'We give the right hand of fellowship to Sarah Mallet, and have no objection to her being a preacher in our connexion, so long as she preaches the Methodist doctrines, and attends to our discipline.'[25]

Mary Barritt (1772–1851; Mary Taft after her marriage) was the most famous female evangelist of the early nineteenth century in Britain. Following the death of Wesley, women experienced increasing opposition. But as Mary's work aroused hostility, her supporters rallied round. 'It is at the peril of your soul that you meddle with Mary Barritt: God is with her – fruit is appearing wherever she goes,' warned one, to a vehement opponent.[26] Letters helped her when she was tempted to despair:

We approve of your preaching the gospel: we have come so to do, for God has blest your labours among us, and made you a lasting blessing to this day. We know that God has called you to preach his word, therefore, fear not; cry aloud, and spare not; lift up your voice like a trumpet, and tell the people the error of their doings. I shall ever love the thought of a woman preaching the gospel. I myself went to hear one out of curiosity, and God made it his opportunity to bless me with his grace, nineteen years ago.[27]

'God himself has sent you,' another friend reminded her, 'like the great Wesley and the great Whitfield; namely, as a blessing to the nation.'[28] How much women of today need those who will similarly affirm and encourage their ministry!

Get out of the way of the women

For some women, encouragement has come from mothers or fathers, husbands or friends. Amanda Smith was much influenced by the example of her mother and grandmother. Like other slave women, they overcame the drudgery of day-to-day toil by sharing their faith with others. They were not preachers, but they encouraged Amanda to see God at work, and after her second husband died she received a call from God to preach and obeyed it.

As she was sitting in church in Brooklyn, listening to a preacher, she became aware that God wanted to speak to her. She leaned back and closed her eyes. 'Just then I saw a large "G", and I said: "Lord, do you want me to read in Genesis, or in Galatians? Lord, what does this mean?" Just then I saw the letter "O". I said, "Why, that means go." And I said "What else?" And a voice distinctly said to me "Go preach".'

Next day she was woken by the sense of a white cross laid on her forehead. She got up to pray, and while praying was aware of the words, 'If any man will come after me let him deny himself and take up his cross and follow me.' And she said, 'Lord, help me and I will.'[29]

After a while she left her home to begin her evangelistic work, and went to Salem. There, struggling to know how she was to proceed, she received encouragement from God himself. Caught in a storm, she cried for calm, and the wind ceased. She went to preach with the message she had prepared:

> I had gone but a little ways when I felt the spirit of the Lord come upon me mightily. Oh! how He helped me. My soul was free. The Lord convicted sinners and backsliders and believers for holiness, and when I asked for persons to come to the altar, it was filled in a little while from the gallery and all parts of the house. A revival broke out, and spread for twenty miles around . . . How God put His seal on this first work to encourage my heart and establish my faith, that He indeed had chosen, and ordained and sent me.[30]

Charles Finney, the American revivalist, encountered opposition for conducting 'mixed meetings' and allowing women to speak. Other evangelists opposed his practice, but because he stood firm, the door was open for women in those churches which stood in the revivalist tradition. It is not surprising that many of the women who were touched by God under Finney's ministry became evangelists, missionaries or leaders in the Church.

Frances Willard (1839–1898), who was converted through Finney, became a prominent temperance leader, the only viable public ministry for many nineteenth-century women in the USA. She was later invited by the evangelist D.L. Moody to work with him on a campaign in Boston, and wrote, 'I deem it one of the choicest seals of my calling that Dwight L. Moody should have invited me to cast in my little lot with his great one as an evangelist.'[31] Yet she encountered open opposition.

All too aware of the difficulties faced by women in public ministry, and the fact that the Church was 'afraid of her own gentle, earnest-hearted daughters', Willard herself became one who encouraged the ministry of other women. She published a book, *Woman in the Pulpit*, which urged other women not to be intimidated as she had been: 'Let me, as a loyal daughter of the Church, urge upon younger women who feel a call, as I once did, to preach the unsearchable riches of Christ.'[32]

Encouragement is the key

In the mid-nineteenth-century revival in Britain, several of the women evangelists began their ministries with the encouragement of men who believed that women should preach. In 1864 Gordon Forlong, a Plymouth Brother active as an evangelist in east Scotland between 1858 and 1862, pushed Jessie MacFarlane on to the platform in an evangelistic meeting, and that began her public ministry, which later extended to the Midlands and London. Geraldine Hooper was encouraged to preach by the curate of Trinity Church, Bath. She went on to preach all over southern England to large audiences, and was referred to as the female Spurgeon.[33]

Fredrik Franson, a Swedish missionary strategist and founder of the evangelical Free Church in Sweden and The Evangelical Alliance Mission (TEAM), is another example of a defender of women's evangelistic ministry. He was thus a great encouragement to women in the Free Churches of Scandinavia and the USA, who encountered opposition to women going overseas. He advocated women's full participation in evangelism, writing in 1897:

> When we realise that nearly two-thirds of all converted people in the world are women, then the question of women's work in evangelization is of great importance. In China each day 30,000 people go into eternity without having heard the gospel. There is no prohibition in the Bible against women's public work, and we face the circumstance that the devil ... has been able to exclude nearly two-thirds of the number of Christians from participation in the Lord's service ... The loss for God's cause is so great that it can hardly be described.[34]

With regard to preaching, Franson was more cautious, advising women at home not to defend it, lest the ensuing dispute should undermine their position.

A late-nineteenth-century Holiness preacher, W. G. Godbey, argued that women had a duty to preach the gospel. We might see his words as somewhat optimistic about world evangelisation, but there is no doubting his sentiments. Give the women a chance, he urged:

> They will rob Satan of his whiskey, confront him on every ramification of the battlefield, fill the saloons and brothels of Christendom, and the jungles of heathendom, with blood-washed and fire-baptized missionaries, marching to the music of full salvation to the ends of the earth, belt the globe with the glory of God, and transform a world groaning in sin and misery into a paradise. Oh brethren, for the sake of the souls Jesus bought with his blood, let us get out of the way of the women.[35]

It was a man who opened the way for Corrie ten Boom's fruitful evangelistic ministry after her release from Ravensbruck. She felt God calling her to take the gospel to America. But then, she discovered, 'No one was interested in a middle-aged spinster woman from Holland who wanted to preach.'[36]

It was not until she was introduced to Abraham Vereide, an influential Christian leader, and asked to address a group of women, that she began to get invitations to speak. 'Abraham Vereide's recommendation brought in calls from everyplace, asking me to come and share my testimony . . . For almost ten months I travelled America, everywhere telling the story that Jesus Christ is reality, even in darkest days.'[37] So began her career as a speaker, which lasted three decades and took her to sixty countries, preaching the gospel wherever she went.

Jill Briscoe tells of how her husband wrote an article on women's gifts and the parable of the talents. 'What would happen if we buried *somebody else*'s talent?' What if he were to stand before God and hear God say, 'You buried your wife's talent, or your daughter's'? Many women were grateful for his affirmation. And despite having a theologically conservative theology he could see that Jill had the gift of an evangelist which was not being used. So he saw it as his job to make sure that she could exercise it:

> And for eight years I preached and taught and saw people come to Christ on the streets. The hierarchy of the mission

was thrilled and affirmed that gift in me. And the place for me was made not by argument or disruption, but by *doing* it, and being a blessing. The people who have set me free to minister to men as well as to women have been *men*, not women.[38]

Women today need the same kind of encouragement if they are to work as evangelists. Those few who exercise that ministry today refer to the value of encouragement, alongside the discouragements. That of husbands and friends is necessary, but particularly valuable is that of someone with some kind of authority. Helen mentioned the support she received from an established evangelist, and the opportunity to work alongside him, which obviously gave weight to her own ministry, and helped to silence critics. Another church leader enabled her to work as an extension evangelist during a Billy Graham mission, and has been very supportive of women preachers. A recent article on women in church leadership concluded overwhelmingly from interviews with a number of women that 'it is obvious encouragement is the key to unlocking potential'.[39]

In Britain, the conferences for young evangelists organised by Springboard (an Anglican initiative to further the work of evangelism in the course of the decade) have seen encouraging numbers of women, around a quarter of the total.[40] In a few years' time we should see these young women exercising their ministry alongside men, and it will be good when all denominations are looking at how women evangelists are identified, trained and nurtured.

Some churches are more equal than others

Besides the encouragement of individuals, some women have been encouraged in their evangelistic ministry because they have belonged to particular churches or religious movements. Women have had more scope for witness and service early in new religious movements, and less scope as the movements become more established, male-dominated and hierarchical. This insight is now well established in mission thinking. Institutionalisation seems to push women to the fringe of the structures. This can be seen with women in the early Church, and more recently in Methodism and the Salvation Army.

Most renewal movements have certain things in common which support equality: Methodism emphasised the value of the individual, the importance of hearing directly from God, the rights of conscience, the need to express faith in the use of individual talents, and the doctrine of the priesthood of all believers, which combined to form an atmosphere conducive to the empowerment of women – hence the many examples in this book.

From the very beginning the American Holiness movement gave a major role to women. Some Holiness churches gave women opportunities to preach, and men encouraged them. Seth Rees, founder of the Pilgrim Holiness Church, wrote in 1897:

> Nothing but jealousy, prejudice, bigotry, and a stingy love for bossing in men have prevented woman's public recognition by the church. No church that is acquainted with the Holy Ghost will object to the public ministry of women. We know scores of women who can preach the Gospel with a clearness, a power, and an efficiency seldom equalled by men. Sisters, let the Holy Ghost fill, call and anoint you to preach the glorious Gospel of our Lord.[41]

Few men have been so blunt about their own sex. The Holiness stance continued into the twentieth century, but as its social status rose and it accommodated itself to the status quo, women have become less visible.

Nineteenth-century women preachers were mostly in movements which were considered sectarian: in England the Quakers, Primitive Methodists and Bible Christians, and in America the Freewill Baptists, Free Methodists and other groups connected with the Holiness movement. In the early twentieth century, women evangelists were important in the development of the Free Church movement. Some of them did itinerant evangelism in sparsely populated areas, and other places where men were less keen to go.

Some Pentecostal denominations have given women more

scope for ministry. Evangelist Jean Darnell, who ministered for over twenty-five years in Britain, comes from that tradition. She had a very fruitful evangelistic ministry, and inspired all who worked with her, including many who did not share her brand of Pentecostalism. She was as at home preaching to crowds as talking to small groups. About four thousand people found faith in Christ through the evangelistic musical *The Witness*, which she organised. Britain has seen few women like her in recent years, and she has no doubt been a role model for many other women.

Today, too, there seem to be differences between denominations. There are few women evangelists coming from the historic churches. This may be because men have often combined an evangelistic ministry with a pastoral one and been ordained, a possibility only recently opened to women in the Anglican Church, for example. Gavin Reid, now Bishop of Maidstone, was called to ordained ministry in the 1950s, and was convinced that his main task was evangelism. 'My own formative years as a young Christian with a sense of calling, was one where evangelism was the top priority, where the gospel of saving grace was the dominating tune of faith, and where the heroes were those who preached and who "won" converts.'[42] Now the same combination of ordained ministry, which gives authorisation, and evangelism, would be available to women. Anglican women have inherited the deaconess model of ministry, which is pastoral rather than evangelistic, but in the next few years this may change.

Other churches see the task of evangelism, and the authorisation of ministers of various kinds, differently. The Catholic Church, for example, does not have a ministry of 'evangelists', preferring instead to work to a model which sees every Christian as called to evangelism. Women cannot be ordained, but priests are pastors more than evangelists, so women are not excluded from evangelism by exclusion from the priesthood. Yet as for so many women, their ministry is almost invisible.

The newer churches vary between those which have a male-dominated authoritarian leadership and others where there is more openness: Pioneer, or Ichthus, for example.

Another way in which there is a difference between

denominations is that some churches separate off 'women's ministry'. This has a long tradition, and continues today in some churches. It is an advantage in that women *are* encouraged to develop their gifts, to be evangelists if God calls them – but they can only be evangelists to women.

A number of churches, past and present, have interpreted 1 Timothy 2:12 in this way. The understanding of what is forbidden as 'authority over men' makes it legitimate for women to address other women, but not men. Ann, who works full time as a children's and youth evangelist, has encountered little opposition to her ministry, partly, perhaps, due to her graciousness, but also for this reason.

Women across cultures

Women evangelists have thus been found more often in particular kinds of churches. They are also more often found in particular kinds of cultures. Missiologist Miriam Adeney has pointed out how a variety of factors determine the status of women, which in turn affects the position of women in the Church.

In the early churches various factors dictated the role of women in society, and these in turn appear to have influenced their role in the Church. In Corinth their position was more free than that in Athens or under Judaism, which may help to account for the role of women in praying, prophesying and general involvement in the worship. In Macedonia, Asia Minor and Rome, women had even more freedom; upper-class women were educated and were active in public life and religious cults.

A historical and sociological perspective also helps to account for women preachers in early Methodism. The cottage preachers were active early in the industrial revolution, and their message helped to provide stability in a time of difficult social change. Thus the culture was more open to acceptance of those who brought it.

In the Philippines there is relative equality between the sexes. The woman's place is in the home and the market – and in the office and the rice field. When women become Christians they use their leadership skills in the Church. Women preachers were especially prominent in the growth of the Foursquare Gospel Church, and other churches use women workers too. Such equality came about partly because Filipina women long had the right to independent ownership and transmission of property, the right to initiate divorce, the right to speak and lead in councils.[43]

In this context the story of Evelyn Quema is less surprising, but still remarkable. While at school she saw thirty of her relatives come to faith in Christ through her witness. Called to serve God, she enrolled in a Bible school, and after three years' work, when she was twenty-four, she had planted four churches, seen over two hundred conversions and taught thousands of children and young people in the twelve Bible classes she had started. She said, 'I would never have been a Christian if a woman hadn't brought the Gospel to me.'[44]

My best men are women

This statement, credited to William Booth,[45] has been echoed by many, in overseas mission and evangelism. It is double-edged, of course: it implies that 'men' are the norm, and some of those who reach the highest standards of that norm are women. But a look at some of those women who have worked as evangelists shows beyond any doubt that women can do the job as well (whatever that means) as men.

There have been two outstanding examples of women being involved early in new evangelistic movements, which set the tone for all that followed. These are Catherine Booth, co-founder of the Salvation Army, and Marie Carlile, sister of the founder of the Church Army. Women have had greater opportunities for public ministry in movements which included women alongside men from the beginning.

As William Booth concluded his sermon at Pentecost 1860, to a thousand or more people in a chapel in Gateshead, his usually timid wife felt prompted to go to the pulpit. 'I want to say a word . . .'

William stood aside to let her mount the pulpit steps. Once there she told the congregation how she had been told by the Spirit of God to preach the gospel publicly, and she had promised

she would. But the time had passed, and she had been silent.
Now she could no longer disobey. As she finished and made
her way back, William announced, 'My wife will preach this
evening.'

Catherine had already written her defence of women's
preaching, in response to criticism of the American evangelist
Phoebe Palmer who visited England to preach in 1859. And there
were other women evangelists around at this time; a weekly
paper, *The Revival*, started by a Christian publisher in 1859,
mentioned women evangelists in almost every number.[46] So
Catherine would have had a few role models. And when in 1860,
at the age of thirty-one, she began her ministry, she opened the
door for women to work alongside men in the new movement
which was soon to be founded.

In 1875, the first woman evangelist was given responsibility
for a Salvation Army centre. This 'daring experiment' was soon
followed up, and three years later forty-one of the ninety-one
officers on the field were women. An early comment stated: 'It
has sometimes been said that female preachers would be the ruin
of the Mission. But on the contrary, it turns out that the
prosperity of the work in every respect just appears most precisely
at the very time when female preachers are being allowed the
fullest opportunity.'[47]

When William wrote a manual of guidance for the expanding
Salvation Army, his chapter on women included the points that
women have the right to an equal share in the work of publishing
salvation, and that a woman may hold any position of authority
or power in the Army.

Among some of the first women to achieve prominence were
Catherine's daughters: Katie, the eldest, preached and conducted
evangelistic campaigns from her teens, and at the age of twenty-
two led the first party of Salvationists to Paris, which saw a
hundred converts in the first twelve months and five hundred in
the second. Evangeline, converted at the age of twelve, in her
teens used to visit pubs to sing and speak of God's love. Then, 'as
captain of a London corps with a large meeting-hall, she managed
to fill it night after night with people eager to hear her im-
passioned appeals for decisions for Christ'.[48] She rose to be a
Commander and, finally, General from 1934 to 1939.

In later years, women found it more difficult to reach the higher positions, and sometimes old prejudices have reappeared. But there are still women in high positions, and the Salvation Army provides more scope for the ministry of women than many denominations. Catherine Booth's example and writings have continued to be an encouragement and inspiration to women from all denominations.

Another example of an early Salvation Army evangelist is Pamela Shepherd. Converted through the Army's ministry, she and her daughters returned from London to her native Wales in 1878. She spoke to drunken men in Aberdare in Welsh, telling them the story of how she had been saved from alcohol and poverty by turning to Jesus. People of the valleys began to come to the meetings where she and her daughter Kate preached. By 1879 crowds of several thousand were coming to listen, and there was a religious revival beginning in the valleys. Women like them contributed to what became the Welsh Revival of 1904.

Marie Carlile and the Church Army

The Church Army was founded by Wilson Carlile, an Anglican clergyman, in 1882. He was inspired by the visits of Dwight Moody, and wanted to use a crusade style of evangelism, with open-air meetings, and to use ordinary working-class men as evangelists. This did not fit the normal Anglican pattern of work; many people were wary of the type of crusading evangelism used by the Methodists and the Salvation Army. The Church Army was founded to provide an alternative model under church auspices.

Carlile's sister Marie (1861–1951) was involved from 1888, and served for fifty-five years with her brother. She believed that women as well as men should be involved in sharing the gospel, and she did not see women's ministry as limited to other women and children. She became superintendent of a training home for women, and from 1887 to 1937 2,000 women were commissioned as Church Army sisters. The women shared some of their training with the men:

> My brother would take all the brothers and sisters to Lisson Grove and they were taught how to divide up into small bands and hold short meetings at different corners, and then rapidly join together again and attack other streets in the same way. As a rule the people used to be most kind, but sometimes we were honoured by being pelted with shrimps' heads, dirty water, and other choice things.[49]

The vital qualification for all the candidates for training was a personal knowledge of Jesus Christ. Social position and educational qualifications were seen as less important. But the women received a comprehensive training. They were not admitted to the office of evangelist until 1962, but from 1921 held the parallel office of Mission Sister, which was virtually equivalent.

In the earliest days of the Church Army much of the work was evangelistic, either in short evangelistic campaigns (missions), or alongside parochial clergy. In 1897 evangelistic work started in prisons. After the First World War some women were involved in mission vans which went round villages in the countryside. Women found themselves meeting practical needs, in nursing and rescue work. Marie believed that the women needed to come alongside people, as Jesus did, not shout the gospel from a distance. Working in the slums, lodging houses and deprived areas was all seen as part of 'preaching good news to the poor'.

After experiencing a new sense of the power of the Spirit in 1892, she was determined that the proclamation of the gospel called for Spirit-filled men and women – as it had done since the Church began. 'When we think of the crying needs of the perishing souls around us, our little band of women seems very small indeed, but inspired by the Holy Spirit we believe, like Gideon's three hundred, they will be used to do great things.'[50]

It is due to the influence of Marie Carlile that women found more freedom and scope for their gifts than in the rest of the Anglican Church, and the Army has always included a large proportion of women, although in recent years numbers have declined, perhaps partly due to the ordination of women to the priesthood.

The female brethren

The history of women evangelists also shows the importance of role models. The lack on the whole of any, for most Christian women, is another significant reason why we see so few women evangelists. Ironically, a century or two ago women in certain situations had more encouragement and more female role models than most women have today! Of course, one may battle on despite everything, but perhaps only the toughest survive.

The early Methodist women acted as role models and encouragers to each other. Ann Mason, for example, acted as role model to other women in the Bible Christians:

> In this neighbourhood I visited a young woman who I believe was called to preach; but being oppos'd by man she omitted her duty, and the distress of her mind had almost destroyed her body. It appears, an old preacher was the chief instrument of her misery: she seemed to feel some relief in telling her sad tale to me. Many females are kept in bondage by those who say, 'we suffer not a woman to teach', thus quoting Paul's words, and not rightly applying them. Man's opinion on this subject is nothing to me; for it is woe unto me if I preach not the gospel.[51]

Sarah Crosby and another woman, Ann Tripp, assumed leadership of a group of women preachers who styled themselves 'The Female Brethren'. Mary Barritt played some part, and many women gained support and confidence from spending time with and working alongside other women. In 1790, Sarah Crosby was encouraging another woman who aspired to preach, and wrote of what sustained her in her own ministry:

> When we know we have our Lord's approbation, we should stand, like the beaten anvil to the stroke; or lie in his hands, as clay in the hands of the potter. Through evil report and good, we pass, but all things worketh together for good to them that love God. Speak and act, as the spirit gives liberty, and utterance; fear not the face of man, but with humble confidence, trust in the Lord; looking unto him who is able,

and willing to save to the uttermost, all that come unto God by him.[52]

Evangelism for a new age

Women evangelists have argued that they were fully scriptural, and their sense of calling, the encouragement of other women and of men, has resulted in the heritage of women preachers who succeeded despite the obstacles in their path.

If we believe that women are called to be evangelists, I believe we have a duty to encourage women in that calling. The report of a consultation held by the Evangelical Fellowship in the Anglican Communion in 1990 concluded that 'Most urgent of all is for the Church to recognise and encourage Christian women as full partners with men in evangelism and mission . . . In too many situations the Church mirrors society in denying the dignity and worth of women and suppressing their dignity and concerns.'[53]

A conference held in 1995, 'Women in Mission', was the first of its kind in providing training and encouragement for women involved in evangelism of all kinds, and was much appreciated by the 150 women who went. What was of concern to the organisers was the pain felt by some of the women, who had been opposed in their ministries and had little or no support and encouragement in their churches. A number of women felt very isolated, and valued the chance to meet people in similar situations, some finding role models and support in the process.

Having proved that they can take their place as evangelists alongside men, women also have something to offer current debates about evangelism. Women seem to be less bound by stereotypes of the way it 'ought to be done'. They are often anxious not to be just like men – although for many their only role models are men. The way women have adapted, altered and avoided the male model of preaching evangelism challenges us to review it. A new generation of evangelists is needed. Now is a good time for men and women to sit down together and rethink evangelists and evangelism. We need a model of evangelist which includes the itinerant speaker model but does not exclude others.

There will be an increasing overlap between the kind of evangelist discussed in this chapter and the last, and that discussed in the next.

Evangelists will increasingly need to start further back and assume less knowledge on the part of their hearers. They will need to work in personal and informal contexts as well as formal ones. They will have to work within the process model as well as the crisis one. They will, according to Gavin Reid, need to operate in more unstructured and uncontrolled ways, be more vulnerable.[54] Perhaps women, more used to working in the kind of area which is the subject of the next chapter, will have much to offer as we plan to meet the needs of the next century.

For reflection/action

1. Peter Wagner reckons that about 10 per cent of Christians have the gift of evangelism. How does your church seek to discover and nurture men and women with that gift? Do you expect women to use evangelistic gifts in preaching roles as well as in small groups and one to one?

2. In some recent missions, ecumenical co-operation has resulted in (for example) Anglican and Catholic evangelists sharing the same platform. How about a man and a woman sharing the platform to demonstrate gender reconciliation as well as unity in Christ?

3. What sort of support and encouragement do you think women in evangelism need? Is there someone you could help in some way?

4. If you think God is calling you to be an evangelist, how can you test your call?

4

Women and personal evangelism

Suppose a woman has ten silver coins and loses one. Does she not light a lamp, sweep the house and search carefully until she finds it? And when she finds it, she calls her friends and neighbours together and says, 'Rejoice with me; I have found my lost coin.'

(Luke 15:8–9)

Jane was one of the keenest evangelists I've ever met. At every possible opportunity she'd be talking to people about Jesus. She'd knock at doors until she found anyone who wanted to talk. If they were interested she'd go back and talk some more. Sometimes she took a questionnaire to initiate conversation. When she found people with problems or burdens, she'd pray with them. Her own testimony was of release from a life of surfing (this was New Zealand) and drugs, then a search through various cults, until she'd finally found Jesus. So she knew what God could do in people's lives. And she wanted everyone else to know how great God is. Her enthusiasm was infectious. Every week she seemed to bring someone new to church.

Is Jane an evangelist? If an evangelist is someone who communicates the good news of the kingdom of God to those who have not received it, then clearly she is. But many women have found it hard to see themselves as evangelists, when perhaps those around them have not always acknowledged their gifts. Penny Frank, who worked as a consultant and trainer on children's evangelism for the Church Pastoral Aid Society, dedicated her book *Children and Evangelism* with some telling words: 'To Dave Richards who first gave me the courage to call myself an evangelist.'

The itinerant evangelist model has a strong hold in our minds. Since, as we have just seen, there have been relatively few such women, and even fewer who are well known, we have tended to see evangelists as those who preach. But as we are increasingly aware of the weaknesses of that model, the real breadth of the gifting of 'evangelist' will become more obvious. Recent research reminds us that only 4 per cent of people become Christians through evangelistic events, while for 15 per cent of men and 24 per cent of women the main factor in coming to faith is Christian friends.[1] Whereas in the past, for example, a town or city might have invited a well-known evangelist and booked the local stadium for a week, today a mission might use teams of ordinary Christians to work with local churches. Preachers have their place, but even more important are Christians sharing their faith with those around them.

In many areas of the world, personal evangelism – spontaneous outreach by converts – has been the main source of growth in the Church. It appears to have been the main source of growth in the early Church. We are given examples of the preaching of Peter and Paul, but the Church grew as each Christian witnessed to the new life they had found, and the same is true whether we think of mission at home or anywhere in the world.

An evangelist challenges people to respond to the good news of Jesus and to join the Christian community. That is the difference between a witness and an evangelist. All Christians are called to share their faith with others and to tell what God has done in their lives. But only some are gifted to challenge people to respond. One plants, one waters, and it is God who gives the growth. It is, of course, dangerous to define an effective evangelist by their results. Nevertheless, a person who finds that their witness repeatedly arouses interest and brings people to respond to God is probably an evangelist.

If women are called, along with men, to be the kind of evangelists we discussed in the last chapter, so they are also called to be what one might call 'everyday evangelists'. Some parts of the Church are beginning to recognise the calling of men and women to this role, and to give them the same kind of recognition that previously only 'preaching' evangelists have received. Some Anglican dioceses run courses which lead to authorisation as lay parish evangelists. In his booklet on evangelists David Sanderson gives some examples of such men and women:

> Amy is a widow and a grandmother. She has been a Christian ten years and has a natural way of gossiping the gospel. A few years ago she felt her Christian life had come to a standstill and during that period was 'given a picture' of an open door. For her, this picture linked with an invitation to join the diocesan evangelists' training course. She is currently involved in evangelism in her parish as a member of the evangelism team.

> Elizabeth [is] a single mum with two young children. She has been a Christian for four years and during that time has led Christian basics groups in the parish. She is an evangelism co-ordinator for her church and is involved in faith sharing and servant evangelism, which includes cleaning cars and picking up litter.[2]

As I have already mentioned, women's contribution to evangelism has often been limited to what has been called 'gossiping the gospel'. What is notable about Amy and Elizabeth is that their effectiveness has led to their being recognised as gifted personal evangelists, and also to appointment to evangelism teams in the Church. Sometimes women are effective in winning people to Christ, but are excluded from making any contribution to decision-making, or from positions where they could also be enablers and encouragers of others. An evangelist who is part of the congregation can be a focus for evangelism, acting as a realistic role model, helping to equip church members and train other evangelists. As we see more evangelists like this in our churches, it is to be hoped that there will be similar numbers of men and women.

One beggar showing another beggar . . .

Down the centuries women and men have followed the example of Jesus in sharing their faith with those around them and those with whom they have been brought into contact. This is necessarily a form of evangelism which has not received as much attention as preaching, and has thus gone unrecorded. But there are some notable exceptions, which may shed light on the work of women as evangelists, and help us in the Church today.

Women in the early Church shared their faith with friends and neighbours. Frequently it was the women who became converts first and brought the members of their families into the Church, as we will see in the next chapter.

In particular situations women could go where men could not. Clement of Alexandria (c. 150–215 AD) tells us: 'The Apostles, giving themselves without respite to the work of evangelism . . . took with them women, not as wives but as sisters, to share in their ministry to women living at home: by their agency the teaching of the Lord reached to the women's quarters without raising suspicion.'[3]

In the apocryphal Acts of Paul and Thecla, we learn of Thecla, a disciple who sacrificed everything to follow Paul. According to the story, Paul commissioned her as an apostle, and she became a model in later years for women who wanted to devote themselves to God. We learn of her evangelising other women: 'So Thecla went in with her and rested in her house for eight days, instructing her in the word of God, so that the majority of the maidservants also believed; and there was great joy in the house.'[4] According to Basil, Thecla won many to Christ, and baptised them.

Other women, such as Vibia Perpetua and Quinta, we learn about primarily because they were martyred. Their attitudes and their lives clearly witnessed to many around. In the past two thousand years there have been many different theologies of mission, and in the early Church mission was inseparable from martyrdom.[5]

Perpetua was taken captive around 202–3 under the persecutions of Septimus Severus. Nothing would persuade her to betray her faith. An eyewitness tells how when the moment of death came in the arena Perpetua 'took the gladiator's trembling hand and guided it to her throat. Perhaps it was that so great a woman, feared as she was by the unclean spirit, could not have been slain had she herself not willed it.'[6]

Quinta was martyred under the Roman emperor Decius. Her captors tried to force her to worship in the idol temple, but she refused, and she was first dragged through the streets, over rough paving slabs, and then stoned to death. Eusebius writes how the women martyrs were 'no less manly than the men', which is obviously meant to be a compliment![7]

Through the first millennium women helped to spread Christianity through Europe. Often the stories preserved are only of the kings and queens and noble families, but no doubt the faith was spread on every level.

Olga was born around 879, and married Igor, prince of Kiev. After his death she ruled the land for her young son. On a visit to Constantinople she was impressed by the hymns of the Orthodox choirs, and on enquiring about them she was instructed in the Christian faith by the Patriarch, and baptised. She returned to Russia with several priests and had the church of St Sofia built in Kiev. Through her influence the message of the gospel began to spread throughout Russia, many became Christians, and churches were established. Her grandson Vladimir was baptised and through him the whole of Russia became a Christian country in 988.

Catherine of Sienna (1347–1380) was called to the religious life and joined the Third Order of the Dominicans, thus choosing to live as a religious laywoman. She is more often known as a mystic, but was an evangelist too. She served the poor in Sienna, and, as she became increasingly concerned about evangelism, she urged them to repent and be saved. She also evangelised many prisoners, and carried on her evangelism through letters to many people, of all kinds, of whom she had heard.[8]

The Reformation did not enlarge the ministry of women as one might have expected, although it did place Bibles within the reach of women as well as men. In many ways, however, there were more losses than gains for women. The Bible was invoked to emphasise the priesthood of all believers, but also to put women in their 'place'. And with the dissolution of the nunneries women lost their only chance of an accepted platform for preaching the gospel. That was left to Catholics until other women found a voice again in different ways.

As missionary work began to expand beyond Europe, some women felt called to the new mission fields. Marie Guyurt was born in 1599, and entered the Ursuline convent in Tours after the death of her husband. She gradually realised she was called to take the gospel to the Indians of North America, and reached Quebec in 1639. 'Marie of the Incarnation' set to work despite the murder of other missionaries, and saw people converted through her witness.

In the years after the Reformation, one of the groups which questioned the limited role of women in the proclamation of the gospel was the Quakers. Equality between all believers and obedience to the inner voice of God were held to be more important than man-made distinctions and rules. In the seventeenth century, English Quaker women carried the gospel to North America, the West Indies, Greece and Turkey.

Exceptional even among them was Mary Fisher, a servant-girl from Yorkshire who was converted, along with the rest of her household, to Quakerism. She felt called to take the gospel to the university of Cambridge, believing the young theologians there to be in need of a more real faith. At Cambridge she and her friend Elizabeth Williams were stripped and flogged, and at Oxford two other Quakers who tried to engage the students in debate were dragged through a dirty pool, and then their mouths were held to a water pump.

In 1656 Mary Fisher went with Ann Austin to Massachusetts Bay, but they were soon deported back to England. Her most remarkable achievement was her visit to Turkey, to take the gospel to the Sultan. After her return from America she set off with five other missionaries to Turkey. Turned back once, she eventually arrived alone. A Quaker historian tells of her arrival at the court of the Sultan in Adrianople:

> The Sultan bade her speak the word of the Lord to them, and not to fear, for they had good hearts and could hear it ... Then she spoke what was upon her mind. The Turks hearkened to her ... Then the Sultan desired her to stay in

the country, saying that they could not but respect such a one, as should take so much pains to come to them so far as from England, with a message from the Lord God . . . She, having no more to say, the Turks asked her what she thought of their prophet Mahomet and she answered she knew him not, but Christ the true prophet, the Son of God, who was the Light of the World, and enlightened every man coming to the world, Him, she knew.[9]

Such a woman was a worthy forerunner of modern mission to Muslims and of all fearless faith-sharers.

The stories of some women who have been notable evangelists have been preserved because of their importance for other reasons. Madame Jeanne Guyon was a French Roman Catholic of the late seventeenth century, whose holiness of life impressed many, including John Wesley. After the death of her wealthy nobleman husband she felt called to do more than helping the needy. A priest challenged her to 'do what our Lord has made you know he desired of you'. Not unnaturally in the circumstances, she questioned his advice:

> I answered him, 'My Father, I am a widow, who has little children four and six years of age. What else could God require of me but to rear them?' He said to me, 'I know nothing of it. You know whether God had made you recognise that he wished something of you. If it is so, there is nothing which should hinder you from doing his will. One must leave one's children to do it.'[10]

Thus Guyon began her itinerant ministry, mainly of personal evangelism, challenging people to live a holy life by placing their faith in Christ. She went to rich and poor alike. Her background gave her access to noble ladies of Paris, and 'some of the most distinguished ladies of the capital of France' began 'recognizing the truths of religion, and rejoicing in the experimental power of piety'. A physician whom she consulted was challenged to consider the place of religion in his life and 'became afterwards a decided Christian'. She also went to the ordinary people of towns and cities, and saw many people turn wholeheartedly to God.

She entered monasteries and nunneries, teaching the importance of faith as the foundation of the Christian life. She also saw many people healed, and in addition to her personal work she wrote forty books.

Selina, Countess of Huntingdon (1707–1791), made the most of her position to share the gospel. She took her friends and acquaintances with her to hear Whitefield, whom she greatly admired, and invited them to meetings in her four homes at which Whitefield and others spoke. A number of aristocrats were converted.

Gossiping the gospel

Christians who share the gospel at a grass roots level can see the good news taken where no preaching evangelist would ever go and preach. And if each person who is themselves converted then shares the gospel with numbers of others, simple arithmetic suggests that this would see the gospel spread more quickly than by using numbers of Billy Grahams. There is a cartoon in Os Guinness' book *The Gravedigger File*. It shows several people (four men and one woman) putting data into a computer and poring over yards of printout at the 'Global Evangelism International Data Foundation'. Another man announces: 'The computer was right! The most effective way is just to talk to people!'[11]

As I suggested in chapter 1, personal evangelism has often been seen as the sphere of women. Women 'gossip the gospel' – and are good at it, so it is assumed. But why should it be seen as a woman's preserve? Is women's seemingly greater readiness to share their faith with others to do with natural talkativeness?

Some women are at home in the day, with young children, as full-time home-makers, working part-time or because they are retired. Their lives often revolve around particular places and people: the shops, the park, the school, parent and toddler groups, clubs, adult education classes, each other's homes. Shared concerns lead to friendships, and friendships lead to the sharing of what is important, including faith. Sharing problems: teething, feeding, behaviour problems of children, being a single parent, difficulties for children at school, illness, worries about other family members, loneliness, can be opportunities for Christian women to share how as Christians they face and deal with such issues.

Particular opportunities are provided by church-based groups: mothers and toddlers, and playgroups. The quality of the group may lead to its being the best one around, which is a good advertisement. Groups vary in how they operate. In some the leaders will just pray for children and parents and perhaps invite them to other events, such as pram services or family services. Others may include spiritual input for the mums and/or the children. Opportunities can be found in personal conversations to present the challenge of the gospel.

More recently some women have put on parenting courses. Parents are increasingly worried about how to bring up children in today's world. So they may welcome the opportunity to learn how to set boundaries, to stop nagging, to give children choice. Parents may be referred through local health visitors or other professionals, or may come through advertisements at primary schools and through parents' groups. A group of parents looking at parenting can be a natural way of bridging the gap with unchurched people. Many women find that events such as this provide natural outlets for developing friendships, and demonstrating by word and action the difference Jesus makes.

Jesus at the school gate

In 1982 Eddie Gibbs, the training director of Mission England, announced that the school gate provided possibly 'the best opportunity for evangelism in Britain today'. One is tempted to ask how many afternoons he has spent at the school gate himself. Nevertheless, he clearly has a point. The school gate has replaced the village shop as a natural meeting place for women (it is still mainly women who collect their children from school). Women congregate there once a day with a few minutes to spare until their children appear. Thus there is the potential for Christians to form friendships with other women, to talk and listen, to give a Christian viewpoint and to share more of one's faith where appropriate.

It has been said that the school gate is the twentieth-century equivalent of the village well. (In many countries of course, the nearest water tap may still have that function.) In the Bible, there are various significant meetings recorded as taking place at wells. Abraham's servant met Rebekah, Jacob found Rachel, Moses met Zipporah. And in the New Testament, one of Jesus' most significant meetings with an individual took place at a well in Samaria (John 4).

The story is frequently cited as a good example of personal evangelism. Jesus was in a public place, and he turned an every-day event into an opportunity for conversation, which in turn led to a challenge to faith. Jesus took the initiative, but he first revealed his own need by asking for a drink. Genuine needs and issues can be the start of conversations which go on to deeper things.

So far so good. But the story is not quite such a straightforward example as the use to which it has been put suggests. The fact that Jesus breaks normal barriers and speaks with a woman in public, and a Samaritan woman at that, is also of note. The rabbis taught that 'a man should not salute a woman in a public place, not even his wife', to drink from the cup would have him made him ritually unclean, and good Jews did not have anything to do with Samaritans. Jesus, here, is not exemplifying how to speak to 'people like himself'. The story is as much an example of how to break with conventions as of how women can meet other women at the school gate.

It is frequently noted that this story is an example of Jesus having a theological conversation with a woman. John 3 shows Jesus sending the religious teacher Nicodemus away with instructions to be 'born again', a female image if ever there was one. In chapter 4 he engages in a philosophical discussion about true worship. Again there is a kind of irony in the use of this story as an example of the personal evangelism at which women are supposed to excel. Women's talk is stereotypically supposed to be 'rapport' talk, not talk about issues. But here Jesus and the woman get into some quite complex discussion.

It is insulting to women to suggest that here is an exceptional woman, one who seems to enjoy a good debate. I would like to suggest that the model of women effectively 'gossiping the gospel' at the school gates needs some modification. What is going on may be far from 'gossip'. It may involve deep 'theological' questions even though they may not be put in theological terms. As happens here, an initial exchange on the basis of shared purpose may lead on to something much more complex, and an invitation to meet the living God.

Jesus was also natural and confident. The Samaritan woman began by being sharp-tongued, hard and cynical. By the end she is so amazed by the conversation that she runs off, forgetting why she has actually come to the well. It is little use to women to expect them to be able to 'gossip the gospel' without helping them have the confidence and the tools to do it. Jesus was sure of what he was saying. In order to be more effective evangelists, women need to be confident that what they are saying is the truth, especially in today's relativistic society. They need guidance on how to relate to people with a post-modern world view. But they also need to depend on God, that he will give them insights, whether from careful listening or by the Spirit, into the spiritual needs of people, just as Jesus stuns the woman by mentioning her marital history. The final irony is that Jesus, a man, is the model of personal evangelism. And the woman, according to some interpretations, is the first 'preaching' evangelist in the ministry of Jesus, whose witness led to many people believing.[12]

The trouble with school gates is that women will only spend five years or so standing at them. And they spend only a fraction of each school day waiting there. Churches need to be much more creative in helping women – and men – find other 'school gates'.

And the story of Jesus at the well is a challenge to those who see it as a story of how to steer a conversation on to spiritual things. What really happens at school gates when friendships arise is that they become relationships. Other mothers at the school gates become friends. Then they watch a Christian's life. They ask a Christian's view on disciplining children, or euthanasia, or which party they'll be voting for at the next election – whatever they are thinking about. That makes evangelism both easier and more difficult: it arises out of real relationships.

It comes naturally?

But do women find this sort of evangelism as easy as some men seem to think? Do women have something men don't have, or do they just try harder?

In a book published a few years ago, Ruth Calver wrote:

> I know that my life should be totally open to God, that I should be prepared to 'gossip the Gospel' to my friends, but I find it far easier to share Jesus with strangers than with neighbours ... We prefer to visit homes on the opposite side of the estate, yet it is our neighbours and friends with whom we have the greatest contact and who can become most open to the Gospel.[13]

Many women might not agree with her feelings about visiting, but would agree that sharing the gospel with friends and neighbours is not necessarily easy. Women who have not had higher education, who have not had much responsibility in their working life and who have spent most of their time looking after children or other family members are often lacking in confidence when it comes to talking about their faith. They feel they have nothing to say. In our tolerant, pluralistic culture, many Christians have lost the habit of seeing those around them as needing to hear the gospel. They receive little support or training.

At least they often have role models, other Christian women leading groups, speaking up in a discussion, sitting over a cup of coffee. But role models without personal encouragement are insufficient. Seeing women who are apparently confident may just make others feel, 'I could never do that.'

As in all situations where Christians seek to win others to faith, a Christian mother at the school gates is a missionary. She needs the prayer and support of her church. She may find the encounter no easier, or more difficult, than it is for those who go into seemingly more hostile places: pubs, clubs, and so on. One woman asked if it is any easier to share the gospel at the school gate than in the places where men meet: the pub at lunchtime or in the evening, the sports club; places where men may actually spend much more time with each other than women have in the five minutes or so at the school gate. It is a good question. I suspect many women do not find it easy. My limited experience of school gates shows some mums busy in conversation, others coming and going without speaking to anyone. It may be just as hard to make the first move here as in any other missionary situation.

Why should someone (a man) suggest that the school gate is the 'best opportunity for evangelism in Britain today'? Does this merely make use of the stereotype that women with children find it easy to talk to each other (which is partially true), and thus easy to share the gospel (which may be less true)? In my experience some women are just as afraid of alienating their friends as many men are. The assumption must have been that this is an opportunity which does not need resourcing; it just happens naturally. But I suspect it only happens, like any evangelism, where women see the opportunity, and make use of it.

Women need training too

If women are to be effective personal evangelists, they need training and encouragement. There are examples in mission history of women receiving quite a comprehensive training in order to equip them to be personal evangelists, and of organisations which have provided support and encouragement.

Early in the modern missionary movement, it became apparent that in countries where the sexes were segregated and women could not be reached by men they would have to be won by women. But there were not enough women missionaries to reach the women. Hence the idea of training women nationals, as 'Bible women'.

At first, suitable women were individually trained by the missionaries, but then training schools were developed. In 1845 a school opened to train women in Constantinople, and by the 1860s there were several training programmes operating in Turkey. By 1900 there were forty female training stations in China, more than thirty in India, and others in Japan and elsewhere.

The courses were quite academic, considering that many Bible women were mothers or grandmothers and not necessarily well educated. In some training schools the curriculum consisted of all the branches of theology except Greek and Hebrew. That might be as much training as today's ministers have, since many now no longer have to study Greek or Hebrew! Such thorough training was thought to be necessary. One missionary wrote in 1918:

> New opportunities inevitably bring new demands and new requirements, and the Bible women of today and tomorrow must not only have the desire to share the glad tidings, but the training which will enable them to adapt the message to the understanding of many types of hearers, to be able to answer many different kinds of questions, to appeal to the minds as well as the hearts of the newly awakened women of the East.[14]

If that was women reaching women in 1918, the words seem very relevant today. In our world, things are changing fast; people, and perhaps especially women, are more 'religious' than ever, but are looking everywhere but to the Church for answers. As then, so now, the first requirement is women full of the knowledge of God, and eager to share the good news. But we also need women who can understand the attractions of the New Age, can refute the claims of astrology and alternative therapies, can explain why Jesus is the only way to God, and who know how to communicate the good news in a post-modern age. Most training in evangelism today is very basic. It usually majors on forming relationships with non-Christians, which many women already have, and on 'apologetics', which often still focuses on the questions of an increasingly outmoded modernism.

There is a danger that training replaces doing. But if women and men are to be more effective evangelists in today's world, more training needs to be available. In Britain several colleges have courses on evangelism available by correspondence; but more could be done at a local level. Admittedly, part of the attraction of the training for Bible women was an education which they would not otherwise have. Our world is very different. Many Christians are very busy, perhaps too busy. But some are retired or unemployed, or mums at home with at least some time on their hands. Women are not so busy as many in the Third World where they may have a job, grow their own food and bring up a family, all simultaneously. Perhaps if we are serious about evangelism we can meet new challenges with new solutions – a variation on an old and extremely effective one.

Women of the good news

One movement involving large numbers of women mobilised for evangelism arose in the 1930s in Nigeria. The 'mouth [is] not wide enough to tell of all the goodness of God' was how the women explained their enthusiasm for evangelism. Methodist women enthusiastic for evangelism developed a volunteer evangelistic outreach to help them to spread the gospel to Islamic women. They organised a variety of events suited to their African context: street processions, city-wide rallies, open air campaigns.[15]

A more recent women's evangelistic movement has been 'Women of the Good News', begun in Zaire in the early 1970s by two women, an American missionary and the wife of a Zairean pastor. They were inspired by another women's evangelistic movement, started in the Central African Republic. In many African churches at that time women were not considered to have a ministry of their own in spreading the gospel, and women were excluded from the leadership of churches. But a para-church organisation gave them new opportunities, and also provided a social outlet.

From a slow beginning, the 'Ade Wene Pangbana' movement grew to 15,000 by 1980, and by 1985 there were 30,000 in one denomination alone. But it also spread to other denominations, so by the mid 1980s there were at least 10,000 women in Grace Ministries churches involved, as well as women in Baptist churches and Assemblies of God. Local groups met weekly for Bible studies, and women were involved in one of five outreach areas: visiting the sick (providing practical help and words of witness and encouragement); evangelising unbelievers; ministering to those who have left the church fellowship; maintaining the church building and grounds; and visiting elderly people.[16]

Involvement in such a movement gave women confidence, so much so that some replaced foreign missionaries in leadership positions. The movement also brought unity to women of different churches and congregations, and a sense of oneness and solidarity, with uniform dresses and headscarves, songs and slogans: 'We the women of the Good News!'

It has been suggested that elements of the movement could be transplanted to North America, where women are spiritually fat and need to apply their Bible study. The same might be said of some churches in Britain. The nearest we have got is perhaps the concept of Cell Church, where small groups are designed to be evangelistic.

Winning Women

In the last few years there have been several initiatives to help women reach other women. 'Women Reaching Women' was founded in 1986 after the Luis Palau Mission to London. Its aim is to enable women to find ways God can use them right where they are, by building women's confidence, sharing expertise, encouraging women to use their gifts and enabling them to learn by involvement. Because what women do at a grass roots level has not been valued by the Church, women do not always gain this kind of support from within their churches.

Women need to know that they have a message to deliver because they have shared the lives of those around them and know what their real needs are. They speak the same language as the people they are talking to, they are real. This was the way Jesus and Paul worked, getting alongside people, listening to them, being vulnerable.

Often the resourcing of evangelism has been done by men. But women are just as capable of coming up with ideas and taking initiatives. WRW enables women to pool ideas and develop new strategies.

Another recent initiative to help women reach women is 'Winning Women', developed by the Women's Ministries department of the Assemblies of God, under the leadership of Jackie Bowler. The aim is to see every Christian woman as a 'winner', reaching her full potential in Christ and winning other women to the Lord. All women, whether single or married, have 'a call to fulfil, a ministry and gifting to release and a commission to go into the harvest'. Being a mother is an important task, but there are times when women have more time on their hands and can fulfil wider ministries. 'A Winning Woman is one who finds her Christian faith leads her to triumph and fulfilment in any circumstances at any "season" of her life. This secret when passed on, wins other women too.'

Resources are provided to give ideas for individual or church-based witness; being a school governor; opening a crisis counselling centre or pregnancy centre; holding coffee mornings in the home; leading groups for girls and young women. Most of these relate to the normal activities of women at home looking after children; thus they suggest not that evangelism is something you might hope to do later, but that evangelism flows naturally out of everyday relationships.

Groups of women are becoming 'winning women': opening their homes for coffee mornings, gaining confidence in sharing their faith. Women are encouraged to proclaim the good news for families; to get alongside single mothers, women who abuse themselves, anorexics and bulimics, those who suffer from low self-esteem, women who are hurting just because they are women, women who feel unloved. Christian women may feel inhibited, but are reminded that through Christ they can win over their own emotions, inhibitions and prejudices, in order that they might win others.

Jackie tells of a young married woman who came to church asking for help. 'She had been an anorexic for fifteen years. She had been abused and felt totally inadequate to live her life to the full. She was locked up in self-pity, resentment, bitterness, fear, and some pride.' Not untypical of many people today, sadly. In the church she found those who would help her in her search for freedom and identity, and help her be free in Christ. Now she is 'rejoicing in God's love and salvation, training for leadership in the church and winning others as a "winning woman" herself'.[17]

The advantage of a 'women's ministry' is that, like the women's missionary societies of the nineteenth century, it can be entirely led by women. Women can be speakers. Women's conferences can be relaxed, freeing places, without the pressure of being in a minority, or having to cope with the kind of atmosphere often created among groups of men.

Such movements, organised and led by women, for women, show the capabilities of women. But they also raise questions about the appropriateness of women reaching women and men reaching men. It has been inevitable in some periods of history and some societies. But is it the right way today?

Women reaching women

One area of evangelism where separate women's work has been essential was in evangelising segregated societies. Kari Malcolm tells of how when her father was working in China, before he was married he could only invite men to meetings in the Gospel Hall. Then women were invited to public meetings as her mother's guests, and the sexes were divided with a green curtain down the aisle. When it came to informal Bible study groups, they were held separately.[18]

When Amy and Samuel Zwemer wrote about Muslim evangelism in 1926, they were aware that despite the attempts of Muslim women to challenge their subjection, most women led lives very separate from men's. Such a situation was either a difficulty or an opportunity. They felt that women's work was one of the keys to this kind of evangelism:

> Owing to the fact that the mother's influence over the children, both boys and girls, up to about ten years of age, is paramount, and that women are the conservative element in the defence of their faith, we believe that missionary bodies ought to lay far more emphasis on work for Moslem women as a means for hastening the evangelism of Moslem lands.[19]

In an article written in 1987, missiologist Miriam Adeney gives a more recent example. She tells of an American missionary to a Muslim country who asserts that women are particularly effective evangelists in Muslim countries. Why?

When a Christian man visits a home in that country, he is welcomed to the front part of the house, the man's part. He is invited to sit down and discuss theology. Local men pride themselves on their knowledge of religion. But when a Christian woman visits a home, she is not invited to the front part. Nor does she have to wade through theology. Rather, she is brought into the back part of the house, the women's section. Here they do not talk about religion, but about life. In this setting, the Christian woman shares how Christ enables us to know God personally.[20]

In that place, over a hundred Muslims have come to follow Jesus Christ. And that includes men as well as women: while women may not go in the front part of the house, men go in the back. And women share the faith with men, with husbands and other family members as well as with children.

In many areas even today, men and women live in separate worlds. There are opportunities for women among segregated poor women and segregated rich women. There are university women in Saudi Arabia who study from their private rooms, who use women doctors, women lawyers and women religious teachers. Women's worlds need women to reach them.

In our society there are some women right outside the reach of usual church activities who can perhaps only be reached by other women. But these, ironically, tend to be forgotten by the organisations resourcing women's evangelism.

Janis works in a church project with unmarried teenage mothers. She wants the church to be a haven, a place where the young women can go. She provides a listening ear, practical help and advice, a link with other agencies. Her model is Jesus, who welcomed people, ate with them, befriended them.

Go to where no one wants to be. That's what a ministry is . . . As you minister, go understanding whom you represent. To these pregnant young ladies, I'm going as an ambassador of Jesus Christ. Although I'm just a vessel in his hand, I'm going to sit here and laugh with these girls, and love these girls. Somehow, with the laughing and joking,

God is going to draw them to himself.[21]

Maria was given a vision which has resulted in the opening of a refuge for women at risk from violence and abuse. Part of the guidance she received was Luke 5:7, where a great number of fish are caught. The refuge is run much as other such refuges, a safe house for women, somewhere where lives can be rebuilt, but part of the aim is to see women come to know Christ.

Another group of women who tend to have been neglected by the Church are feminists. While many women would not own that label, they have been influenced by feminist ideas. 'Of all the unreached people in the UK and USA, feminists outside the church rank high on the list,' wrote Kathy Keay in 1988.[22] I have discussed some of the issues raised by feminism in my booklet *Liberating the Gospel for Women*.[23] Some feminist women, such as theologian Daphne Hampson, argue that it is impossible to be a feminist and a Christian: Christianity is a dangerous patriarchal myth. Where are those women who will communicate the gospel in such a way that it can be heard as liberating good news to women?

Barbara worked as a Church Army evangelist among prostitutes and women at risk, and was able to share Jesus with women from many feminist groups.[24] Getting involved in women's groups, or groups working on 'women's issues' such as domestic violence, pornography and ecology, putting some Christian input in International Women's Day events (remembering that many of the early feminists in the nineteeth century were Christians); only women can do these things – but few women seem called to this mission field at the moment.

So separate women's work is sometimes essential, and it has some advantages. On the other hand, men and women are not so different. Is it right to divide men and women so rigidly? Can only women reach women? Should we not, rather, recognise that as men's and women's lives have become less segregated in society, so they should be less segregated in church life?

Side by side for the faith of the gospel

Women may reach women through home-based or children's activities, or through work with particular groups of women, and men may reach men through special events for men. But some women are good at evangelising men, and men have always evangelised women.

Other women who are missed out in traditional 'women's work' are those who work in what used to be called a man's world, the public world of work. But that is now becoming the world of men and women. Do men and women have more in common than not in this context, so that gender is less relevant? Churches, and organisations which help women in their evangelism, have been slow to realise that working women have just as many opportunities to share the gospel with work colleagues as do other women with the women they meet around their home, school and so on. Have our churches changed their 'businessmen's breakfasts' to 'business people's breakfasts'? Do we remember that men and women work together in all kinds of jobs?

I remember arriving for my one and only night shift on a hospital ward. It was an emergency, and there was no one else who knew the residents and could do it. I met my fellow-nurse, who soon established that I was a Christian. He had had a Catholic upbringing in his country of origin, and having let it lapse had been thinking about it again. He was, in fact, delighted to have a whole twelve hours to ask me all his questions about God!

That kind of work is ideal for sharing faith. Christians who have white-collar jobs sometimes forget the kind of opportunities afforded in jobs where the work is mainly physical, but which has opportunities for talking while you work, and tea breaks. I recently visited a factory. Men and women were working alongside each other, operating the machines. Everyone knew everyone else's name, and people knew who the churchgoers were. What potential for evangelism! But offices provide opportunities too. Wherever they work, Christians who witness by their whole way of life and the way they go about their work soon find conversations about faith opening up with colleagues, who may be men or women.

Christiana Tsai is one remarkable example of how faith can overflow first to family and then to work. Christiana was a high-born Chinese woman, converted from traditional ancestor worship to Christianity early this century through reading the Bible and hearing preaching at a mission school. Very soon, despite their early hostility, members of her family were converted:

> So the brother who tore up my Bible and persecuted me in the early days at last confessed my Lord. In all, fifty-five of my relatives, adults and children, have become God's children and expressed their faith in Jesus. I have never been to college, or theological seminary, and I am not a Bible teacher; I have only been God's 'hunting dog'. I simply followed at the heels of my Master, and brought to His feet the quarry He sent me after.[25]

And it was not only relatives who were converted. When Tsai left high school she began to teach in a government school. Parents were outraged when they heard of her attempts to share her faith: she talked personally with pupils during break times and held Bible studies at her home. Out of her two hundred pupils, seventy-two professed faith in Christ, and their faith was so infectious that the dean of the school who confiscated New Testaments from the dormitories and threatened to expel any pupils attending Bible studies was herself converted.

It is somewhat ironic that this woman could achieve such remarkable things in China early in this century, but that any woman teaching today in Britain, a so-called Christian country, who tried to share her faith in such ways would probably be dismissed. Yet Christian teachers are uniquely placed to influence their pupils, and can be very influential through helping with Christian Unions in schools as well as letting their faith be known to others. Churches need to support Christian teachers – women and men – and Christians in all kinds of work situations, as they seek to share their faith.

Sharing in Christ's mission

Some Christians would see the witness of lives lived for God as the primary model for evangelism. The Catholic Church, for example, does not have 'evangelists' as a specific ministry within the Church, although there are a few Catholics who might use this title. But the main emphasis is on the whole Church participating in the task of evangelisation. *This is the Laity*, a simplified version of *Christifideles Laici*, issued by Pope John Paul II in 1989, puts it like this:

> Every Christian therefore can say
> as Jesus said of himself:
> 'The Spirit of the Lord is upon me
> because he has anointed me
> to preach good news to the poor.'
> Thus, every baptised person
> shares the same mission as Jesus . . .
> The laity share Christ's mission
> as Prophet-Teacher.
> This gives them the capacity
> to believe the Gospel
> and the responsibility
> to proclaim it with courage.[26]

For the Catholic Church, word and deed are closely bound together. This may have strengths and weaknesses: actions may not always have words which explain them, but words are never used separately from actions. Thus, no Catholic woman – and every Catholic woman – is an 'evangelist'. But in practice many who seek to share their faith at a grass roots level experience just the same challenges and pressures, and the same lack of encouragement and resourcing, as their Protestant sisters. As, increasingly, churches of different denominations, men and women, work together in the task of evangelism, perhaps both women and men will gain more courage to proclaim the good news to all with whom they have contact.

An old bible and an old bicycle

Behind all the stories in this chapter is the simple model of 'one beggar showing another beggar where to find bread', as Asian theologian D. T. Niles defined evangelism. One person talking to another – still the most effective method. Some women just get on with it. They read 'do the work of an evangelist' (2 Tim. 4:5), and do it!

Evangelist Daisy Osborn tells the story of an eighty-year-old woman in Uganda. She had little but an old Bible and an old bicycle.

> She asked God to show her where she might bring the good news of Jesus, and God showed her an area of the country-side where there were no churches or Christian leaders. Soon she had started seven little churches, each in a separate village. Now with her message of grace, she pedals the rickety old bicycle around to a different church each day of the week . . . She has no teeth, but she smiles. People can tell that she really cares about them.[27]

For discussion/action

1. If Luke 15:8–10 shows the seeking love of God in the representation of a woman, how might that help you or women in the Church today who have evangelistic gifts?
2. What other 'school gates' do women have? What 'village wells' do men have today? How could your church equip women (and men) to be better evangelists in the workplace, and in other places where people spend time with each other?
3. How can the Church reach women influenced by feminism?

5

Women and their families

A wife of noble character who can find?
  She is worth far more than rubies . . .
Charm is deceptive, and beauty is fleeting;
  but a woman who fears the Lord is to be praised.

(Proverbs 31:10, 30)

The story is told of a woman many years ago who went to a mission meeting led by the preacher Gipsy Smith. She wrote to him afterwards: 'Dear Sir, I feel that God is calling me to preach the Gospel. The trouble is, I have twelve children. What shall I do?' Gipsy Smith replied: 'Dear Madam, I am delighted to hear that God has called you to preach the Gospel. I am even more delighted to hear that he has provided you with a congregation.'

When I first heard that story I felt quite angry. It seemed a real put-down to a woman who might have had a genuine call from God to be a preacher. Or she could have been right about the calling, but wrong to move towards that role before her children had grown (though Gipsy Smith hardly gave her any indication of how she might have tested such a calling). Or, as people who tell that story usually intend, perhaps Gipsy Smith was right. For a woman who is a mother, there is no higher calling than that of 'evangelist' to her children.

We have looked at women as preachers, and the opposition many have encountered. We have looked at women sharing their faith one to one, 'gossiping the gospel' as it has been termed. Now we move on to look at the sphere where women's evangelism has been least controversial: in the home.

It seems that throughout the history of the Church women have tended to be more receptive to the gospel than men. Thus women have often been converted first, and then won their husbands. And many have also taken the evangelism of their children very seriously too, seeking to bring them up in the faith and praying that they will make the faith their own.

Won over without a word?

Right from the beginning, wives with unconverted husbands were a concern for the Church. Peter tells women in his first letter, 'Wives, in the same way be submissive to your husband so that, if any of them do not believe the word, they may be won over without words by the behaviour of their wives, when they see the purity and reverence of your lives' (1 Peter 3:1–2).

Some women have taken this literally, attempting to witness silently; others have seen that there must also be a place for words, for answering questions and explaining faith. In most of the examples we have of women down the ages winning their husbands we do not know how they were won; probably by a combination of things, and above all by prayer. As in the examples in the last chapter, the only extant early stories are of queens or noblewomen, but no doubt Christian wives of every class sought to win their unbelieving husbands.

The Acts of Peter (second century) tells of a Roman woman, Candida, who became a Christian through the witness of Paul. She then 'instructed her husband' Quartus, and he believed.[1] Early church history reveals a number of examples of prominent non-Christian men with Christian wives. Julian the apostate complained about those whose wives gave money to the poor. Some women tried hard to persuade their husbands not to go to pagan altars.

With the fall of Rome in 410, the gospel was spread by refugees to all parts of Europe and the known world. The practice of royal families making marriage alliances between countries also helped spread the gospel, because in those days a whole tribe or people took the religion of their ruler. Clothilde, born around 471, daughter of the King of Burgundy, married Clovis, King of the Salian Franks. Within four years she had converted him to Christianity by her prayers and her example – and her words. She told her husband, 'The Gods you worship are no good . . . They haven't even been able to help themselves let alone others.'[2] Victory in battle after he prayed to his wife's Christian God brought his conversion.

In the sixth century, Bertha, another Christian princess from France, married the pagan King Ethelbert of Kent. He eventually became a Christian through her witness and encouraged his subjects to follow in his footsteps. Ethelbert and Bertha welcomed Augustine to Canterbury, and thus it became the centre of the Roman church in England.

Their daughter Ethelberga married the pagan Edwin, King of Northumbria. The marriage was agreed only on condition that she was free to live according to her beliefs, and when she went to Northumbria she took her chaplain Paulinus with her. And she too was determined to win her husband to her faith. In 625 Pope Boniface wrote to Ethelberga:

> Our paternal responsibility moves us to urge Your Christian Majesty, imbued with the force of divine inspiration, not to avoid the duty imposed on us in season and out of season, in order that, with the assistance and strength of our Lord and Saviour Jesus Christ, the King may also be added to the Christian fold . . . My illustrious daughter, persevere in using every effort to soften his heart by teaching him the commandments of God. Help him to understand the excellence of the mystery that you have accepted by believing and the marvellous worth of the reward that you have been accounted worthy to receive in this new birth. Melt the coldness of his heart by teaching him about the Holy Spirit, so that the warmth of divine faith may set his mind on fire through your constant encouragement and remove the numbing and deadening errors of paganism. If you do this, the witness of the Holy Spirit will most certainly be fulfilled in you, that, 'the unbelieving husband shall be saved through the believing wife'.[3]

More was involved for Ethelberga than merely living out her faith. She had to teach it too. Two years later Edwin was baptised, together with Hilda, Edwin's niece, who was brought up as a Christian by the queen. Many others in the family were converted through Ethelberga, and Edwin set about winning his kingdom for Christ.

As I have already mentioned, the Reformation did not bring women increasing scope for ministry, as might have been expected. Married women were urged to be good wives and mothers, and with a few notable exceptions that is what they did. Sometimes, though, ministry outside the home was closely connected with ministry inside it. The early-nineteenth-century cottage preachers flourished in a pre-industrial society when public and private worlds were still merged within the domestic framework of labouring life. Women could be wives, mothers *and* preachers. Later in the century, as the middle-class ideas of the home as women's primary sphere of action began to influence working-class women too, women were expected to preach to their children instead of the entire community.[4]

In the United States early in the nineteenth century, wives of unbelieving husbands were often taught that the only verse applying to their situation was 1 Peter 3:1. The only way they could seek to win their husbands was to live exemplary lives. The revivalist preacher Charles Finney, however, suggested that wives could do more. They were not to be passive. They should talk to their husbands, guided by the Spirit: 'I have known women who felt that they ought to talk to their unconverted husbands, and pray with them, but they have neglected it, and so they get into the dark. They knew their duty and refused to do it: they went around it, and there they lost the spirit of prayer.'[5]

If women found their duty, they would see God's Spirit in action through their lives. Some saw their husbands converted. And if they could see their husbands converted through their witness, why not others? No wonder the mid-century revival in America was a time when the ministry of women blossomed.

At the end of the century, too, one man who encouraged women to serve God overseas, if God called them, also encouraged wives of non-Christians to speak about their faith. For Fredrik Franson, it was not a matter of actions *or* words, but both were necessary:

Some have objected that Peter has said that the husbands would be won without words through the wives' quiet conversation (1 Peter 3:1). It is clear that a wife cannot incessantly talk (nag) her husband into conversation. Her word in that way loses its power and in such situations her conduct speaks louder than her words . . . The Word should of course be the first means that the wives should use in order to win them, but if that does not succeed, they should believe that through their quiet conduct they can bring blessing to their husbands.[6]

Starting at Jerusalem

Why were such words necessary? Surely the Church has always encouraged, and taken for granted, the witness of wives to husbands? But Finney and Franson had to speak this way because American women were not witnessing. Many women had, it seems, been silenced altogether. Witness was the task of someone else. They were not encouraged to use whatever gifts they might possess.

Some Christians have written about the 'separate spheres' of men and women, the witness of women in the home but not outside it. But much of the evidence seems to go against that sort of distinction. Again and again we can read stories of women who started to witness in the home, and whose ministry then spilled over beyond it. Those who witnessed effectively in the home witnessed outside it. Starting at 'Jerusalem' soon leads on to 'Judea', and the ends of the earth. By contrast, other women, taught that witness should be left to men, have often never got started.

In mid-nineteenth-century England, Catherine Booth was aware that many women were reluctant to 'in any manner bear testimony for their Lord', that the same forces and circumstances which kept women from sharing their faith outside the home might equally work inside it. Women's 'false, God-dishonouring timidity' was, she argued, made to seem a virtue by a Church which seemed determined to stifle the talents of women. To her it was the same whether it was praying in a prayer meeting, speaking up at a meeting or preaching. Women need to be serious in their discipleship of Jesus Christ. God gives gifts to men and women equally. 'I believe it is impossible to estimate the extent of the Church's loss, where prejudice and custom are allowed to render the outpouring of God's Spirit upon his handmaidens null and void.'[7]

She spoke against 'tattle and tea-parties', and 'light reading'. Women must be encouraged to use the gifts God gives them, to throw off 'the swaddling bands of blind custom', in order that the gospel may be spread. How can women be effective in winning their husbands if they are too timid to share their faith? Surely that is not to God's glory?

As *Finding Faith Today* tells us, for nearly a quarter of men finding faith the 'main factor' was their partner, while for women their partner was the 'main factor' for only 5 per cent.[8] The stories told in the book show that women's witness was usually a combination of words and action. 'When someone you love and respect starts talking about something you oppose it makes you think about it,' said one husband. 'My girlfriend was a Christian, so I thought I'd give it a try although she never forced it on me.' 'I wished to share in the comfort and peace of mind which it obviously brought to my wife.'[9]

Stories of Faith, which tells other stories of faith used for the research, includes the story of Jack, for example.

> Shortly after we had moved to X my wife joined the local Anglican church. Within a short period of time I noticed there was something different about her when she returned from the morning service . . . She was always anxious to tell me about the wonderful preaching and fellowship. One Sunday I decided to see what was going on.[10]

He found the church both welcoming and challenging, and soon became a regular churchgoer, and later had a marked experience of the Holy Spirit. He was clearly attracted by the change in his wife, but her words about what went on drew him to see for himself.

Even in cultures where men and women lead separate lives,

women may still be the most effective evangelists of the men. Missiologist Miriam Adeney tells how, when an Indian woman recently set up Christian ashrams for Brahmin women, they ran to tell their menfolk and bring them too. The solidarity of groups of women, such as those mentioned in the last chapter, can provide confidence which helps women to share their faith.

A recent book by Marion Stroud, *Loving God But Still Loving You*, deals with many issues faced by Christians (often women) whose partners do not share their faith. 'What shall I tell him?' What is the best way to talk to a non-Christian husband about faith? 'I said very little to John about it for a long time,' said Anne. Then John went with her to church on Easter Day. On the other hand, when Lorna discovered what it meant to be a Christian, 'I was so excited that I ran home from church with a grin from ear to ear. I blurted it all out to Terry, and to be fair to him, he did listen.'[11]

There are no right ways. What is important, as is evident from many stories, is that women in this position need support and encouragement. Many feel isolated, coping with opposition or conflict at home, and feel second-class Christians because they are unable to be as committed to the church as those whose husbands share their faith. The words of Pope Boniface to Ethelberga quoted earlier, 'persevere in using every effort to soften his heart', ring down the ages: a reminder of the importance of witness, the privilege of witness, some guidance on how to do it sensitively, and a reminder of the power of the Holy Spirit, who alone brings people to faith.

'I sometimes think that Kevin is being awkward just for the sake of it. However carefully I try to explain what I believe, he either can't or won't understand. Talk about a closed mind!'[12] Witnessing to family can be the hardest kind of evangelism of all. Our family members know us too well. One step of inconsistency and our faith is thrown back in our face. In a culture where religion is often seen as a woman's thing, and we think men need strong Christian men witnessing to them, it is all the more surprising that so many men are won primarily through the witness of those who are closest to them – and are women.

And no doubt those women have learnt a lot in the process. How to answer all the criticisms of church, the taunts, how to answer the genuine questions, how to tell what God has done, how to live a consistently Christian life under constant scrutiny. What experience such women have to use when witnessing to friends, to neighbours – and more widely! Other women need to hear what God has done, to see what God can do. 'Where are the men?' is a matter of some concern at present. Most churches have more women than men. If women are so effective at winning men, why does no one ask *them* how to do it? Church leaders and church committees need to hear from wives who have done it how to win men to Christ.

Teach them to your children

The Bible makes it clear that children should be brought up in the faith of their parents. In the Old Testament the people of Israel are commanded to pass on the faith to their children: 'These commandments that I give you today are to be upon your hearts. Impress them on your children. Talk about them when you sit at home and when you walk along the road, when you lie down and when you get up' (Deut. 6:6–7). In Psalm 78:3–4 the psalmist asserts:

> . . . what we have heard and known,
>   what our ancestors have told us.
> We will not hide them from their children;
>   we will tell the next generation
> the praiseworthy deeds of the Lord,
>   his power, and the wonders he has done.

The New Testament carries on this tradition. Paul wrote to Timothy, 'I have been reminded of your sincere faith, which first lived in your grandmother Lois and in your mother Eunice and, I am persuaded, now lives in you also' (2 Tim. 1:5). Timothy's father was Greek. There is a difference of opinion among commentators as to whether Lois and Eunice were Jews or Christians, but it is likely that both were Jewish, and were then converted through the ministry of Paul at Lystra (cf. Acts 16:1). As Jewish women, they had instructed Timothy from childhood in the 'holy

Scriptures' (2 Tim. 3:15), and when converted would have taught him the Christian faith. Thus, as Calvin wrote, Timothy 'was reared in his infancy in such a way that he could suck in godliness along with his mother's milk'.[13]

There is no reference to Timothy's father, so he was probably not a believer. But presumably he left his wife to follow Jewish custom and be responsible for the teaching of children at home. This passage shows the importance of this spiritual heritage. Of course people can come to God at any age, and many are converted from non-Christian backgrounds in their teens or twenties, or later. But there is nothing like the stability of a Christian upbringing to give a young person the best possible foundation of faith.

Jesus himself would have been taught by his parents, and assuming that we regard his knowledge as natural rather than supernatural, it is clear how well he was taught the Scriptures. He has a good understanding of the faith even by the age of twelve (Luke 2:47). Jesus in turn placed a high value on the spiritual understanding of children: 'He called a child whom he put among them and said, "I tell you the truth, unless you change and become like little children, you will never enter the kingdom of heaven" ' (Matt. 18:2; cf. 19:13–14).

A recent survey of fathers, conducted for Woolworth's, revealed that a large number feel that moral and religious education is not the responsibility of either parent. Many parents today, even Christians, have abandoned their responsibilities. 'We will not influence our children in making choices and decisions in matters of religion,' some say. But why not? The ads will; the press will; TV will, computer games and the Internet will; their friends will. Should parents let these things influence their children more than they do themselves?

Or some Christian parents think it is up to the Church to provide their children's Christian education. There is a good Sunday School at church – is that not enough? But when Mary Lar was addressing the first ever Pan-African Christian Women's Assembly in 1989, she assumed the home was the primary place for the evangelism of children. Christian parents are given this task.[14] Similarly, at the Anglican conference on the Decade of Evangelism in 1995, Mary Bulla of Ghana reminded delegates from around the world of the God-given command in Deuteronomy to teach children. Children need to be evangelised.

Do not reject your mother's teaching

While Scripture gives parents joint responsibility for bringing their children up in the faith, in most cultures it falls to the mother to do most of this work. 'Educate a man and you educate a person. Educate a woman and you educate a nation' (Kenyan proverb). 'A man's church will last for one generation. Mothers are the conservators of religion, bringing up their children in their own faith.'[15] Most children see more of their mothers than their fathers. We see in examples of children in the Bible that it is often their mothers who have most influence, and who are seen seeking to bring their children up to know God.

Early in the story of God's people there is a mother who saw the importance of bringing her child up in the ways of his people: Jochebed, the mother of Moses, whose story is told in Exodus chapter 2. Had Pharaoh's daughter not rescued him from the basket, Moses would not have lived. But Jochebed's faith allowed her to see the importance of saving her child's life. And it would have been her teaching, as she assumed the role of his nurse, which gave Moses a sense of identity with his own people, and a knowledge of their God, which was obviously stronger than anything he subsequently learned in Pharaoh's household. It is surely no accident that all three of Jochebed's children, Miriam, Moses and Aaron, became special servants of God.

Hannah is another mother who wanted her son to be brought up to love and serve God. Admittedly it was as a gift to God in thanks for answering her prayer, but her devotion to God, the faith to pray in the first place, is real enough. The Jesuits have a saying, 'Give us a child until he is seven and he is ours for life.' Samuel was perhaps only three when Hannah took him and left him with Eli. Eli did not seem to have made too good a job of bringing his own sons up to love the Lord (1 Sam. 3:13). Was it those three years in which Hannah brought up her son which made the crucial difference?

There have been many examples in church history of godly

mothers. Some of the early church fathers, John Chrysostom, Gregory Nazianzen, Basil, and Gregory of Nyassa, celebrated the influence of their mothers. Perhaps the most famous example is Augustine, who attributed his conversion to the influence of his mother Monica. The story has encouraged many mothers who have seen their children turn away from God, but have never given up hope that they will turn back again.

Monica was a north African woman of the fourth century. She was married to a difficult pagan husband, often drunk and unfaithful to his wife, but who became a Christian just before his death. According to Augustine, Monica 'had wept over me for many years so that I might live in your sight', and she was exultant when he turned away from his old life to follow Christ: 'She saw that much more in regard to me had been granted her by Thee than she was wont to ask with her unhappy and tearful laments.'[16]

One remarkable woman in the gallery of eminent women in church history is Ludmilla. Born in 860, the daughter of a Slavic prince, she married Borivoy, Duke of Bohemia. She followed her husband in becoming a Christian. Her son Wratislav became a Christian, but was married to a princess whose family hated Christians. Ludmilla was responsible for bringing up her grandson Wenceslaus. Her Christian influence angered pagans in the court, and when Wenceslaus' father died and his mother became regent, Wenceslaus was taken away from Ludmilla, who was murdered in 921. But Wenceslaus' faith was firmly established, and when he became king at the age of eighteen he ruled as a Christian until he was murdered only four years later by his jealous brother.

The spiritual strength and determination of another mother may have helped to convince her son, James Hudson Taylor, of women's capacity for mission. His parents, James Hudson and Amelia Taylor, both had a strong faith, and their son was taught about God from an early age. But it was to the prayers of his mother (and sister) that James attributed his conversion at the age of seventeen. One day, when his mother was away from home, she felt an urge to pray for him.

She went to her room and turned the key in the door,

resolved not to leave that spot until her prayers were answered. Hour after hour did that dear mother plead for me, until at length she could pray no longer, but was constrained to praise God for that which His Spirit taught her had already been accomplished – the conversion of her only son.[17]

In the meantime, James had been reading a tract, and had fallen on his knees and 'accepted the Saviour'.

Neglect of the great privilege of bringing up children in the faith was partly what prompted Mary Sumner, wife of an Anglican vicar, to start the Mothers' Union. When her own children had grown up, she started to invite younger mothers to the rectory, and they began meeting regularly. They were given membership cards which bore the words: 'Remember that your children are given up, body and soul, to Jesus Christ in Holy Baptism and that your duty is to train them for His service.' At a church congress in 1885, several years later, Mary spoke of the opportunities that mothers had to bring up their children in faith and prayer, and the Mothers' Union was founded. The prayer she wrote acknowledges the different ways in which Christian mothers may touch the lives of those they meet: 'All this day, O Lord, let me touch as many lives as possible for thee; and every life I touch, do thou by thy Spirit quicken, whether through the word I speak, the prayer I breathe, or the life I live. Amen.'[18]

Mary Sumner's idea of women was the traditional one. Their place was in the home, training their boys and girls for their future place in society. But today, in the Church in parts of Africa, for example, Mothers' Unions are important and very strong, providing fellowship, support and a common purpose.

Your father's instruction

But while mothers do most of the practical tasks of bringing children up, even today when there is some shared parenting, are mothers supposed to be solely responsible for seeing to a child's spiritual upbringing? According to the Bible that is not only the job of the mother. It is implied in both Old and New Testaments that the job of bringing up children in the faith is the joint task of parents, wherever that is possible. The verse in Proverbs which says, 'Do not forsake your mother's teaching', is a parallel second half of a verse which begins, 'Listen, my son, to your father's instruction' (Prov. 1:8).

Similarly, Moses was speaking to the whole assembly (not just mothers) at the end of his life, when he said: 'Take to heart all the words that I have solemnly declared to you this day, so that you may command your children to obey carefully all the words of this law' (Deut. 32:46). The role of fathers is specifically mentioned on several occasions:

> When I was a boy in my father's house,
>   still tender, and an only child of my mother,
> he taught me, and said,
>   'Lay hold of my words with all your heart;
>   keep my commands and you will live.' (Prov. 4:3–4)

Even the reformer Martin Luther, who tended to see women in a traditional way, nevertheless emphasised the role of a father in the upbringing of his children. This extends from when he 'washes diapers [nappies] or performs some other mean tasks for his child', which some may think makes him an 'effeminate fool', to Christian education. 'Most certainly father and mother are apostles, bishops, and priests to their children, for it is they who make them acquainted with the gospel.'[19]

A story is told by Ingrid Trobisch, whose father was a pioneer missionary in Africa. There was a time when he lived at home in the USA because his church had no money to send him back to Africa. A friend asked him, 'Are you not sorry that you cannot be working on the mission field?' He replied, 'Don't you see, my family is my mission.' Ingrid tells how he spent many hours each Sunday teaching his ten children one by one. And twenty-five years after his early death, five of his sons and his widow were serving as missionaries on five different continents.[20]

In the early Church there is a contrast between the words of Paul, addressed to believers irrespective of their sex, and some of the instructions in writings of the apostolic fathers. Even in Ephesians 5, where Paul briefly addresses husbands and wives separately, he then commands children to obey their parents – fathers and mothers, as in the Ten Commandments – and tells fathers: 'do not exasperate your children; instead, bring them up in the training and instruction of the Lord' (Eph. 6:4). Polycarp, on the other hand, writes this: 'After this we can go on to instruct our womenfolk in the traditions of the faith, and in love and purity; teaching them to show fondness and fidelity to their husbands, and a chaste and impartial affection for everyone else, and to bring up their children in the fear of the Lord.'[21]

The Bible stresses joint responsibility, whereas many of those since have followed their culture in making child-rearing and spiritual instruction the mother's task. But fathers who ignore Ephesians 6:4 and leave the evangelism of their children to mothers because they are out doing more important things in the public sphere are quite simply ignoring Scripture.

An ounce of parent is worth a ton of priest

How do parents set about this task? Children need to experience a loving Christian home and to be taught to understand the faith.

Children are receptive. They can understand the gospel as soon as they can understand right and wrong, and we all know children who can date their first commitment to the age of six or seven. In some circles there is debate over whether children are unsaved pagans until they make a definite commitment, or whether as children they are under grace until they are old enough to opt out of it. Either way, children need to be taught right from the beginning. An eighteen-month-old child can say, 'I love Jesus.' Then as a child grows, their faith matures. Some will come to a specific decision point. Others will simply know that they cannot remember a time when they did not believe.

But what happens if the mother is a Christian, but the father is not? How is the Christian mother to act then? Clearly it depends on the attitude of the father. Some may be hostile, others very happy for children to be brought up to know about God. Even if a husband is opposed to direct teaching about Christian faith, the children will learn a lot from experiencing the faith of their mother, and from natural conversations which will arise.

Other mothers (or fathers) face the challenge of being the only parent. Support from their church, and from other Christian parents, is also vital – as it is for all parents faced with this awesome task. But in the end it is God who brings people to faith, and whatever difficulties parents may experience – being on their own, opposition from partners, rebellion in their children – they have all the resources of prayer. And as the example of Lois and Timothy shows us, it is not impossible for one Christian parent to raise their children as Christians. And today too, we can benefit from the help of Christian grandparents or other relatives.

Hearing God's Word

Yet if fathers are to be more active in the home, the mother's sphere, where does that leave women? That might leave mothers feeling even more useless. They would not have even one area of service which is uniquely their own. But, as this book suggests, women are gifted with many and various gifts, and are called to exercise them in whatever sphere they find themselves. If men and women together share in parenting, both children and parents will benefit. And mums as well as dads can then use their God-gifts in the 'public' area too. Ministry in the more private sphere of home and family will often overflow into the public arena.

I would not want to devalue the contributions which women down the ages, left with only a limited area in which to exercise their gifts, have made to the spiritual nurture of their children. This would be true of Judaism, in its more traditional form. It would also be true of some Christian groups. The Brethren, until recently, have been noted for their prohibition of women's public ministry. In the absence of any public role, mothers have seen their ministry and service of God in terms of their home life. I can remember hearing from a friend of mine how his mother saw her calling as to have a large family and to bring them up to follow God: church growth by natural birth!

But do these examples, and those of mothers I gave earlier, really reflect God's intention for women? Mothers spend more time with their children in their early years than fathers do. But as we have just seen, God did not intend to leave the job of bringing them up in the faith to women, while men were to use their gifts in the 'public' sphere. Scripture gives both parents responsibility. Furthermore, motherhood, in the West at least, now takes only a small proportion of a woman's life. Is being a mother a primary identity? Or is it one identity among many, a temporary focus of energy?

What, according to Scripture, is a mother? A mother has the biological role of bearing children. But what other implications does this have? In his Gospel, Luke tells us of a time when the mother and brothers of Jesus came to him. 'Someone told him, "Your mother and brothers are standing outside, wanting to see you." He replied, "My mother and brothers are those who hear God's word and put it into practice"' (Luke 8:21). In other words, the biological bond of motherhood is less important than the responsibility of discipleship.

The same point seems to be made in Luke 11:27–8: 'As Jesus was saying these things, a woman in the crowd called out, "Blessed is the mother who gave you birth and nursed you." He replied, "Blessed rather are those who hear the word of God and obey it."' Mary is not so much blessed among women for the fruit of her womb (Luke 1:42) as for her obedience to the Lord's will for her life: 'Blessed is she who has believed that what the Lord has said to her will be accomplished!' (Luke 1:45). And so it is for all mothers who are heirs of the Kingdom.

Somewhat more than I do

A Christian woman now has many options open to her. For some, that is more of a burden than an opportunity, but all women, as all men, are different. There may be some women involved in the Lord's work who ought to be spending more time with their children, and others who never look beyond their family, or who hang on to their children when they should have let go and moved on. Different mothers will have different views about work outside the home and about combining motherhood with ministry. But even for those who choose for a time to make their central focus their children, it is possible that what may seem a difficult time of life can also be a preparation and rehearsal for wider ministry to follow.

One might think that an emphasis on women's domestic role would lead to a closing of other options for them. That is partially true. The Reformation, and the Puritans in England and America, elevated women as wives and mothers, at the same time denying them any public ministry on the grounds of scriptural prohibition.

But it seems from the history of the later eighteenth century that the opposite is also true. According to one historian, 'the evolving recognition of mothers as the primary spiritual nurturers of children and the idealization of the hearth eventually provided the rationale for women's new public role'.[22] Women were seen as the guardians of religion. It was even claimed that women were by nature more religious than men. This had interesting implications when it came to mission.

As we have seen, the first missionaries of the modern missionary movement were all men. Then their wives began to play an active role, domestic duties permitting. But men and women alike soon began to see the potential for missionary work among women and children. This could best be done by women, hence the field opening up to single women missionaries. Mission to women was arguably even more important than work with men, if women were the keepers of a community's values, including spiritual ones. If this were the case, a whole culture would be more effectively reached through the conversion of women than through the conversion of men. In the USA it was partly this reasoning which resulted in the start of the women's missionary movement.

But this sort of thinking had its disadvantages, for women as well as for men. It reinforced the stereotypes of women's nature. It contradicted the ideas of other women who maintained that women could do the same things as men, that they could take their place alongside men in the 'public' world. And the idea that women are more religious may have contributed to the association of the Church with women which continues to hinder the mission of the Church to this day.

But the possibility that what mothers did in the home might

spill over outside it has also had more far-reaching and healthy results. One important example of such a mother is Susanna Wesley.

To save the souls of their children

Susanna Wesley (1669–1742), the mother of John and Charles, was brought up in a nonconformist household, by parents who gave her an excellent education which included biblical and classical languages. At the age of twelve she converted to the Church of England, and she later married Samuel Wesley, an Anglican minister.

She bore nineteen children, of whom nine lived to adulthood. She took the task of bringing them up very seriously, teaching them herself from the age of five. They learned to say the Lord's Prayer as soon as they could speak, and learned passages of Scripture as soon as they were able. They were brought up according to her own 'method', which included half an hour a week with each of them, talking on spiritual matters. The words in which she describes her commitment make strange but challenging reading today:

> No-one can, without renouncing the world, in the most literal sense, observe my method; and there are few, if any, that would devote above twenty years of the prime of life in hopes to save the souls of their children, which they think may be saved without so much ado; for that was my principal intention, however unskillfully and unsuccessfully managed.[23]

Her ministry seems to have begun when her husband was called away to Parliament during the winters of 1710–12. As she considered her responsibilities,

> At last it came into my mind, though I am not a man, nor a minister of the gospel, and so cannot be engaged in such a worthy employment as they were, yet ... I might do somewhat more than I do ... I might pray more for *the*

> *people*, and speak with more warmth to those with whom I
> have an opportunity of conversing. However, I resolved to
> begin with my own children.[24]

Her home school began to extend to the children in her neighbourhood. Then, it seems, her reputation began to spread, and
others came. Evening prayers for the family became religious
services. 'Other people's coming and joining with us was merely
accidental. One lad told his parents: They first desired to be
admitted; then others that heard of it, begged leave also: So our
company increased to about thirty; and it seldom exceeded forty
last winter.'[25] As people sought her spiritual advice, she began to
teach them, and her gatherings, to listen to her reading 'awakening sermons', grew to two hundred, with others turned away.

Susanna had doubts about what it was proper for women to
do, whether it was right to offer the prayers, for example, but at
the same time, it seems, she was impelled to preach the gospel to
those who came to her. Yet she did not neglect her own children.
When they were grown up she continued to support them, and
her letters to her sons reveal her own theological awareness and
her desire to continue helping them in their spiritual growth,
correcting and advising where necessary.

Susanna Wesley's capabilities, her sense of inner calling and
the fruit of her work no doubt helped to convince John of the
appropriateness of women preaching the gospel. He had seen his
own mother in action as a 'preacher of righteousness', and seen
the results in people's lives. And no doubt, if the age had allowed
more freedom, her schooling of her own family in the ways of
God would have developed into a public ministry of evangelism.

Beforehand with the devil

Catherine Booth is the best-known example of one who combined
the upbringing of her children with a public ministry. She preached
publicly a few months after her second daughter was born, so
her two ministries of family and public evangelism developed
together, and she wrote that once she had started preaching she
felt more at home on the platform than in the kitchen.

But public ministry did not stop her from paying a great deal of attention to the upbringing of her children. As her preaching aimed at seeing adults saved so getting her children 'saved' was her first priority at home. Another mother apparently asked her how she had managed to get her children converted so early. She responded: '*I have been beforehand with the devil.* I have not allowed my children to become pre-occupied with the things of the world before I have got the seed of the Kingdom well in.'[26]

Having seen her children come to faith, Catherine trained them for ministry. They all served in the Salvation Army. Words spoken on the marriage of her daughter Katie sum up her commitment to her two ministries, and the connections between the two:

> Mothers will understand . . . a side of life to which my child is yet a stranger. Having experienced the weight of public work for twenty-six years, also the weight of a large family continually hanging on my heart, having striven very hard to fulfil the obligation on both sides, and having realised what a very hard struggle it has been, the mother's heart in me has shrunk in some measure from offering her up to the same kind of warfare . . . The consecration which I made on the morning of her birth, and consummated on the day that I gave her first to public work, I have finished this morning in laying her again on this altar.[27]

Churches need to help parents learn how to evangelise their children. Those not brought up as Christians will have no experience themselves, and even for those who were, society has changed so much that old methods will not necessarily work today. Children need lively Sunday Schools that they want to belong to, and which provide a Christian peer group, and services in which they are welcome. Parents need resources for helping children at home: Bible stories to tell, books and videos. They need ideas on how to pray and worship as a family, to explain what is going on at church, and to find spiritual connections in everyday experience.

Some parents today assume that even children brought up in Christian homes will rebel. But should it not be true that each generation of believers is stronger than their parents? Christian parents should train their children to know God, first so that they come to know God personally and second so that they can grow up to reach their generation for Jesus.

Better together

It will not do to separate out the roles of men and women in evangelism. Women can preach, men can evangelise their children. In times past, the only role allowed to many women was that of influence over their children. So it is not surprising that we have more stories of women passing on the faith.

But it is here that the attempt to make rigid role distinctions breaks down most obviously. If women are unfitted to teach, why should they be entrusted with the teaching of the most vulnerable and malleable audiences, young children, but not fitted to teach those who are older and can evaluate the teaching for themselves? It must be because there is a very deep, cross-cultural assumption that women stay in the home while men go out of it. One is also tempted to wonder whether such prohibitions have been invoked, subconsciously at least, because ministry in the public sphere seems easier than ministry in the home, or because men seek to justify their absence from the family.

Our society is beginning to recognise the need for hands-on fathering and the damage caused by absent fathers: absence through irresponsible abandonment or through irresponsible devotion to 'more important' matters. Some families have only one parent, who must bear the full responsibility, and God will give special help to a parent in that position. Family and church members may help share the load. But where children have two Christian parents perhaps it is not too late to return to a more scriptural way: joint parenting and the recognition that at Pentecost God poured out his gifts on men and women alike. Then women and men will be free to be a partnership inside and beyond the home, enabling each other to follow God's calling, whatever that may be.

For reflection/action

1. What support and help does your church give to women with unbelieving husbands? If you are one of those women, do you have an opportunity to talk about your needs?
2. How might the experience of women in reaching men be used to help your church in its outreach to men?
3. What could your church do to help parents pass on their faith to their children?

6

Women and gender difference

Little girls are allowed to dream wild impossible dreams. Mine were about Joan of Arc and Boudicea and other women warriors, of being chosen by God to carry out superhuman tasks, which I achieved with superhuman strength. It was all a far cry from marriage to a responsible God-fearing man who would protect me from life's dangers, and supply me with a nice house and a brace of children. At some point little girls are intended to stop dreaming and make the transition into the real world where dwells the Ideal Woman, who turns eventually into a beautiful Wife and Mother, achieving Ultimate Contentment.[1]

Dear God,
Are boys better than girls. I know you are one but try to be fair.
      Sylvia.

There is no doubt about it. There is a bias in the world towards boys. Boys seem to get a better deal in life. So many girls and women wonder, with the writer of this often-quoted letter from *Children's Letters to God* by Eric Marshall and Stuart Hample, (Fount, 1977), whether God thinks boys are better than girls.

And boys, it seems, often assume that 'different' equals 'better'. Anne Atkins tells of a conversation with a friend who was explaining that he preferred an all-male Bible study group as a teenager.

'We wouldn't have discussed our problems in front of girls,'
he said.
'Why not?' I asked him.
'We wouldn't have admitted our failings.'
'But *why*?'
'Why?' He pondered for a moment. 'They're beneath us.
They're lesser,' he said simply. 'That's what we really felt.'[2]

Such feelings are rarely articulated as clearly as this, but they are
buried beneath many of the assumptions we inherit. So are boys
not only different from girls, but better than girls? Is that also
part of God's intention?

It will already be apparent that the issue of gender difference
is crucial to this exploration of the role of women in evangelism.
As the previous chapter suggested, one role for women in
evangelism has always been that of evangelising their husbands
and children. Some Christians have argued that this is all they
should be doing, because it is their 'sphere' – women and men
being different by design and destined for different roles in society
and in the Church. In the nineteenth century this role was en-
larged, for middle-class women, to philanthropy, but only as an
extension of their maternal and domestic instincts outside the
home. Women were different from men.

At the same time, other women were claiming a place for
themselves alongside men in the public world of preaching. In
overseas mission they were doing pioneer work and planting
churches as well as teaching and filling more traditional women's
roles. They were also beginning to start missionary societies, and
to write on the subject of mission, as we will see in a later chapter.
If women and men could do the same things, perhaps women
and men are not so different after all. Whether they are different,
and what implications any differences may have, is the subject of
this chapter.

First, are there differences, beyond the obvious biological
ones? And second, if there are, what implications should that
conclusion have? Should we try to minimise the differences? Or
should we apportion jobs and roles in society and in the Church
according to sex? Is the job of evangelist a 'male' one, or can

women do it too? Many of the arguments and debates around the role of women in the other chapters of this book depend on the kind of answers we give to these questions.

Some Christians argue that men and women are naturally different, and that these differences are God-given. So when it comes to evangelism, we should not attempt to blur those distinctions by letting men have jobs or roles which were intended for women, or vice versa. A recent book, *Women in the Church: A Fresh Analysis of 1 Timothy 2: 9–15*, begins with the following words:

> The battles over gender issues in the church in recent years are signs of a world that has strayed from God. Whatever God's design was for a humanity made up of men and women, it was not one of division and strife, but one of beauty and harmony. Since God exists, and since he made human beings male and female, these distinct genders must have been created for a purpose, and we should be able to understand this purpose.[3]

Thus, the Church will function as God intended when men and women fulfil the roles God intended for them.

Others will assert the existence of such differences too. But they will argue that differences should not be used in a rigid way to determine what men or women do. Others again would contend that there are really no ways in which men and women are fundamentally different. There is no evidence that God made men and women different, though they are complementary. When Christ came he broke down the barriers of division between men and women which were caused by the fall. The battle between the sexes has continued because human sinfulness has meant the continued domination of women by men and the continued manipulation and deviousness of women. The more biblical equality we see, the more the harmony intended by God will be restored. Roles and responsibilities in the Church should be allocated according to gifting, not according to gender.

The book by Gilbert Bilezikian, *Beyond Sex Roles*, is one influential book which takes this view. Bilezikian argues that we are called to be set free from bondage to the sex-role stereotypes which come from our socialization: 'Nowhere does the Scripture command us to develop our sex-role awareness as males or females.'[4] Rather, we are called to proclaim our sameness in Christ, a sameness which yet allows for complementarity.

Men are from Mars, Women are from Venus

Some people have no doubt, when they look at men and women, that they can see many differences between the sexes. Men are strong, aggressive, they win arguments, they exert power, they strive for independence and avoid vulnerability. Women share, create connectedness, minimise difference, find it easier to be vulnerable and more difficult to be independent. Boys will be boys, whether it is little ones getting dirty and being rude, or older ones failing to control their sexual drive or failing to understand women. Women – oh, what do you expect from a *woman*?

We all know there are exceptions. But those stereotypes are very persistent. Girls brought up in a non-sexist way still want dolls to play with. For all the women who want to move on in their careers or areas of service, there are many others who seem lacking in that kind of ambition.

What do we make of it all? We know the stereotypes are there. But do all people across the world have the same ideas? Have they always thought men and women are different? And have they always thought that those differences should dictate what men and women should do with their lives?

The discussion about difference is not as new as we might think. It would be easy to assume that this debate is another manifestation of the recent movement for women's liberation. It is true that in the past the relatively separate spheres and roles of men and women in our culture were generally accepted. But there have been dissenting voices. And such voices were usually raised by women who were prevented from using their talents to the full, in society or in the Church, or by men who saw that women were capable of far more than they were allowed to do.

No such great difference?

The subject of women's nature was raised at the time of the Renaissance. Agrippa von Nettesheim wrote a treatise in the early sixteenth century, 'On the Nobility and Excellence of Women'. He observes that Eve was God's last and hence greatest creation, and argues for the equality of women:

> The only difference between man and woman is physical . . . In everything else they are the same. Woman does not have a soul of a different sex from that which animates man. Both received a soul which is absolutely the same and of an equal condition. Women and men were equally endowed with the gifts of spirit, reason, and the use of words; they were created for the same end, and the sexual difference between them will not confer a different destiny . . .'[5]

It is a remarkably forward-thinking argument.

One of the few voices of women of this era which has been preserved for us is that of Mary Ward (1585–1645), who founded the Institute of the Blessed Virgin Mary, the first unenclosed order for active apostolic women religious in the Roman Catholic Church. But her vision to give English girls a Catholic education did not go down too well in the predominantly Protestant climate of the seventeenth century, and she moved to the continent, there establishing convents and schools for women.

'There is no such great difference between men and women, yet women, may they not do great matters also?' she wrote. 'And I hope in God it will be seen that women in time to come will do much.'[6] She was accused of 'wishing women to rival men in the ministry'. If, as she believed, they are not so different from men, why should they not? But while she must have raised the sights of those women she educated, there was little chance in those days that they would have such opportunities.

In the next century, Dorothea Christiana Erxleben, born in 1715, was the first woman to gain a medical degree at the university of Halle. Erxleben did not believe, as some thought, that women lacked the intellect necessary for study. What held them back was lack of schooling. She published a book on the subject of women studying, dealing with the prejudices and self-imposed obstacles which prevented them.[7] Such ideas were remarkable. But there has never been a shortage of remarkable women who have proved exceptions to all the rules.

Later in the century, in 1792, Mary Wollstonecraft published *A Vindication of the Rights of Women*. Arguing for universal co-education and women's right to work in the trades and professions, she asserted that femininity is a social construct. Women are born equal but are taught to be subordinate, weak and feather-headed. 'How many women thus waste life away, who might have practised as physician, regulated a farm, managed a shop, and stood erect supported by their own industry, instead of hanging their heads?'[8]

In the nineteeth century, the debate became more common-place. Should women be educated? Should they have the vote? Could they vote for parochial and other church councils? All these milestones in history aroused passionate advocates and detractors. Those arguing for the fuller participation of women in society argued on the basis of justice and equality.

The growing 'equal rights' position contrasted with the dominant view of women in Victorian times. As I have already suggested, this view of women's essentially different nature opened up new avenues of service for women. If women were these superior beings, with noble spiritual and maternal qualities, should they not use these attributes for the betterment of society?

It was the latter view which was invoked by many of the middle-class women who became involved in philanthropic and evangelistic activities. Catherine Booth, for example, thought that women as well as men were needed in ministry partly because what they brought to it was different. According to Booth, 'God has given to woman a graceful form and attitude, winning manners, persuasive speech and, above all, a finely-toned emotional nature; all of which appear to us eminent natural qualifications for public speaking.'[9] Women are different, she argued, but none-theless called to ministry and nonetheless equipped for it.

Maude Royden (1876–1956), on the other hand, a campaigner for women's suffrage and a noted preacher, took Jesus' attitude to women as evidence that there are no 'male' and 'female' spheres:

> It is part of the amazing originality of Christ that there is to
> be found in his teaching no word whatever which suggests
> a difference in the spiritual ideals, the spheres, or the
> potentialities of men and women. There is no classification
> of virtues assigning some to men . . . and others to women.
> There is no limitation of sphere . . . If the words of Christ
> were isolated from their context and read to one to whom
> the gospels were not familiar it would be absolutely impos-
> sible for him to guess whether any special word or phrase
> was addressed to a woman or to a man.[10]

Some men also argued against the 'natural' differences between
men and women. John Stuart Mill, in *The Subjection of Women*
(1869), argued that men and women are fundamentally equal. It
was the enormous differences in their upbringing and education
which accounted for their seemingly different abilities. 'What is
now called the nature of woman,' he wrote, 'is an entirely arti-
ficial thing.'[11] The revolutionary socialist Engels argued from
history that women's social status had not always been inferior,
but was due to changes in the way society and the family
operated.

Some women found that experience taught them that they
could do the same things as men. Sojourner Truth (1797–1883),
born a slave, and later an evangelist with the African Zion
Church, could silence anyone who said that women were, for
example, too frail for public life. 'I could work as well as a man
and bear the lash as well – and ain't I a woman?' The stories of
women in the nineteenth-century missionary movement show
that women, given the opportunity, could withstand the difficulties of life in remote places, and could be pioneers, Bible
teachers, preachers and leaders, things which some people
thought women were not able to do.

Debate continued. In the Second World War, millions of British
and American women went to work for the first time, as men
went off to fight. Women working in factories or on the land
discovered that there were plenty of 'men's jobs' that women
could also do. But when the men came home, they were expected
to go back to 'women's work' in the home.

It eventually became clear that equal education alone was not the key to making men and women equal. While there were increasing exceptions, the differences seemed well entrenched. And as the debate became more heated with the beginnings of modern feminism in the 1970s, those on both sides turned to science for an explanation. A number of scientific tests were conducted in the 1960s and 70s, and research into psychological differences was joined by brain and hormone research, in attempts to find a biological source of sex-role differences.

Sex and gender

The concept of sex roles is a modern sociological tool for describing the way men and women fulfil appropriate functions in society. Feminism considered sex role not to be linked to biology but to be assigned by society, hence a commonly held distinction between 'sex' to describe a person's biology, and 'gender' to relate to society's roles and expectations. In the early 1970s, feminists tried to eliminate sex roles, but soon discovered that such roles were not so easy to change or abandon. Hence there has been an ongoing dialogue among feminists between those who would see the whole concept of difference to be oppressive, and those who have tried to re-claim so-called 'feminine' characteristics such as emotionalism, vulnerability and intuition, and instead have them more highly valued by society.

The debate between 'essentialism', the idea that there are basic irrefutable differences which are inherent, and 'relativism', which sees differences as a matter of upbringing and culture (nature vs nurture), continues. Argument has become more fierce in recent years in the Church, in relation to the suitability of women for leadership, teaching and priestly roles. Some of the debate has had to do with tradition and history, or the Bible, but it has also related to what women and men are 'naturally' suited to do. Those who have invoked particular Scripture passages, as indicated in the Appendix, have also, sometimes, invoked the idea of natural, God-given difference. They have set out the case that men and women were created and intended for different spheres, roles and responsibilities.

In the next few pages I will attempt to outline such arguments, and those of Christians who disagree with them. Ultimately, as Christians, we seek to be true to Scripture. So we need to take seriously an argument which claims that it was never God's intention that women should have the same roles in the Church as men. If this is true, many of those who have done so, and do so today, are being disobedient to God. If, on the other hand, such differences as there may be were not intended to predetermine the role of men and women, then women are free, and should be encouraged, to be evangelists, teachers, leaders or whatever God calls them to be, in his service.

Let me list five arguments which have been put forward in support of the claim of natural God-given difference between men and women.

1. Difference can be traced back in Scripture to the account of creation.
2. Jesus also recognised role distinctions.
3. Differences in role are accounted for by biological difference, in particular in the brain and/or hormones.
4. Similar differences between the roles of men and women can be found in all cultures.
5. Fundamental differences between men and women are obvious.

Different by design

A book published in 1991, *Recovering Biblical Manhood and Womanhood*, edited by John Piper and Wayne Grudem, asserts, as its title suggests, 'biblical' difference. Difference stems from creation. Men and women are fundamentally different:

At the heart of mature masculinity is a sense of benevolent responsibility to lead, provide for and protect women in ways appropriate to a man's differing relationships . . . At the heart of mature femininity is a freeing disposition to affirm, receive and nurture strength and leadership from

worthy men in ways appropriate to a woman's differing
relationships.[12]

These differences were instituted by God at creation, and remain
permanent aspects of human existence. The book argues against
the long-held view that the domination of men by women is a
consequence of the fall.

One of the key texts cited is Genesis 1:27: 'God's naming of
the race "man" whispers male headship.'[13] Then in chapter 2 it is
made plainer. According to Ray Ortlund, God shows man all the
animals to name, and then says, 'I have one last creature for you
to name.'[14] The naming of the animals and of Eve is said to show
the headship of Adam. And Eve, meanwhile, is simply created as
a 'helper'. This shows woman's position in relation to man.
Woman is a helper, not a leader.

A final set of arguments comes from Genesis 3. The fall is a
demonstration of the results of sex-role reversal. Satan knew
where to strike: at Adam's headship. 'Eve usurped Adam's headship and led the way into sin. And Adam, who (it seems) had
stood by passively, allowing the deception to progress without
decisive intervention – Adam, for his part, abandoned his post as
head.'[15] Ortlund asserts that this interpretation is borne out by
the fact that, though Eve took the fruit first, God speaks to Adam
first in verse 9; and that God mentions Adam's sin, his lapse of
headship, in verse 17: 'Because you have listened to the voice of
your wife . . .'

What do we make of this? I would suggest that the reasoning
throughout is faulty. First, too much is claimed for Genesis 1:27.
If anything, this verse is usually interpreted as asserting the
essential equality of men and women. The Hebrew word used is
adam, which is used to mean undifferentiated 'human being' as
well as 'man'. (When man as opposed to woman is meant, the
word *ish* is used.) Hence the 1996 edition of the NIV translates,
instead of 'God created man in his own image', 'God created
human beings in his own image'. The verse goes on, 'male and
female he created them', referring back to *adam*.

Next, chapter 2. What Ortlund says about naming is simply
untrue. When God brings the animals to Adam to name, he does
not bring Eve and ask him to name her. He only brings the

animals. Then he creates woman. There has been a great deal of scholarly debate about whether Adam's 'naming' gives him superiority over Eve. He names the animals before the rib is taken from him to create Eve, so it could be argued that he is still acting as an undifferentiated human being. He calls her 'woman' in 2:23, but he does not name Eve until after the fall, in Genesis 3:20.[16]

The other issue here is about the implications of Eve as a 'helper'. Numerous commentators have sought to demonstrate that the word *ezer* is used elsewhere in the Old Testament of God, and therefore cannot automatically imply an inferior status as the word 'helper' tends to do in English.[17] Nor does the passage anywhere set out a role for Adam as leader. Adam's reaction in verse 23,

This is now bone of my bones
    and flesh of my flesh;
she shall be called 'woman',
    for she was taken out of man

speaks more of sameness than of difference, and the same can be argued for the making of Eve from one of Adam's ribs.

And so to chapter 3. Ortlund tells the reader to mark well what the text says. But he himself does not, in my view, do this. The text does not say anything about Eve 'usurping Adam's headship'. Indeed, the word 'headship' does not appear in the Bible anywhere. Furthermore, there is no way of showing that the mention of male dominance in Genesis 3:16 ('Your desire will be for your husband, and he will rule over you') is anything more than a prediction of how male sinfulness would actually manifest itself after the fall. In other words, the verse is a prediction, not a prescription for post-fall behaviour.[18]

Ortlund indulges in some imaginative reading of the thoughts in the serpent's mind. But there is nothing in the story that indicates why the serpent approached Eve first; we just do not know. The idea that the serpent approached her knowing that she would want to usurp Adam's headship seems to be a remarkably modern interpretation. In truth, the whole idea of headship is an anachronism. There is no reason to separate out the first clause of verse 17, as if 'you listened to your wife' is the sin. Surely the sin is disobedience. The sin is that Adam listened to his wife instead of to God, and 'ate from the tree about which I commanded you, "You must not eat of it" '. In his letters Paul makes no reference to the way in which Adam's sin was letting his wife usurp his headship.[19]

In conclusion I would argue that the case has not been made for pre-fall 'headship' and strict gender roles. The creation account is not concerned with delineating roles, or the forms of ministry that are appropriate to the different sexes. Such evidence as we have, I would argue, points in the opposite direction. Men and women are created equally in the image of God, and equally given the command to be fruitful and multiply, and to have dominion over the rest of creation. It is true that the results of the fall relate in the woman's case to childbearing and in the man's to tilling the soil. But when they were in the garden, it seems that both were looking after it. It will not do to read more into the text than is there. Much is simply left unsaid.[20]

In addition, it might be argued that if difference is embedded in creation, we would expect to find more evidence of differentiation in the Bible than there actually is. It is curious that the Ten Commandments and the New Testament letters, for example, treat men and women together rather than separately. There are no separate ethical instructions for men and women, such as one might expect if men and women are naturally so fundamentally different. Men as well as women (or women as well as men) are told to be gentle, self-controlled, humble and compassionate (e.g. Gal. 5:23; Col. 3:12–14; 1 Pet. 3:8). Scripture does not imply that these things come naturally to one sex but not to the other.

Jesus and women

In another chapter of *Recovering Biblical Manhood and Woman-hood*, James Borland aims to show that Jesus recognised role distinctions for men and women. This is demonstrated by Jesus 'choosing only men to serve as His apostles with their primary tasks of preaching, teaching, and governing'.[21] Women served Jesus in other important capacities, but not these ones. It is argued that it was not for cultural reasons that Jesus chose only men. He could have challenged the status quo if he wanted to. No, it was his intention to choose only men to be leaders, rulers, and to receive special revelation.

The argument assumes that the early Church had no women leaders. This of course depends on how certain verses in Acts and Paul's letters are understood, and how you understand early church history. But is the premise that Jesus intended this all-male leadership true? The Twelve clearly had a special significance, but Borland claims too much for them. First, he says, they were to be with him, to learn and to be trained first hand. But then so too were some women, according to Luke 8:1–3. Jesus encouraged women to learn (Luke 10:39, 42, and John 4:21, for example), and they were expected to recall their lessons (Luke 24:6). Second, apostles were to be the leaders in the early Church. Yet almost from the beginning the designation 'apostle' was used of others, including James, the leader of the church at Jerusalem, Barnabas and Andronicus. Moreover, it also appears to include women, such as Junia (Rom. 16:7). Lastly, special rulership is committed to the apostles (Matt. 19:28). But whether this special privilege in heaven has any relation to earthly leadership is another matter. Jesus' main emphasis on the character of earthly leaders is servanthood (John 13; Mark 10:42–4), not rulership.

Borland also argues that Christ has promised the apostles special revelation (John 16:13–15) and a special teaching ministry of the Holy Spirit (John 14:26), which women could not have. These assurances of the work of the Holy Spirit do, of course, apply first to those present with Jesus at the Last Supper (not necessarily just the Twelve but possibly including women as well as other male disciples). But the emphasis of the verses is not so much on an exclusive teaching ministry, as that the Spirit will assist these apostles in a special way. If Jesus meant to be so exclusive in these verses, what of Paul and other non-primary 'apostles' who wrote letters or who taught? And if by 'you', in chapters 13 to 17 of John's Gospel, Jesus meant only the Twelve, then those chapters do not apply to anyone else, and have no relevance today.

Initially, those who were with Jesus and enlightened by the

Spirit at Pentecost would be considered the primary teachers. But once this first period was past, the situation would change. Men who were not witnesses are not necessarily more qualified to teach than are women; the question is whether they faithfully teach what has been handed down to them.

Thus I would argue that Borland's argument does not stand up in the way he claims it does. He ignores many other aspects of Jesus' ministry and attitude to women. He ignores Jesus himself, who challenges male–female role distinctions on a number of occasions. Jesus cooked a meal: didn't he worry about doing a woman's job? Jesus wept: can a real man cry? Jesus told Martha there were more important things than housework: wasn't that her job? Jesus discussed theology with a woman: can women think? Borland's claim that Jesus chose 'only men to write the New Testament Scriptures' is simply untrue. Jesus did not 'choose' anyone. Neither is it clear that Jesus 'affirmed a clear and abiding role distinction between men and women and an abiding leadership role for men'.[22] Jesus left no words to indicate the sex of those who might, two thousand or even twenty years hence, be leaders in his Church.

There is no verse in Scripture to justify the idea that males and females have distinct and immutable spiritual responsibilities based on sex. Male leadership is never made a principle in Scripture, and there are numbers of exceptions to it, from Deborah in the Old Testament to Phoebe in the New.

Sex and science

What does science tell us about differences between men and women? Do differences in biology account for differences in behaviour? Are men innately aggressive (and therefore supposedly more fitted for leadership!) because their brains or their hormones are different?

Sheila Stephen, in a chapter in *Men, Women and Authority*, writes: 'Many secular researchers are publishing data that does not support a unisex model.'[23] She gives as one example the work of Doreen Kimura on neural and hormonal differences in intellectual functioning: 'Women and men differ not only in physical attributes and reproductive function but also in the way they solve intellectual problems.' According to Stephen, Kimura's research on brain symmetry and brain organisation shows that men's and women's brains are organised on different lines from early in life.

Research such as this is often cited to support the view that there are real differences in emotional response between men and women. And these differences are seen in women's greater ability to express emotion in words, their greater innate sensitivity to personal and moral aspects, and so on. These differences in turn predispose women and men to the different roles and responsibilities that God has laid down for them.

Gregg Johnson, writing in *Recovering Biblical Manhood and Womanhood*, cites studies in biology and psychology. In some research, for example, males score higher in levels of aggressiveness, dominance, self-confidence and activity level. Females score higher in verbal ability, compliance, nurturance and empathy scales. He notes the caution needed in relation to studies based on animal brains, but asserts that the data is in favour of 'a divinely ordained and biologically rooted division of gifts between the sexes'.[24]

He finishes by saying, 'We should not conclude automatically that because men and women may have different gifts, traditional roles are the only way these may be expressed. Yet it seems very significant that these different gifts correspond very well to the different roles given to men and women in Scripture.'[25] Men and women need to accept their God-given gifts and not seek to become what they are not. This line of reasoning underlies the argument that God did not intend women to be evangelists, pioneers or leaders in the Church because those jobs are for men.

There has indeed been a great deal of research from which some scientists have concluded that there is biological evidence of difference which is linked to behaviour. And this, it is maintained, accounts for the differences between men and women which are popularly identified. However, there are also a number of reasons, from both a scientific and a Christian point of view, for viewing these conclusions with caution.

First, as these authors allow, other scientific study comes to the conclusion that there are no such differences related to biology. The psychologist and author Mary Stewart van Leeuwen claims that both psychologically and biologically men and women are more alike than they are different. 'Men and women are not biologically different enough (or simple enough) to justify the explanation of behavioural differences on the basis of biology alone.'[26]

There is often much less difference than is popularly supposed. One discussion of cognitive tests (one way of testing such differences) cites textbooks which talk about 'the well-known difference in spatial ability' between men and women, but notes that according to an extensive survey of such tests, 60 per cent indicated no sex differences and of the rest only 35 per cent showed males to be superior on average, while 5 per cent showed females to be superior. It also points out that such tests may be biased by the different education received; people trained in technical drawing are more likely to do better in tests for spatial ability.[27]

Even if research seems to suggest some difference, there is often more than one way of interpreting the results, or more than one way of accounting for the difference. 'If we are to explain or justify separate spheres for men or women . . . we must look more to economic, social, and world-based explanations.'[28]

Attitudes towards men and women affect how a child is treated from birth, so it is impossible to separate off nature from nurture. It is also known that nurture can affect nature; attitudes towards the menopause, for example, can affect the physical experience. Van Leeuwen examines the evidence concerning genes, hormones and brain structure. In all these, she concludes, nature contributes less to male and female behaviour than is popularly supposed. Male domination, and the related division of men and women into separate spheres in all cultures, is, she argues, traceable to the fall, and there are various different anthropological explanations which help to account for the situation we see.

She also points out some of the dangers, for a Christian, of supporting the 'essentialist' theory of natural, God-given difference. To hold someone responsible, she reminds us, 'we have to be able to say, "You could have done otherwise, even given your past and present biology and your past and present social circumstances" '.[29] We are all aware of the arguments which have been used to justify male violence and sexual exploitation: 'men can't help it, it's part of how they're made'. If, as society usually says, they must 'help it', then how much of that behaviour is really attributable to biology?

Related to this, there are some serious criticisms to be levelled at arguments made in popular books like *Brainsex*, which is cited approvingly in *Men, Women and Authority*. *Brainsex* brings together a mass of scientific research which comes to the conclusion that 'the brain is sexed in the womb'. Brains are male or female according to relative amounts of various hormones. It concludes that although we should try to tame such things as male aggression, ultimately, 'we are still subject to the biological imperatives of our bodies'.[30] But Christians believe we have free will, to follow either God or our fallen human nature, and in Christ we take on a new nature.

The argument in *Brainsex* takes into account people who do not fit the stereotypes of male and female behaviour. It considers that this is the result of their mothers being treated with some hormone during pregnancy which upset the usual balance. The book gives examples of girls who are tomboys, show no interest in dolls or in babysitting, and have no interest in motherhood when they grow up. Could it be that Boudicca was dosed in the womb with male hormones? the authors ask. Or Joan of Arc, or Florence Nightingale?[31]

But experience suggests to me at least that it's just not like this. I know two sisters, one of whom showed no interest in dolls or babysitting yet has grown up to be an excellent mother, and the other who played with dolls, loved babysitting, yet has no children and displays a number of what might be termed male characteristics of behaviour. Their mother was not in either case under the influence of hormone-related drugs. The evidence cited in the book does not fit the reality of experience. Many women missionaries and evangelists would fit the description of 'masculine behaviour', but it is ridiculous to believe that this is attributable to the presence of male hormones.

Further, when the supposedly masculine and feminine characteristics are examined individually, we could take issue with many of them. Take, for example, intuition. Is this really natural and biological? Many women have a particular way of processing the information they receive, which is labelled as 'intuition' by those who are less well able to do it. It is seen as a gender-appropriate way to describe a mode of behaviour which seems non-rational and therefore non-male. But in fact it is partly a result of women's exclusion from public spheres and relegation to the margins where they are observers. People who are very shy, and who find it hard to speak, may develop a finer intuition to compensate. Men can be intuitive too.

Some have also argued that intuition is associated with the way women experience God. Women have traditionally been associated with the mystical and non-rational, men with the rational. But does a woman experience God differently from the way a man experiences God? Is intuition a unique constituent of women's consciousness? This is the question considered by philosophy professor Elisabeth Morelli.[32] She asserts that 'intuition' is a term for 'a set of conscious and intentional operations that is neither distinctly intuitive nor specifically female'.[33]

She concludes that if women do have a peculiar mode of access to God, then either woman is not quite human or there must be two distinct human natures. If men and women are so fundamentally different, there would be a good case for saying that, as some radical feminist theologians have said, women cannot be redeemed by a male saviour. And that is something that the supporters of natural difference, among others, would certainly deny.[34]

The persistence of patriarchy

Some Christians assert that what is often called 'patriarchy' is common to all societies, and that men and women have particular roles in all cultures. Therefore this must be the way God meant it to be. But while patriarchy is indeed very persistent, there is more than one way of accounting for it. There are also significant differences in behaviour in different cultures. And just because patriarchy is persistent does not mean that it is inevitable.

Various theories have been put forward to account for the universal lower social status of women. If the natural/biblical argument is unconvincing, there are alternative explanations, and Mary Stewart van Leeuwen examines some of these.[35] One possibility is that women are seen as closer to nature than men are, and men as more involved with culture. The public world has more respect than the domestic, and men are associated with the public world and women with the domestic, so men's activities are valued more highly than women's. There may be some truth in this. Then there is the theory that it is because men are physically stronger and more mobile, and used to hunt to supply food, and so gained higher status as food suppliers. In most societies, though, the majority of food is gathered locally by women, not hunted by men.

She proposes a third theory. This is the physical and psychological absence of fathers from the process of child-rearing. Children of both sexes usually see far more of their mother than their father. A boy then struggles to learn masculinity, but a role model is unavailable. He is forced to look to stereotypes rather than a real man, and, in order to make himself feel more secure, finds his identity as a man by rejecting everything which is associated with a woman. If this analysis is correct, it is not surprising that women's desire for equality is seen as a threat by men. If women are equally intelligent, enterprising and able, what is left for men?

Thus, she argues, men have sometimes found their security in being other than women, which has led them to devalue women. But if they are able to find their security fully in God, then they may be able to participate in the breaking down of male dominance and rigid role casting which hinders them as much as it hinders women. And this will be done by integrating men into the domestic sphere as well as allowing women to participate in the public world. To some extent that is beginning. It is no longer unusual to see men out pushing prams, or changing nappies, or washing up, or doing the shopping or cooking. Some men are finding it as liberating to spend time with their children, or cooking meals, as women are to be able to do other things. So perhaps patriarchy is not so inevitable, after all.

If, to return to Genesis, patriarchy is one of the consequences of the fall, one would *expect* it to be widespread. It is part of the 'curse', one of the many distortions in the created pattern. But

Christ came to reverse the effects of the fall, and to the extent that we see the kingdom evident among us already, we should expect to see equality between men and women, rather than male domination.

The naturally nicer sex

Finally, defenders of natural difference assert that difference is natural because it is obvious: you only have to look at men and women, boys and girls, or groups of them, to see that they are different. I have already referred to some of the so-called masculine and feminine traits. Women are said to be 'responsive, compassionate, empathetic, enduring, gentle, warm, tender, hospitable, obedient, trusting, sweet, delicate, quiet ... and weak, passive, slavish, weepy, vain, chatterbox, moody, petty, catty, nagging, spiteful.'[36] For each sex there are positive and negative traits. The positive ones are how God made us, and the negative ones are distortions caused by sin.

But if most of us would come up with a list similar to this, most of us would also think immediately of many exceptions. Sometimes I enjoy upsetting people's expectations because I do not conform to some of the stereotypes of women. At other times I find it painful. Women are supposed to be good at listening, while men frequently interrupt conversations. A couple who are friends of mine are the exact opposite. He never interrupts, but is a good listener, while she interrupts all the time. If there are many exceptions to the stereotypes, does that not disprove, rather than prove, the rule?

A recent Gallup Poll on the roles of men and women in society shows that many of the supposed universal stereotypes of male and female behaviour do not apply quite so universally. The poll was conducted in twenty-two countries in 1995. If differences are innate and clear, some of these findings seem surprising. In nearly half the countries surveyed, people thought men and women to be basically similar, and only just less than the other half thought them to be different. 'Only a minority of most nation's populations believe that men and women are basically different and that those differences existed at birth.'

Furthermore, 'large numbers of women in most countries feel resentful about the expectations that society places on them *as a woman*'. Large numbers of men also feel resentful about sex-role expectations. One might want to attribute the numbers of women to the consciousness-raising of the feminist movement. But the figures for men might suggest a challenge to the idea that these roles are innate, 'natural'.

Perceptions about various character traits were surveyed. In all countries, more people said that 'emotional', 'talkative' and 'affectionate' apply to women more than to men. But when it came to ten 'male' traits, none was ascribed unanimously as 'male'. Both men and women in Iceland, for example, ascribed 'aggressive' more to women than to men. In fourteen of the countries, at least 40 per cent of the public said that 'ambitious' applied equally to both sexes, 'implying that the consensus about men being more ambitious than women is hardly solid'. 'Courageous' also elicited a varied response, from being a male trait to being claimed by a majority of each sex for itself.

So much for male and female traits being obvious, fixed and biological. These figures suggest such great areas of 'exception' that the case that they are natural and God-given seems to me to be untenable. Interestingly, most people believed that their country would be better governed if more women held political office. Might this also relate to women in leadership in the Church?

If all was fixed biology, we would not expect to find changes over time. But we do. Society is constantly discovering that women can do things that a few years ago women 'couldn't do'. Women now run marathons. Recently, in Britain we hear that football, that very 'male' sport, is now so popular with women that a women's soccer magazine has been launched. Women playing football presumably play to win as much as men do. And no doubt we will continue to witness such changes.

Furthermore, there are uncomfortable implications about making certain characteristics the possession of men or women. If it is characteristic of women to be 'obedient', for example, where does that leave men? As Anne Borrowdale has argued, to assert that some desirable characteristics are 'natural' to women is first to let men off the hook and second to deny the effort which women make to be obedient or hospitable or gentle or nice.[37] Again, if all these traits have their roots in biology, where is our God-given freedom of choice? Next, will we hear that there is a gene which determines our response to the gospel? That might make the task of evangelism a whole lot easier!

One book which is commonly cited is that by Deborah Tannen, *You Just Don't Understand*.[38] She analyses the differences between the ways men and women tend to communicate. Men interact with 'report' talk, women with 'rapport', for example. Women find it difficult to make themselves understood by men and vice versa because they communicate differently. But it will be interesting to see what happens as time passes. My guess is that more and more women will find it easier to operate in a 'man's world', and as it becomes less of a man's world, patterns of communicating will also change.

I would want to see such patterns of mis-communication as part of the results of the fall. Men and women fail to understand each other because we still live in a world where the 'battle of the sexes' has not yet been replaced by gender reconciliation. In my church recently some children were relaying to the rest of the church what they had learned in Sunday School. They had been thinking about Solomon's wisdom. It turned out that they had been listening to the story told in 1 Kings 3: 16–28 of the two women and their babies. It set me thinking. The story is the ultimate test of kingly wisdom. And Solomon is able to bring true speech from the real mother of the live baby, when one might expect such women both to lie. But does this story also tell us something about God-given understanding? Solomon's wisdom lies in his ability to understand a mother's love, how she would feel, how she would speak. Perhaps he gives us a picture of how true godly insight transcends gender difference.

Split image

Clearly there is much more which could be said around these arguments, and there are many loose ends and unanswered questions. If 'natural' differences are minimal, what is masculinity and femininity? Men and women are not clones of each other.

We will probably always see men being more physically aggressive than women, women more relational than men. Society seems to have an important role in explaining differences between men and women, but that is not the whole answer. We are more than the product of our environment.

And there is more than one way of working out the implications. If we believe in God-given differences, do we maintain them or minimise them? If there are no such things, then why are they so persistent? Is it because polarisation is founded on insecurity, and men, who tend to have the power, want to maintain some areas of life for themselves?

An alternative way is to look at the evidence we see in human behaviour. As I have suggested, there are many cultural variations which cut across supposed biological arguments. There seem to me to be so many exceptions to any kind of generalisation about innate gender difference that it ceases to have meaning. On the other hand, it is possible to make some generalisations about men and women because there do seem to be some distinctions between how men and women behave or react in particular situations. For example, some recent research suggests that gender plays an important role in conversion.[39] Carol Gilligan's research on moral development suggests that men and women often have different modes of thought. But she notes that these differences arise in a social context where social status and power combine with biology to shape the experiences of men and women.[40]

Elaine Storkey has suggested a way out of this impasse. We should stop worrying about whether there are essential differences or not and consider men and women relationally. At creation, Adam stressed his one-ness with Eve, not his difference from her. Each sex needs and complements the other.

'In rejecting the essentialist and relativist explanations of gender differences, the Christian understanding of creation affirms that the difference between men and women is *total*, but paradoxically that the difference is indefinable. It claims that the differences can only be understood at all in the context of unity.'[41] Men and women are like the two halves of a coin. They seem different, but they have no meaning or existence without the other.

In the context of this book, that means that men and women need each other, need to work together in evangelism, but there are no rules about who does what. There is something incomplete about a team of women, or a team of men, working alone without the other sex. An Adam needed an Eve. The two were to be complementary. God did not intend groups of men and groups of women to separate themselves off – even though in historical terms this has sometimes been inevitable. God's intention was for men and women together, bringing their individual skills, experiences and perspectives, to carry out the task of taking the good news to the world.

But one sentence from *Brainsex* is pertinent: 'As things are arranged at present, women are only going to get a halfway equal chance in the male world of work if men choose voluntarily to emasculate its predominantly macho ethos.'[42] The Church is still a male world in that it is men who have always done the thinking and made the rules. If women are to work alongside men in evangelism, some things will need changing.

To talk of 'men' and 'women' as if each sex is distinct is to take away from the personal uniqueness which God has given each of us. Some women are called to be evangelists, pioneer missionaries or leaders, others to fulfil their calling on a less public level. Men and women can be pioneers, leaders. But men and women are also made to be dependent, to be vulnerable, to be weak – and that is right, 'because they are creatures, ultimately dependent upon a Creator who upholds and sustains them all'.[43]

This book attempts to explore the variety of ways in which women have sought to fulfil the Great Commission. Their roles have often been restricted. But it is clear from the biblical, historical and contemporary evidence that they have broken all the stereotypes. Women have proved that, given the opportunities, they can fulfil all the same roles and functions as men. They can do things as well as men. I hope that this in itself is evidence that God never intended the rigid role distinctions which society and the Church have sometimes imposed on women. Who knows what will be achieved when women are free to be themselves?

Some women involved in evangelism have freed themselves from the stereotypes by breaking new ground for the gospel and planting churches. And that is the subject of the next chapter.

For reflection/action

1. If sexual hierarchy is not part of creation design, but the result of sin, what implications does that have for the Church and society today?
2. In a group, how far can you agree on male and female qualities? Do you attribute any differences you identify to nature, or nurture?
3. Are spiritual gifts gender-related?
4. 'For every woman who is tired of being a weak person when she knows she is strong, there is a man who is tired of looking strong when he feels vulnerable.' Do you believe this is true?

7

Women and church planting

As regards the evangelisation of the Gobi oases there was everything to learn.[1]

'Why not?'

I can well remember a very significant conversation I had in 1988. I was involved in a mission at a university, working with a male colleague for the week in one of the colleges, where our job was to help the students with their evangelism. We got on well and made a good team, and in that particular college it was a fruitful mission week. In between talking mission, we each talked about where God was leading us; my job contract was coming to an end, and John was about to take his family to London for a year to do a church-planting course. He was excited about returning after that to his home city and planting a church.

'Why don't you think about that church-planting course?' he suggested to me.

'But women can't plant churches,' I responded.

He replied, 'Why not?'

That was one of many things which set me on the path towards ordained ministry. I was more used to being told what women *couldn't* do in the Church. But here was someone giving me a new idea about what women *could* do. And since it was a personal conversation, it was also about what *I* could do. It was one of the most affirming moments of my life.

Can women plant churches?

Coming back to the subject of evangelism a few years on, I started to think again about church planting. Can women plant churches? What sort of contributions are women making to this aspect of evangelism today? There is currently a renewed interest in church planting. Has this allowed women to be involved without being hindered by old assumptions and traditions?

Amid the spate of recent books and articles on the subject of church planting, virtually no attention has been given to the issue of gender. So I decided to do some original research, on which this chapter is based. This included contacting a number of women involved in church planting, the majority of them Anglicans but including some from other denominations, and consulting some men and women with an overview of the church-planting scene in Britain, as well as reading books and articles.

'The best evangelistic method under heaven'

Church planting is a subject which has begun to excite churches in the last few years, and is seen as a strategic aspect of evangelism. Peter Wagner, a leading proponent of church growth thinking, calls the multiplication of new churches 'the best evangelistic method under heaven'. In 1989 Jim Montgomery published *DAWN 2000*, the story of a vision to plant seven million new churches by the year 2000, in order to have a church 'within easy access of every class and kind and condition of person in the world'.[2] Across the world, there has been significant growth in church planting in the last few years.

Of course, church planting is no new thing. It's as old as the apostolic Church. When Paul went on his missionary journeys, he was planting churches, and the gospel has been spread by church planting ever since. Mission history is full of examples. In every area to which missionaries took the gospel, they planted churches. Church planting has also been a way of reforming and reviving the Church. At the time of the Reformation, while some churches were reformed, many new churches were planted.

And in Britain, church planting has continued to be a feature of every denomination. In my own (Anglican) denomination, for example, 2,475 congregations came into existence between 1900 and 1989, many of them in areas of new housing. I am currently curate of a church on a 1950s council housing estate. The church was planted in the early 1950s, and it in turn sent a team to plant another church as the other end of the estate was being built in the 1960s. But while Anglicans have established around 2,500 churches this century, many more than that number have been planted by other denominations, mainly the newer ones.

And so church planting has continued to be a means of church growth. But the current phase has important differences. Church planting is now also seen as an opportunity for churches to explore what 'church' really means. For example, do churches need to meet in special buildings? Do they need to meet on Sundays?

What is church planting?

So what is church planting, as we use that term today? One current definition of a church planter's task is this: 'the founding and forming of a new, locally relevant worshipping and witnessing Christian community'.[3] Another definition of church planting is 'creating new communities of faith as part of the mission of God to express His Kingdom is every geographic and cultural context'.[4]

Churches are still being planted in new areas of housing. But at the same time, churches have begun to plant for a variety of reasons. My last church wanted to plant because the church had grown and the building was full. Some parishes have realised that their parish church serves one part of the parish but is making little impact on another part. Other church plants arise within existing buildings and existing churches, new congregations to meet particular needs, of young people, for example.

Apparently, the ability of a church to reach the people surrounding it diminishes significantly when that number exceeds 2,500 people. But most urban Anglican parishes have a population of anything between 6,000 and 20,000 people. We are unlikely to have smaller parishes, but some parishes have begun to plant additional worship centres focusing on smaller geographical areas. As our culture changes and people no longer belong to one geographical area, there may also be scope for planting different kinds of congregations, or churches based on factors other than the place where one lives. Church planting is likely to become increasingly important.

In 1992 when the first Challenge 2000 conference was held in Britain, none of the historic churches had church planting officially on their agenda. The conference set a goal of planting 20,000 new churches in the UK by the year 2000, with various denominations setting their own targets. Partly as a result, all the historic churches are now involved in church planting.

There have been various attempts to categorise church plants, and to suggest recipes for church planting. But in reality all church plants are different. Some are planned, others have happened by accident.

Most churches are planted by a team, but with some kind of leader. I am not aware that any attempt has been made to record numbers of women and men involved; some women have planted churches virtually alone, others have led teams, and others have taken over leadership in the early stages. I came across one plant which is nominally led by a man, but most of the leadership and energy comes from a woman; there may be other examples, which it would be almost impossible to discover.

Church planting vs church extension

Martin Robinson, one of the foremost writers on church planting, draws a distinction between church planting, which has a missionary intention, and church extension, where new buildings and clergy are provided to care for the needs of existing believers.[5] The true focus of church planting is on mission. In the past many churches planted in new areas of housing tended to be church extension. But I know of one church planted in a large new owner-occupied estate seven years ago, which has grown to about 150 people mainly through conversion, rather than transfer growth. It continues to grow – in the first four months of 1996, for example, sixteen people became Christians – and it is thinking about planting another church. So this would be true church planting.[6]

Insights from church planting are contributing to wider thinking about evangelism. At the Anglican Church Planting Conference held in 1991, Archbishop George Carey stated, 'I actually believe that church planting is taking us back to the proper theology of evangelism in the New Testament.' The concept of 'missionary congregations', associated particularly with the name of Robert Warren, the Church of England's National Officer for Evangelism, is challenging many churches to move from maintenance to mission, and for that to take place there is much that might be learnt from the experience of church planting.

So what about women?

As I have noticed the growth of church planting over the last few years, my initial impression has been that women have not made much contribution to it. Church planting usually involves teams, men and women working together. I knew of a couple of women leading church plants. But otherwise, from the books I possessed and my general awareness, I had concluded that most of the ideas, energy, theology and training came from men. Would I find any evidence to prove me wrong? How were women involved, particularly as leaders, and what might I discover to contribute to wider questions of women and evangelism?

Paul had female co-workers as he planted churches: what part did they play? Were there any other women in the New Testament who planted churches? There are many stories in mission history about women who planted churches. Do their stories relate in any way to the experience of women today?

If, towards the end of the Decade of Evangelism, the Church is now moving on from 'doing evangelism' to being 'missionary congregations', is church planting a fresh opportunity for the gifts and insights of women to be incorporated, or will it be as male-dominated as most of our previous mission thinking? And are there any particular gifts which women bring to this aspect of evangelism? Can women plant churches?

Paul and his fellow-workers

What does the Bible tell us about church planting and the role of women? When Jesus commissioned his followers, no limits were set on the involvement of women. Men may have taken the lead in the early Church, but after Jesus' profound influence, women could never stay in the background again. As women were converted to Christianity they discovered that they were expected to be disciples in their own right. God might call them to his service just as he called men.

When it comes to church planting, we do not have a lot of biblical material to go on. But it is clear that as Paul travelled and planted churches, he worked with teams of co-workers. Among these were the couple Aquila and Priscilla, who appear to have been active in planting both in Corinth and Ephesus. Priscilla is usually mentioned first, perhaps because her role in the church was more prominent, but it was unusual for a couple to be mentioned in this way at all. Neither is ever mentioned alone. The couple head the list of those whom Paul greets as he writes to the church in Rome. As 'co-workers in Christ Jesus' who 'risked their lives for me' (Rom. 16:3, 4), perhaps they had a special place in his heart.

Their role was important. They must have been quite well-to-do people, mobile and able to support a church in their home. When Paul arrived in Corinth, he went to stay with the couple, and worked with them, as they were also tentmakers (Acts 18:3). They had recently been expelled from Rome, perhaps because they were Christians and active in the church. They may have founded a church there, and by the time Paul wrote to the Roman church, they had returned there (Rom. 16:3–5).

Nothing is said of their involvement in the church in Corinth, but they must have been a crucial part of the team, since in Acts 18:18 we read that Paul sails for Syria, taking them with him. He then goes on to Ephesus and leaves them there (18:19). Presumably their role was to repeat in Ephesus the kind of work they had done alongside Paul in Corinth, an advance team to get the work started before he returned. Priscilla and Aquila come across Apollos, a keen evangelist, but deficient in his understanding of baptism and the Holy Spirit. By this time they have established a church in their home, and the believers are mature enough to encourage Apollos to move on to Corinth, and to write a letter of recommendation (18:27). This also suggests that the work was growing sufficiently for them to be able to spare him. They could not afford to wait for Paul to rejoin them. Who knew when Paul would return?

There is no suggestion that the couple have roles allocated according to gender. Priscilla is presented as a teacher fitted to teach the evangelist Apollos, and they appear to have worked side by side in establishing the church.

Later Paul came back to Ephesus, and he taught in the synagogue and then in the lecture hall of Tyrannus (Acts 19:8–10). As the church grew there would have been plenty for Priscilla and Aquila to do, looking after the church in their home (1 Cor. 16:19) and others. Not long after this they seem to be back in Rome (Rom. 16:3), with yet another church in their house, one of at least five cells of believers. Some cultures were more open to the ministry of women then others, and judging from the number of women mentioned in Romans 16, Rome was one such place. In the early centuries of the Church, women continued to play a major role in the leadership at Rome. Perhaps this openness at Rome, where Priscilla began her ministry, accounts for her unusually prominent role.

It is also possible that Junia (Rom. 16:7) and Andronicus were another wife and husband ministry. Some Bibles still make this person a man, Junias, yet that name is unknown, whereas the name Junia is common; early commentators such as John Chrysostom understood Junia to be a woman. Presumably it was too much for some more recent translators to have a woman designated as an 'apostle'. Paul describes the two as 'relatives' who had been believers longer than he had. Since they had been imprisoned with him, and are said to be 'prominent among the apostles', perhaps they were also involved in itinerant evangelism and church planting.

Church planting in Philippi

Another woman who had a church in her home was Lydia. She

was the first convert in Europe, a Jewish proselyte who was open to Paul's message by the river in Philippi (Acts 16:14). Not finding a synagogue and any men to whom he could preach, yet knowing that God had pretty clearly directed him there, Paul seems to have had no problem adapting his style to a group of women. It would be fascinating to know what he said! What started as Lydia's grateful hospitality became a church in her home (16:40).

Macedonia, like Rome, appears to have been a culture open to women having prominent positions in society and religion, which would have paved the way for women to be involved in the emerging church. It is difficult to establish Lydia's role in the church, but there were certainly women in leadership in the church when Paul wrote to it (Euodia and Syntyche: Phil. 4:2–3), so it seems at least possible that she played a prominent role. She was originally from Thyatira, a dealer in purple cloth, which was a luxury industry. It seems she was in Philippi as a kind of business agent. Purple was associated with wealth, and as a business woman she would have had contact with the elite of Philippi, among whom to spread the gospel, besides the influence she had over her own household.

It may also have been Lydia, returning to her home town of Thyatira, who took the gospel there. That was the area where Paul was intending to go before he was summoned to Macedonia, so it would be particularly appropriate. If Lydia was a prominent member of the church, why is she not greeted in Paul's letter? Other women are mentioned, but not her (Phil. 4:2–3). She could have died, but she could also have returned to her home town and taken the gospel with her, perhaps planting a church.[7]

But the story of the church at Philippi is seen rather differently by Charles Chaney, a writer on church planting from a Southern Baptist perspective. He not unnaturally sees Acts 16 and the Philippian letter as the most central biblical texts on the subject of church planting. But he regards Lydia merely as someone responsive to the gospel, a woman with circles of friendship and a home to provide hospitality. Women, he notes, tend to respond more readily to the Christian message and thus can be a significant factor in the planting of churches. He overlooks the active role which women played in evangelism in the early Church.

Chaney makes No. 9 of his ten church planting principles, 'Do not discount the place and effectiveness of women in church planting', which suggests that his book is intended for men-only reading. As a Southern Baptist he wants to deny women leadership roles on 'biblical grounds' (which he does not elaborate). But at the same time, his own experience of women doing rather more than providing hospitality forces him to admit that some women do have other gifts. Some have the shepherding or pastor gift, and can lead small groups and congregations (within the larger Church). Some (he cites Priscilla) have the gift of apostle, needed for pioneering, and he gives an example, Delores Thomas, who continued her husband's church-planting ministry after his death. 'She gathered the nucleus of new congregations, helped to find and orient pastors for the new congregations, and provided advice and support for young pastors coming to serve the new churches.'[8] But if Priscilla had these gifts, why not Lydia?

'Do not discount the place and effectiveness of women,' he says. Presumably there are some who would . . .

Other women are mentioned as having churches in their homes: Nympha (Col. 4:15); the 'elect lady' of 2 John. It is hard to establish from mere mentions what their roles were. Were they, as people like Chaney would have us believe, merely opening their homes to provide hospitality? Or does the idea of wives as hostesses owe more to the recent, and Western, view of women as primarily homemakers, than to a biblical one? Could it have meant, as seems more likely when letters are addressed to them or they are picked out for mention by name, that they had some real involvement in the planting of the church? There is a good case for believing the 'elect lady' to be a real woman who was a leader in the church.[9]

She is a great man

Women clearly contributed to the task of planting some of the earliest churches. How have they contributed to the task of church planting in more recent history?

The Celtic church-planting movement allowed more scope for women than the Roman one; Brigid has already been mentioned, and other women were involved in founding and leading monastic settlements. At the time of the Reformation, Anabaptist churches were sometimes planted and led by women. Later, when the mission field began to open up to women, many women planted churches.

'She is a great man.' So exclaimed King Louis-Philippe of France in 1833, congratulating Mother Anne-Marie Javouhey on her tremendous achievements in the settlement she established at Mana, Guiana. When a woman exhibits gifts such as pioneering and leadership, which are thought stereotypically 'male', she is sometimes described in masculine terms. But why could she not be a 'great woman'?

Mother Javouhey founded an order which was intended to be missionary, and might thus be justly described as church planting. Like many church planters she experienced a specific call, in the form of a vision: a crowd of people calling out to her. She also felt that St Teresa had spoken to her, telling her that God had special plans for her. This gave her the courage to go, despite opposition from her family and church authorities.

Her understanding of mission was based on compassion. She worked for the liberation of African slaves, and to provide work and education for ex-slaves. She built houses, churches, a hospital, and cleared forests for agriculture. She pressed on despite opposition. 'The male sex are to be feared because of their ambition to rule: but if God is on our side, what have we to fear?'[10]

At one time the authorities deprived her order of the services of a priest, but she determined to carry on with whatever she could do: baptising people, arranging marriages, discussing the faith in homes. She broke the stereotype that strenuous pioneering work is only for men. She was an administrator, a visionary, a planner.

Pioneers of the weaker sex

Sometimes it is difficult to remember that just over a hundred years ago men were still arguing that education for women was dangerous because over-exercise of their brains would damage their reproductive systems. Women were held to be innately fragile and weak; middle-and upper-class women, that is – not women who worked long hours in the factories at the same time as raising their families! As we have already seen, women had to overcome considerable opposition just to be allowed to go on the mission field. Once there they had to adjust to the expectations of their missions regarding women. So the achievements of women in these circumstances are considerable. Despite the obstacles women have shown themselves just as capable of planting churches as men are.

Eleanor Macomber worked alone as a single woman in Dong-Yahn, Burma. Within a few months, she saw more than twenty conversions and the beginning of a church. Undeterred by opposition from Buddhist priests and the local authorities, she preached, held worship and prayer meetings and formed a training school. But she had to wait until 'brother Osgood came up again' before converts could be baptised. Through the 1830s before her early death at the age of thirty-nine, she visited all the families within six or seven miles, and trained and sent out converts to nearby tribes, going out with some of them herself, so that they could learn by apprenticeship.

Lottie Moon (1840–1912) was one of the women who, more than most, challenged the role that women were given on the mission field. Arriving in China in 1873 as a Southern Baptist missionary, she saw herself as an evangelist, but instead was assigned to teach in a girls' school. 'Can we wonder at the mortal weariness and disgust, the sense of wasted powers and the conviction that her life is a failure, that comes over a woman when, instead of the ever broadening activities she had planned, she finds herself tied down to the petty work of teaching a few girls?'[11]

What Moon wanted was opportunity to use her gifts to the full, to do the same things as men were doing, evangelism and church planting. 'Simple justice demands that women should have equal rights with men in mission meetings and in the conduct of their work.'[12] She was forbidden to 'preach' to men. But she found a way round it. How could she help it if men were so interested in the message she was giving that they came along to her women's meetings and studied along with them?

In 1889 her work in P'ing-tu was described as 'the greatest evangelistic center' of the Southern Baptists in China. She was not qualified to lead the churches she planted, but this made it necessary for her to train indigenous ministers quickly, which in turn helped church growth. The Chinese pastor at P'ing-tu baptised more than a thousand converts in two decades. A missions journal paid tribute to Lottie Moon by calling her 'the best man among our missionaries'.[13]

Evangeline and Francesca French and Mildred Cable were all called to China in the late nineteenth century. After a number of years in more traditional work training teachers and running a Bible school for women, they felt called to the unevangelised areas, and volunteered to go, hoping to evangelise the area before it closed to missionary work. They set off as travelling evangelists, in a couple of carts, crossing the Gobi desert several times and planting small communities of Christians along their way. 'Six times, in missionary journeys, the Trio had covered the North-West area and now the witness was to be carried once more into Turkestan. The Gospel had been preached through Inner Mongolia and in the Tibetan lamaseries.'[14]

Winning the hearts of the people

Incarnation: 'to send Jesus down your street', as Martin Robinson puts it,[15] is an essential part of modern church-planting thinking. Apparently few missionaries surpassed Malla Moe's close identification with the Africans in Swaziland where she served for fifty-four years. She had emigrated from Norway to Chicago, where she was recruited by the founder of the Scandinavian Alliance Mission, Fredrik Franson, who, as we saw earlier, was a strong supporter of women in ministry. She founded one of the early stations of the Scandinavian Alliance Mission. At a time long before such principles were recognised, she accepted African culture, ate African food and lived in native kraals, and her dependence on Africans contributed to her success.

Malla Moe (1863–1953) was not only a pioneer; she was also innovative and imaginative. In 1927, at the age of sixty-five, she began a new ministry, travelling from place to place in her 'gospel wagon', preaching to the men and using Bible women to reach women. Accompanied by a band of local helpers she planted dozens of churches among the Swazis. Although not ordained she apparently functioned as a bishop, assigning pastors to the churches she founded and overseeing their continued growth and development.

But when she returned to Norway on furlough she was not permitted even to speak, and officials of the state church 're-minded her to read Paul's instruction that "women should keep silence in the church" '.[16]

For Ruth Watson, a medical missionary ('Kanchi Doctor'), it was her medical skills which won a hearing for the gospel. She was one of a group of six women who helped to plant the church in Nepal when the country re-opened in 1951. In 1936 Lily O'Hanlon had seen Nepal from India, and God had told her that one day she would enter the forbidden land. She and another woman waited near the border, ran a clinic to help Nepalis and collected a team to enter Nepal. They worked with a small group of Nepali believers (converted from Hinduism) so that the church would be indigenous.

There had been no missionaries in Nepal for two hundred years. Government permission was given to start medical work. And as Nepalis were cured they begun to understand the God who healed. Evil spirits were driven out. Ruth found herself more and more in charge of the work and eventually 'senior mis-sionary', with many newer missionaries under her. Faced with a seemingly impossible task, Ruth knew that 'the God who had called her would enable her,'[17] and gradually a Nepali church was established. Doctors came and went, and Ruth died of cancer in 1976. The church continued to grow on those foundations, until by 1984 there were 150 groups with 15,000 members, and there are now over 100,000 Christians.

Another woman whose pioneering work depended on incar-nation is Jackie Pullinger. At an early age she thought about being a missionary, and had a dream in which she saw Hong Kong. Turned down by missionary societies because she was too young, she was encouraged by her vicar to set off where God seemed to be leading. That turned out to be Hong Kong, and she soon found herself ministering to drug addicts in the feared 'Walled City', which sheltered a network of vice and corruption run by notorious Triad gangs.

In the midst of many challenges and difficulties, she soon began to see young men coming off heroin, becoming Christians, and themselves telling others the good news. The work developed, safe houses were set up and a rehabilitation centre established in a former resettlement area, Hang Fook camp. In the 1980s Jackie began to see that the work was not just about seeing people freed from drugs, but about planting new churches and building up the church for the future, when Hong Kong would be returned to China. Churches have been planted and Christians prepared to be 'church' in networks of homes if necessary. The work goes on.

Planting churches on home ground

Women have been responsible for some of the churches planted in Britain by the newer denominations. Miss Reeve and Miss Fisher were brought together through a campaign by evangelist George Jeffreys. They felt called to serve God in India but were thwarted by the Second World War. So instead they hired a room in Hockley, Birmingham, where they lived, and a room for prayer was turned into a Sunday School as children started to gather. Immigrants from the New Commonwealth were arriving in the area: God had brought India to them! Out of this Sunday School grew Hockley Mission, an AOG church.

Miss Fisher was a dynamic evangelist and organiser, especially gifted in praying for the sick and leading seekers into the baptism of the Spirit, while Miss Reeve was a quieter pastor and teacher with an ability to hear from God. Neither woman was particularly well educated or trained, but they depended on God. Through forty years of ministry both women lived by faith and led the church on the same principles, taking no collections. Their approach to evangelism was that if people saw God's Spirit at work, they would be won to Christ, and exuberant praise and worship was a feature of the church, which has influenced many hundreds of lives.[18]

Stories that were never told

According to some mission histories, one would think women had barely contributed to the task of mission. But fortunately the stories of some have survived, while others are remembered almost by accident. Ruth Tucker grew up in a rural community in northern Wisconsin in the 1930s. She might not have become a Christian had it not been for the ministry of two women. In one of her many books on church history and women's issues she tells the story:

> Enter two 'lady preachers' – Miss Salthammer and Miss Cowan – convinced that they were called to plant a church where there was no gospel ministry. In the years that followed they did just that. First they opened a Sunday School, and then they initiated church services. They evangelised, visited the sick, taught classes and preached sermons. Finally, when the little church was on a solid footing they moved on to plant other churches, and a succession of male pastors took over the work.[19]

The women used to return occasionally to teach vacation Bible school, and that was how Ruth Tucker came to know them. And they became her role models as she grew up. Their story, like that of many other women, might have been forgotten. The women lived and died in poverty, and when Miss Cowan died she was buried in a pauper's grave. Not even the church acknowledged what they had done. Perhaps they ended up in that area because no one else wanted to take a gospel ministry there. The standard histories of mission – by Stephen Neill, for example – have been the stories of men. If Ruth Tucker had not met God through a church planted by two obscure women, the stories of many women would still lie untold, as unknown as the other stories which have been lost for ever.

So much for the ministry of women in church planting from New Testament times until today. What contribution are women making to church planting today? Is there any resistance to women in a pioneering or leadership role? Do women bring particular gifts or styles of ministry to the task? What difficulties and challenges do women face? The following are some of the stories of women currently involved.

'A church plant? That's an excellent suggestion, Miss MacAdams. Perhaps one of the men would like to make it'

That was Jackie's version of a cartoon which summed up some of her feelings about being leader of a church plant. A women puts forward an idea and it is as if she is invisible. A man suggests the same thing, and everyone takes notice. 'But I just said that!' she thinks.

Jackie is leader of a suburban church plant which has in turn planted several more churches. Her husband was leader of the original planting team, then felt it right to step down and hand over to someone who was more of a team person. The church prayed, and Jackie's was the name that emerged. Jackie, initially reluctant, prayed that God would show her if it was wrong, and felt that if God was calling her she must get on and do it. The church soon doubled in size, and continued to grow. Her aim is to facilitate others, to see others move on, to make herself not needed. She is thrilled by seeing people who were formerly tongue-tied start to take some part in the service. She sees everyone in the congregation as a potential leader.

As a woman heading the leadership team, she is aware of the challenges and pressures for women in church planting. There are few role models. Women need to find their own style. Not having many other women around, she knew that she needed a strong sense of assurance and confidence in God which would withstand the knocks and challenges: like the visiting preacher who looked past her as she greeted him, saying, 'Could you just introduce me to your leader?'

As someone who spends four days a week in a management job, Jackie thinks that women can do the same things as men – but they might do them their way. Of course it is hard to divide personality from gender, but her desire to empower people, to work as a team, to relate to the local community, seems to be characteristic of many women. The first plant launched by the church which Jackie leads started running Sunday meetings and doing all the things that the planting church did – and found it had little energy for evangelism. So as plans were made for a second plant, an action group was sent to the area, making contact with people, networking, inviting people to meals, before beginning to meet for worship. Jackie's philosophy of church planting is echoed by most of the other women whose stories I have heard: what one woman called 'bottom up' rather than 'top down'.

Take Sue, for example. She saw the potential for a church plant in one part of her parish which was a distance away from the parish church. Few people came to church from the flats in that area; it was up a hill, and the church was quite middle class. In a previous church she had seen a laywoman leading a congregation, so that helped her to have the confidence that she might do something similar. 'I grew up with a heart for evangelism, but I never realised I could be involved fully, rather than just with things like giving out leaflets.'

She shared her vision, and a team was formed. She and another woman started a toddler club, and it succeeded, through much perseverance, where a social services one had folded up. It was a way of meeting people and telling them about the church which was meeting in a nearby hall once a month. They could tell the mums, 'We'll pray about that for you.' Services became twice a month.

Sue spent hours walking around the flats, just smiling, listening and talking to people. Three years of doing this, and people knew about the church, and that people cared for them. People were sent cards on their birthdays, flowers from the church when they were ill. The team got to know the caretakers, the cleaners, the tenants' association. The toddler club closed as it was no longer needed, and an evening friendship group started, a place to share and chat, with some prayer and Bible reading. More and more people learnt to pray aloud. For those people who came, that group was 'church', even though it was meant to be a stepping stone to church. An afternoon group started, doing a simplified version of the Alpha course, and continuing like a house group. Some people who started in groups like this did move on to church, which was carefully designed to be nothing like worship at the parish church, but more appropriate to a non-book culture.

An enabling style of leadership, some reluctance to take the role on, challenges when they do, lack of role models, a 'bottom-up' method of working – these are some features which seem to be common to many women involved in church planting, especially as leaders. And women seem to be doing some very creative things. Perhaps less of a sense of what church ought to be, and more sensitivity to what is needed, enables women to break out of old models of church and try new things.

Can women plant churches? They can, and they are doing so. Most church-planting teams have men and women on them, often in roughly equal numbers, or perhaps more women than men. After all, there are more women in most churches than men. But whose idea was it to plant? And who is the pioneer, the visionary? Is it always men who have the ideas?

For six of the women I contacted, the vision to plant was theirs. For at least two of these it was a particularly attractive idea, since it meant an opportunity to exercise their leadership skills which, stuck as a deacon (before the priesting of women in the Anglican Church), were underused. Some saw themselves as 'getting things going' people, pioneers, and would look to hand over to someone else to do the growing. Patricia Wick pioneered a plant in Hull, Ann Wooderson on an estate in Tamworth, Judie Horrocks in Moss Side.[20]

As always, encouragement and having role models seems to be crucial. Jackie was encouraged by her church. Another woman wrote, 'I think I have been very fortunate as I have always had people around who have believed in me and have encouraged me to make the contribution they believed I had.' A good role model opened up possibilities for Sue. In Ichthus, where at the time of writing there were at least eight significant women church planters, women take all the same roles as men. Having Faith Forster and Sue Mitchell as models no doubt has helped this. Kensington Temple has a similar openness to the ministry of women as church planters, and a quarter of the leaders of its satellite churches are women.

So women appear to be challenging stereotypes about ideas and pioneering. There are a few Miss MacAdams who are credited with their ideas. But according to one man with wide experience of church plants, 'Women are allowed to have the ideas – so long as that does not threaten men's power.'

'When a field was found too difficult for a man, a woman should be sent'[21]

' "Do anything you like at the margins, but not where it might be a success," is the message women are often given,' the same man added. In other words, men will let women be used in places which are marginal, but not in places which are central to the Church's mission, which are likely to succeed and give the planter prestige. Where success is important, a man will be found to do it. In places which are difficult, where men may have tried and failed already, then women are welcome to have a go.

Some women have been given situations like this and succeeded. Ann Wooderson, mentioned above, has been cited as one example. A man might try to plant with a team, find it hard, and blame failure on the 'difficult area'. A woman might go in by herself, or with a smaller team and a different approach, and a church emerges. Of course some do not succeed. But many of the women surveyed reckoned they had more stickability, more patience than men. They made comments like: 'No one would have gone to X if they wanted to make a name for themselves', 'I've spent three years just being there', 'We need to resist the numbers game.' Women have 'servant hearts' and 'endurance', some reckoned.

Chris, who planted a church in one part of a large parish and two further churches in old people's homes, commented: 'It certainly is true that women are not given many opportunities and I always felt that I had had this opportunity almost by accident and certainly by the back door. Nobody expected that I would plant a church that would be successful.' I was told by one man who had seen both men and women leading church plants that for women numbers seemed to matter less than the quality of the work, which might well be invisible, whereas men need to see visible results. He also felt that men given responsibility for a church plant in their curacy might see it just as a step on the career ladder, whereas women would be more committed to the place, and to people.

'Surely God isn't asking me to do this?'

'Women have often been their own worst enemies and not wanted to take on anything that is pioneering,' suggested Marion, a very modest woman, who had pioneered in two very difficult situations. Several women told me how hard it is to be a leader when you are a woman. Many women are more used to being in a serving/supporting role, and struggle when called to take the lead. This is hardly surprising, given the mixed messages women can be given in the Church, and the lack of opportunity they usually have to develop leadership skills.

Jackie assumed leadership because she was the person whom the church had felt was called to do it. Women like her who were aware of a specific call recognised by others seem more confident. For many women who have had to contend with challenges to their role in evangelism from within the Church, on top of the struggles involved in pioneering, it is their call which has kept them going. Others have drawn on the confidence gained in their secular work.

'I was head of the science department in a school and I've been ordained for ten years, so being in a man's world is not a problem for me,' said Shirley, working with a small team on an estate with no community provision. She'd spent three years 'just being there', getting involved with building a community centre. After meeting people where they were, they were beginning to ask, 'When's the church coming?' So it would soon be time to start worship. She was in no hurry, but content to wait for God's timing; there were no grand plans and not much of a vision, so she had no one to let down, nothing to prove.

But Louise found herself vulnerable in a way she had not expected. 'I've worked in business and teaching, and I was asked to take a major role because I've been quite involved in the church and I'm a getting-things-going person.' But when the vicar's initial involvement ended and people looked to her by default, 'I felt uncovered. I felt God had drawn me into the plant. But there are no role models.' And planting from a church where women would not be permitted a leadership role, she was left with an uncertain status. Was she not really a leader, or was the plant not really a church?

Lose your cat and plant a church!

Patricia described how she was working in an area to build bridges with the local community. It was an area of new housing and she lost her cat in the first week she was there, so after wandering around looking for it she soon knew all the other residents! She began to listen to people and find out what their needs were. Nearly everyone came to a wine and cheese party at her house, and she started a mothers and toddlers group.

> After a year I decided to get a group of non-church-goers together and find out why they didn't go. I knocked at twenty houses and invited them to my house for an hour. They all came! I asked them to imagine we could start with a clean sheet of paper: what would you like to see? Sundays were out. What about Wednesdays at 7 p.m.? By the end, people were beginning to talk about 'our church'.

She aimed to grow a local leadership, not bring in leaders from outside. She drew women into (secular) community groups which she started, and they began to gain confidence and leadership experience and discover what their gifts were; then as they were drawn to Christ and converted, they were able to take on a leadership role in the growing church.

Women tend to work closely with the local community, building relationships. Margaret drew some wonderful diagrams. 'Very often church plants seem to have a group which goes in like this: $\vee$. We felt our growth was more like this: $\wedge$. Very few people came in from outside.' Then she added: 'I am told ∇ is a male shape and Δ is a female shape. I know which one looks more stable to me!' She told me:

> I was given an area of new housing. I visited and got to know people as they moved in. From this a house group was formed. We started praying. More building included a block of sheltered accommodation for the elderly with a social room. They invited us in to do a monthly Sunday evening service. At the same time I joined up with the local Methodist deaconess. When a school was built we began

monthly family services using ten of the original house group as the core. Forty people came to the first service and the next year we were formally declared an ecumenical partnership church and began weekly services. The pace of that early growth was breathtaking. We didn't really know what order to do things in – we felt we were trying to catch up with God all the time!

Janet agreed that women tend to use bottom-up rather than top-down methods. 'They communicate their vision through small groups or one to one, casually. With many women being home-makers, maybe some of the same tools for creating a safe and welcoming environment for a family come into play.' Men, on the other hand, used to meetings as places where statements are made and information is exchanged, would tend to summon people to a meeting. I was reminded by one man I talked to that committees are a male invention!

Barnabas ministry

One of the central characteristics of church planting is that it releases ordinary church members into ministry through the use of teams. Men and women tend to find their gifts better used in the new church than they might in the planting church. Thus church planting is intrinsically enabling.

If church planting is about enabling then this is certainly a gift that many women seem to be able to offer. The largest number of comments I received about what women bring to church planting concerned enabling leadership. Almost all the women alluded to this in some way or other. Clearly some women are defensive and hold leadership to themselves, but it does seem that women often have a more inclusive style. Many women work better in teams than men do, and have gifts of team building.

Women saw themselves as tending to draw out the gifts of others, mobilising people and identifying gifts, rather than being lone rangers, doing everything themselves. This might at times mean delegating the things they most enjoyed or were good at; perhaps women are more practised at making such sacrifices.

Patricia described how she shared leadership of the plant: an informal group for 'prayer and planning' to which anyone was invited, and which was then split down into task groups.

'My own lack of skills for the task proved to be the most powerful tool in the hands of the Lord,' wrote Monica Hill, in her account of church planting in the East End of London. 'I had to discover and use local people to whom I acted as an "enabler" and "encourager" – a Barnabas ministry.'[22] Pauline Boland, in her section on women in leadership in *Local Church Planting*, mentions how women may enable men as well as women. Some men need to be given permission *not* to be leaders.[23]

One man who had been vicar of a church with several plants confirmed that enabling and permission-giving was greater with a woman leader than with a man. But he noted that a woman particularly enabled women, eliciting a much higher level of participation and more initiatives. If the woman leader were then replaced by a man, these women would retreat back into a subservient role and allow the man to be 'vicar'. Of course cultural factors may have contributed to this, but it is a comment that is quite telling.

Women are doing more interesting things

'Women are doing more interesting things than men are', one writer on church planting told me. 'Women work in teams better, they come at problems differently. Women are broadly prophetic to what God is doing,' he said.

Hey, I thought, would you mind repeating this? Are you really saying that women are doing church planting better than men are? Why didn't anyone tell me this before?

Of course he did not mean there were not exceptions. And it seemed like another set of stereotypes. But I think he meant that in his extensive experience of evangelism, this is a pattern he has seen. Women have seldom been asked for their ideas. Put men and women together and new things happen!

As I have listened to what women are doing, I have been excited by their varied approaches. Sometimes they have almost been forced to be creative, because they have been working in places where the usual strategies would not work. As they have adapted their style and strategy to the situations they found, they have come up with interesting new things. One of the conclusions from a discussion on church planting held by the Council of the British Church Growth Association in 1993 was that 'women often have more radical ideas for church planting'.[24]

Women have been involved in creative forms of church planting overseas. In parts of Uganda women reach other women through personal evangelism, and form a 'church', then ask for a leader. In Mexico City an 'accident' led to the use of home Bible studies as a basis for church planting. A group of women got together to say goodbye to a single woman missionary in 1974, and some of them decided to meet weekly with another missionary. By 1985, five churches had been planted through the establishment of thirty-five women's home Bible studies, and eight years later there were ten churches. The aim was to establish local leaders, and middle-class Mexican women were found to be natural in this role.

The goal of the church planting was growth by conversion. That way, there was no one in the church to say, 'We've never done it that way before.' While the studies aimed at women, sometimes, while the study was going on, young adults or husbands were converted while 'listening in' upstairs, and whole families ended up coming to church.[25]

In an article, 'New Churches for a New Challenge', Martin Robinson writes: 'Church planting offers an opportunity to think afresh about the kinds of structures and communities of faith which will be able to rise to the missionary challenge that the new Europe brings ... It may mean thinking afresh about the cultural clothes in which we present those ancient truths.'[26] In other words we want 'new church plants', not 'old church plants'. In the same article Robinson also notes that many church planters are unusually gifted people. The Church has often found it difficult to use such creativity, other than in new initiatives such as church planting – and in the past such people often became overseas missionaries. Now creative people are needed for creative new church plants, in Britain and around the world. Perhaps many of these creative people will be women.

'Dads come because there's a role for them in shifting chairs'

Some people have been concerned that women in leadership will lead to an even greater proportion of women over men in the Church than there is already. Does female leadership make a difference in terms of the balance of men and women in the church plant? The evidence seems variable. Yet it must be remembered that women seem to have predominated in the Church for at least the last 150 years, despite male leadership. Culture and other factors have quite a part to play.

Only three women noted that the plants they led had more women than men and saw this as a problem. For Hilary, women's leadership worked both ways: as a woman on the doorstep she was less threatening, but a woman did not cut a lot of ice with men – she felt it needed men to reach men. Teresa commented that because there were more women than men in her church, to some people it did not seem a 'proper' church. Sue was doing much of the pioneering herself, reaching mainly women, and felt that more men needed to be involved, to reach the men. Clearly, where women feel they are most gifted at reaching other women, that will initially draw in more women than men. But to my mind none of these situations are peculiar to church plants, and I am not convinced the problem, if it is one, is attributable to women's leadership.

Other women noted how they succeeded in attracting both men and women. For Margaret, the biggest growth area was with young families. Her Methodist woman colleague had started a mums and toddlers group. 'The mums begin to come because of their children. The dads come because there is a role for them in shifting chairs.' Ann Wooderson pioneered on her own, but at the first confirmation service in the new plant the bishop laid hands on twenty-two people, many of whom were burly miners and working men, brought to faith through her work. Teams went into homes with 'Good News Down the Street', a six-week introduction to the Christian faith, and reached men as well as women.[27]

The accusation of 'feminising' the Church cannot be laid against women evangelists. Where plants are successful in attracting women into church, those women need to be given confidence and equipped to reach their husbands, brothers, fathers, and to bring their children up to know God. But as earlier chapters suggest, where women are allowed to minister without restriction they have seen as many men come to faith as women. Perhaps it is because women's involvement in evangelism has often been restricted to 'women's work' that we have seen more women than men come into the Church. Set women free, and maybe we can reverse the trend.

In a different voice

Some women do feel that women have particular things to contribute to the task of church planting, particularly in children's work, prayer and pastoral care.

Chris, who was given a free hand in an area of a large parish and found herself with the opportunity to plant a church 'almost by accident', believes that she has a 'female' way of going about evangelism: lingering and loitering, chatting, 'wasting time with people'. But this female way is not valued as much as 'male' ways, she feels. 'I believe that we complement male ministry but I would wish that our gifts would be recognised . . . I believe we have a long way to go in convincing our male partners of our ability to complement the ministry which we share together.'

But some of the women I spoke to made the point that they work through pastoral care or children's activities because it's what they are gifted at rather than because they are women! And churches do need people who are good at pastoral work, are sensitive, listen to people and relate to those who are marginalised.

As the previous chapter shows, the debate about 'difference' between men and women is complex. Whatever our conclusions, a Christian perspective requires us to resist the use of difference as a basis for hierarchy, which is what has so often happened. Different individuals will have different ministries but this cannot be specified in advance simply on the basis of gender. Women are called to evangelism; some will find themselves in pioneering or leadership roles, others in ones which harness their experience of being wives and mothers.

My research shows that many women do feel they have particular gifts which they think of as 'women's gifts'. But other women take on roles which have often been thought of as men's, and feel their ministry depends entirely on personality and gifting, not gender. These variations may be due partly to differences between churches, between those which emphasise gifting and calling and those which are more institutional.

'Give me a hundred men . . .'

So – can women plant churches? The answer ought to be obvious, Since the early Church, women have played a part in church planting, Women have continued to experience the call of God down the ages to plant churches, and have used their varied gifts.

There is no lack of women involved in church planting. That being so, one might expect the role of women to be given a higher profile in books on church planting, especially since most of them have been written in the last ten years. Some recent books use inclusive language, and talk of 'men or women' leaders. But examples of women church planters tend to be rare. The following are some of my conclusions arising from the research on which this chapter is based. I hope they will be a challenge to the Church.

In his book, *Church Planting: Our Future Hope*, Charlie Cleverly changed Wesley's 'Give me a hundred preachers . . .' into 'Give me a hundred men . . .' for his chapter on leaders,[28] and showed no awareness of the possibility of women as church planters. None of the books I have found are written by women, unless one counts the one edited by Monica Hill. At the time of writing, Challenge 2000 had only one woman on its steering committee, whose responsibility was – prayer! The only women speaking at the DAWN Congress in 1995 were one on 'How women plant churches' and one taking half a session on 'New forms of Church'. Some women have been visible at Anglican conferences, but tending to share 'women's experience'. There is much more which could be done to include women.

Lack of role models is disempowering to women, and a barrier to women becoming involved in church planting, especially in less traditional roles. That will improve as women take risks and move out. But the women who are there need support and encouragement. Young women studying evangelism or working in churches need to see other women in action.

Women's ministry has been further hampered by rigid expectations regarding the proper place for women, or by literalistic interpretations of Scripture. This may mean their leadership is not fully accepted by those in their church, or in other churches. They may know that they can exercise leadership in the plant which they could not in the main church, which is a blessing with a sting in the tail. It is the hypocrisy of allowing missionaries to do things they could not do at home one step nearer.

Women may end up as lone pioneers, either because they are 'sent' by someone else or by default if not supported properly by their church. And whether with a team or not, they are likely to end up in marginal places. This will only change when there are enough situations to tell a different story. It was a man who told me that men need to learn to celebrate women's success.

The evidence of church history suggests that women are often more active in the first generation of a new movement, but by the third or fourth generation, when it has become respectable, men have taken over and institutionalised it. It is too early to see whether that is what will happen to church plants, those successfully pioneered by women, for example. I have one example of a woman pioneer now replaced by a male curate, but it is too early to tell if that is part of a trend. But it will be a tragedy if this happens. Can we make sure it does not?

On the other hand, a standard feminist observation is that when an idea/concept/task is new, interesting or challenging, men tend to keep it to themselves. When it becomes mundane, routine and has lost its original charisma, anyone can do it. When the typewriter was invented, it was a new and complex machine which could only be operated by men. When typing was perceived to be dull and repetitive, it became a woman's job. My perception is that church planting has so far been 'owned' by men. If and when it ceases to be the latest thing, will it be fully opened up, or even left, to women?

Finally, when genderedness is fully integrated, 'women's perspectives' will become obsolete. But I think we still have a little way to go before that happens. If the Church can focus outwards to mission, then perhaps the question of what women can or cannot do will fade away. Men and women must work in partnership to get the job done. And as that begins to happen, partnership, complementarity, teamwork and service will become features of the whole life of the Church, and men and women will both be freed to exercise the gifts God has given them, in his service.

For reflection/action

1. If you are involved in a church plant, does the leadership team have numbers of men and women which reflect the church membership?
2. If a woman can preach/lead in a church plant, can she do the same thing in the 'planting' church? If not, why not?
3. Are women allowed/encouraged to take initiatives in your church?
4. How can women in evangelistic ministry find more role models?

8

Women as thinkers and decision-makers

United wisdom and mutual consideration between men
and women can alone adequately plan for proportionate
advance.

(Missionary society report, 1912)[1]

While I was researching women's involvement in church planting
for the previous chapter, I was invited to a meeting of local church
leaders concerned for evangelism in my city. There were three
other women, out of a group of twenty-five or so, and as we
were waiting for the meeting to begin one of the other women
expressed relief at my presence. Much of the meeting was for
information, and then several of the men were invited to contribute some insights, things they felt God might be saying. The
chairman announced an event to bring leaders together for prayer,
planning and encouragement. 'Perhaps we could open it to
leaders' wives,' one man suggested.

If I had been a fly on the wall I would have described some of
the contributions as showing off, attempts to outdo the rest in
the 'spiritual' stakes. Those who spoke had come prepared, but
they also seemed to be those 'in the know', and with a hot line to
God. The gathering felt far too intimidating for a newcomer –
and a mere woman – to venture a comment.

We concluded with a time of prayer, in which the sense that
I'd somehow wandered into a men-only meeting continued. I've
been to many meetings in my life, including quite a few male-
dominated ones, and I thought that nothing would surprise me.

But this one I found harder and harder to take seriously. Does God really answer prayer according to how much noise we make? Was this how men behave when there are no women present? Was this how to be a real Christian with a heart for God's world? I began to wonder.

As the meeting finished, one of the other women, whom I'd met once before, came over to me. 'How about a coffee?' she asked. 'Or a stiff drink?!'

I had felt pleased to be invited to a meeting where evangelism was to be discussed. I was keen to meet those who are leaders in various churches, who are working to see the kingdom of God extended. I hoped to be inspired, and perhaps to find a place where I might be able to make some contribution. Instead, I felt, here was a group of men who displayed the worst excesses of male competitiveness – and clearly did not regard women as having anything to contribute.

Why is so much thinking about evangelism dominated by men? Are there any women who want to make things happen? And will men let them get involved? As we have seen, women have always been involved in sharing their faith. So why have they made so little contribution to decision-making, to thinking, to training, to strategy, to writing, on the subject on evangelism? That is the subject of this chapter.

The work of those who sit on committees, teach evangelism, write books or make decisions may not be very visible, but it is crucial. If, through the years, most of the decisions about the direction of evangelism have been made by men, it is not surprising that women's involvement in evangelism has been seen from a male standpoint, and that women have done only what men considered they could do.

Training the gossipers

If women are considered better at 'gossiping the gospel', personal evangelism, how is it that most training sessions on personal evangelism are led by men? The question about the absence and potential of women has been raised recently by Robert Warren and Clive Calver, who, from their different perspectives, have a broad awareness of the Anglican Church and the evangelical scene. They have noticed an absence of women. Why should this be? Is it about the absence of women as speakers and trainers in the Church generally? Is it that women have nothing to contribute to the subject of evangelism, or is it that they have never been listened to?

I was interested to compare personal evangelism taught by women and that taught by men. I must have experienced the latter many times and the former rarely, but in the past year I have sampled both. I know which I preferred. Again I struggle to avoid stereotypes, but on these occasions it seems to me that they were at their most obvious.

Frances professed no expertise and agreed to do it 'after much arm-twisting'. She was teaching a group how to train others in personal evangelism. David works for an evangelistic organisation and spends his life as an evangelist, as well as teaching friendship evangelism and preparing churches for mission. He was teaching a group of Christians from different churches in preparation for a mission.

Frances started by asking two questions: what do people need to know, and how are we going to deliver it? For her, training covered knowledge, skills, attitudes and experience.

For David, there was no opportunity to find out what people needed to know. The assumption was that they needed knowledge, and that knowledge would be translated into skills and attitudes. Wherever he taught, Christians got the same package, because what he was teaching was already laid out in a booklet, with blank spaces ready to fill in.

Frances' model of training involved flexibility. It involved teaching Christians to listen to non-Christians, to hear their stories, to look for a word for the individual person. David's model was the same for everyone.

Both models involved learning to use testimony. But David's model of a testimony seemed to assume a story of sudden conversion, which John Finney's research has shown is generally inappropriate. Only 37 per cent of people experience such a conversion. For 63 per cent of people, becoming a Christian is a gradual process.[2]

Frances' model involved using role play, building confidence, enabling people. David's model attempted to allay fears, but at an intellectual level. There was not even a break in the monologue for the audience to discuss with one another. What I found particularly irritating was that David had made no effort to make sure his anecdotes were relevant to the audience – with the result that many were inappropriate.

Subsequent investigation revealed that I was not the only one who thought his training style was inadequate. He had, I discovered, been asked to make changes for a subsequent occasion. But he is not an isolated example. I have experienced similar training by other male evangelists. Evangelists are often asked to lead evangelism training, but a woman with wide experience of evangelism suggested that they may not be the best people to do it. They tend to talk too much, and to tell story after story; they may be good preachers, but they do not know how to train people.

To some extent the lack of women in teaching and training roles reflects the general lack of expectations and opportunities for women in the Church. There are few women involved in training, and those we do have tend to be confined to the family and pastoral areas. One of those few suggested to me that with regard to teaching in a church context, 'The more important the subject is, the less likely a woman is to be doing it.'

But there are exceptions. For two women who have become accepted as teachers and trainers in evangelism, their involvement had started through men opening the way for them. Men had the 'power' – and the opportunity to delegate it to women as well as to men. Once they had been given the opportunity, the expertise of these women showed itself. This had led to further responsibility and experience, so that now both are highly respected. One of them is clearly a gifted evangelist as well as a good trainer, has seen many friends and neighbors come to Christ and has had a significant ministry on the radio. When her church saw how gifted Mary was, they sent her to Bible college, so that she would be better equipped.

But many women have never had that kind of encouragement. Some have had the opposite. Women who have taught evangelism to mixed groups have had to contend with Christians who cited 1 Timothy 2 against them. Some women who have stood up to speak have had men shout to them to stop, have been publicly rebuked, have had people walk out. Anne Graham Lotz, an evangelist and Bible teacher, tells of one occasion where, as she got up to speak, some of the men got up and reversed their chairs so that they had their backs to her. Yet she persevered. On another occasion, when she spoke to an international conference of itinerant evangelists, a young African evangelist came to her and said:

> 'I thought God had called me to come to this conference, promising to speak to me here. I went to every meeting, to every workshop. I fasted and prayed and wept and pled with God. But he still did not speak. I thought I had come halfway around the world for nothing. I was in despair, deeply discouraged, until this morning, when you spoke. Through you, I heard God speaking to me again and again.' His eyes widened as he looked at me with astonished wonder, and he concluded, 'And I can't believe God spoke to me through a sister.'[3]

Women teaching mission and evangelism

There is a heritage of women teaching mission to women. This was one of many ways in which the separation of women's work enabled women to play a fuller part in every aspect of mission than they would otherwise have done. From the 1860s, as the women's missionary movement sent women to the mission field, women became involved in missions education. Women produced textbooks, educational programmes, courses on missions. But with the demise of women's societies, and the loss of leadership roles to men, women stopped being involved in training.

Florence Allshorn (1887–1950) is one example of the kind of women who were involved in training women for mission. After serving with CMS in Uganda, she became warden of St Andrew's Hall, a CMS training college for women. And along with the academic subjects, Bible study and prayer, she focused on the need for students to deal with their weaknesses. 'We must send out people who are growing into the kind of personality which will react, as a living stimulus, to every possible condition. We must look for the signs of a conquering personality.'[4] Everything must flow out of a student's relation to God. It was what we would call today a wholistic approach to training, with those doing the training setting an example, being the kind of people they wanted the missionaries to be.

With the merging of women's and men's training colleges, those responsible for the training were predominantly male. Most Bible school and seminary mission faculties are comprised mainly of men. Does this matter? Do women have a different style?

It is dangerous to generalise, and there are not enough women teaching to draw any clear conclusions. But from those who are involved in teaching mission and evangelism it seems that perhaps women are more honest about difficulties, thus giving a more realistic picture of mission. That is not say that women are 'different', just that men and women tend to be socialised differently: it has been more acceptable for women to show weakness than it has for men. One woman said she personally acts more relationally as a teacher than men do; she is more involved as a person, and less concerned to 'know it all'. In contrast to the concept of education which sees teaching as depositing knowledge in the brain of the student (what a friend of mine calls 'jug and mug'), women's teaching is likely to be more learner-centered, experience-based, open-access and co-operatively oriented – all of which would be true of Frances' teaching of evangelism. Some of the workbooks and booklets for group study on evangelism (written by men) do use a more learner-centered and experience-based approach. But often this seems to go out of the window as soon as men stand up to speak!

In recent years, more women have begun to take up positions teaching mission and evangelism. However, one woman told me that in colleges married women are sometimes pulled in as stop-gaps, so tend to be on the fringe of things, never fully involved. Until there are more women teaching evangelism at colleges or in churches, the Church may be missing out on some essential perspectives to complement the approaches usually taken by men.

Men make decisions, women make the tea . . .[5]

Just as there are few women teaching evangelism, so there are relatively few women involved as leaders in organisations, as strategists, or on committees which consult and make decisions.

Sarah was appointed to a strategic position in an evangelistic organisation. She was well qualified, having had responsibility for evangelism in her church and considerable other experience. But her appointment was viewed as unusual, and some people did not think a woman could have the role of evangelist. Fortunately, she has been able to overcome any doubt in people's minds about her ability. If people ask, 'What does a woman know about evangelism?' they soon find out, 'Quite a lot.' Such a position has also provided her with a platform for teaching and training on evangelism, for producing training material and for contributing to wider thinking.

Nevertheless, Sarah is still a rarity. She would not see herself like that. She is a women who just wants to get on with the job God has called her to do. But many women who have a passion for evangelism, who want to make things happen and who find themselves gravitating towards leadership positions find themselves struggling. Women are a threat – or, to put it more accurately, men feel threatened by women. Women are sometimes given the impression that to be a strong, capable woman is ungodly. While women are increasingly rising to positions of responsibility in the secular world, the Church fails to use their full potential.

Much church culture has encouraged women to be passive, so it is not surprising that relatively few have been strong enough to buck the trend. The opposition women have experienced has sometimes been almost overwhelming. No wonder if some have taken the advice of Jane Austen: 'A woman, especially if she should have the misfortune of knowing anything, should conceal it as well as she can.'

But there are a few exceptions. By 1997 the Church of England had seven women diocesan advisers in mission and evangelism (out of about fifty), not many, but a slowly growing number. More women might have the ability to do the job, but many lack confidence and underestimate their abilities. Not many women apply for such jobs. They do not think they could do them. One woman, however, twice short-listed for diocesan evangelism jobs, was concerned that it may have been prejudice rather than lack of ability which meant the door shutting on both occasions. There are two women working for the Board of Mission, who are thus involved with mission advisers and a whole variety of meetings and activities concerned with the mission of the Church.

Two women have been appointed diocesan representatives or advisers in church planting, which is quite significant given that there are only about half a dozen such diocesan posts. However, the steering committee of Anglican Church Planting Initiatives has only one women out of ten, and its board of reference has only one woman out of thirteen. The Churches Together in England Group for Evangelisation, with a membership of around thirty-five evangelism officers from different churches, has only four women. The Salvation Army, which has seen women involved from the very beginning, has recently appointed someone to be responsible for mission and evangelism in each of its eighteen divisions. But only three of those eighteen are women. In other denominations there are a few similar appointments, but such women find themselves very much in a male world.

It can be hard being the only woman in a meeting. 'People tell me to push my ideas forward,' Clare told me. But women are branded 'pushy' if they are assertive. They thus find themselves in a great dilemma. Most women do not want to play power games. Some find their style is at odds with men's, find it hard to operate in meetings when the only way to be heard is to interrupt aggressively. I was told of one discussion where the women, in a minority, fell out of the discussion one by one. And yet to push their ideas forward may be the only way they will be heard, when that is how everyone else operates.[6]

We don't want to blow our own horn

So how can women be enabled to make a contribution to thinking on evangelism? If God's intention is for men and women to work together, the voices of women need to be heard. They need to be heard by men as well as by women. But on an all-male committee, who notices and suggests that women be invited to join? In many situations, women need men to open the way. Women who have become the first one to sit on this or that committee have usually had the way opened by men. Many women gratefully acknowledge those who have empowered them, invited them to participate and ensured that their contribution is heard.

Sometimes denomination affects the style of participation for women. One might not expect the Catholic Church to allow women much prominence at decision-making levels. But it seems precisely because the church does not ordain women that it has made more effort to involve laywomen in leadership roles. The Catholic Missionary Society is staffed entirely by priests, but a woman is Director of the Sion Catholic Community for Evangelism. A woman who represents the Catholic bishops at ecumenical meetings finds that almost all her equivalent colleagues are ordained men. And when the church sends women to other national level bodies, they find that most other churches are represented by men.

Is it that women do not have the vision or the capabilities, or is it that they are not given the space? Women have shown that they are as capable of thinking and making decisions about mission as men are. And there are some signs that women are starting to be included.

Women's missionary societies held their own conferences in the nineteenth century, but after they were amalgamated with the main societies women had only a small representation. In 1946, when women accompanied their husbands to a conference in Geneva, they were shocked to find that though they might have started global mission work or managed large budgets, they were expected to go shopping while their husbands took important decisions.[7]

At the first Lausanne Congress on World Evangelization in 1974 no women were plenary speakers, and women made up only a few hundred of the thousands invited. At the second Congress in 1989, four of the forty plenary speakers were women, and nearly a quarter of the participants. But Robyn Claydon, an Australian who co-ordinated workshops on the subject of women in evangelism, pointed out where the problem starts. 'Unless the church recognizes and releases the gifts of women and allows them opportunity to speak we will never be able to find enough women for our public platforms,' she said.[8] Women are not on the platform because they do not have the necessary experience.

Within the Anglican Church, an international conference was held in Kanuga, North Carolina, in 1995 to assess the Decade of Evangelism at its mid-point. Initially only one woman's name was among those submitted by primates and archbishops, but a number of others were subsequently invited to attend. Clearly Kanuga was slow to learn from Lausanne. A presentation at that conference on women's involvement in evangelism noted how involved women are, but how much of women's involvement has been invisible and marginalised.

One of the most fascinating parts of the presentation was where women handed over to let men speak about women and evangelism. Henry spoke about how the church in Uganda trains and empowers women; Felix gave three examples of the Mothers' Union in Burma, varying from selling rice to pay for the advance of the gospel, to an effective evangelist called Kathleen; Don spoke of six women who had been influential and had changed his views and his life.

It seemed very odd to see (as I saw on video) men speaking in a presentation chaired by women – until I remembered that men speak for women nearly all the time! In this context, though, it achieved several things. It prevented the whole presentation from being the 'women's slot'. It began to model a partnership between men and women which was surely what God intended. It modelled for men what needs to be done all the time in reverse: men making room for women. It allowed men to affirm the value of women's contribution; in a context where men have the power, this was empowering. And it was very moving.

It was good to have some women speaking at Lausanne and Kanuga. It was better than having no women. But the danger is that such conferences put women into a compartment called 'women and evangelism'. This implies that women's evangelism is somehow different from 'men and evangelism', which was the concern of the whole of the rest of the conferences, and enabled the insights of women to be excluded from the rest of the sessions. Surely what is needed is not sessions on 'women and evangelism' but the participation of women alongside men in whatever area of evangelism is being discussed, whether it is church planting, personal evangelism, mission strategy, the work of evangelists or the evangelism of children. If such integration was made, there would be no need for books like this!

The world was made for women also

What is best way to allow the fullest participation of women in the Great Commission: to separate out men's and women's work, or to hold them together? This was one question which came to the fore at the beginning of this century. It is time to ask it again, in the light of the lessons they learnt.

In the time of the women's missionary movement of the late nineteenth to early twentieth century, women were largely confined to their own circles. Women wrote for women and spoke to women. That era allowed women to gain responsibility, to speak, to think, to train missionaries, to have role models, and so on. The missionary societies gave women places to use their talents and to make a difference. By 1900 there were three million American women involved in over forty denominational women's societies.

At the same time, numbers of women in the Church Missionary Society, for example, had grown from 100 in 1866 to 743 in 1904. By the turn of the century, with such large numbers of women involved, it seemed logical to bring about fuller co-operation between the work of men and women, and the matter began to be discussed. In 1912, not long after the Edinburgh missionary conference of 1910, where the work of women was discussed, Minna Gollock wrote an article entitled 'The Share of Women in the Administration of Missions'.

In the article she noted the desirability of co-operation in the administration of missions at home and abroad, but observed that most societies overlooked this in practice. She drew attention to the emphasis, in a recent report on the co-operation between women and men, on the need for the gifts of women to be used: 'No woman with her heart on fire to serve her generation according to the will of God should find her sphere more readily outside the Church than inside.'[9] She also highlighted the facts that a committee which can select members from the best men and the best women will be better than if selected from men alone, that the insights of both men and women should be applied to the varied issues of missions work, and that recent advances in education for women meant that many women were just as capable of the task as men. The report had concluded that the united work of men and women would prove more fruitful than their separate work. Women felt that Jesus was asking more of them than in other days, 'but not more than His own attitude towards them and His own expectation from them indicated from the first'.[10]

But there were also dangers in amalgamation. These were not seen by everyone, but one women who saw what might happen was Helen Barrett Montgomery (1861–1934), one of the most notable leaders of the women's missionary movement.

She was a woman who grew up knowing that her gifts were in thinking and debate – certainly not then the spheres in which women were expected to operate. But the women's movement gave her the scope to use her gifts. As a Baptist minister she was involved in the organisation of the movement, encouraging ecumenical unity among mission societies and fostering missions' educational work.

She was also a missiologist, and among other things she wrote a history of the women's missionary movement from 1860 to 1910, *Western Women in Eastern Lands*. This included many insights into the scope and extent of women's work. Part of the achievement was raising the dignity of women. ' "The world was made for women also," said a Hindu woman after a month's stay in a hospital where she had seen all women, caste or outcaste, treated with respect as human beings.'[11]

The book ended with the hope that this was but 'a feeble beginning of what they can do and will do, when the movement is on its feet'.[12] But soon came calls that women's societies were no longer needed. A few men like A.T. Pierson advocated an equal role for women in the amalgamated societies, or even as board director: 'If Priscilla be the equal of Aquila, let her take rank with him, and if by superiority Priscilla outranks Aquila, let us not fear to put her name first.'[13] But he was in a minority. Where are the Piersons of today?

Helen Barrett Montgomery's book addressed the question of amalgamating the missionary societies: 'Would it not be better to have one great organisation of the entire Church to which men and women contributed?' Not, she argued, if that meant women were to raise the money for mission and men to decide how to spend it! Women, as well as men, needed the opportunity for self-expression and responsibility. So, what if the plan was to have men and women on the board, men and women in the work? That sounded ideal. But, she argued, 'are men ready for it?'

> Are they emancipated from the caste of sex so that they can work easily with women, unless they be head and women clearly subordinate? Certain facts seem to indicate that in spite of the rapid strides made in this direction we have still a long stretch of unexplored country to be traversed before the perfect democracy of Jesus is reached.[14]

When the decisions about amalgamation were made, women were powerless to resist the takeover. The co-operation which Minna Gollock and A.T. Pierson hoped for did not happen. As women's societies were amalgamated with men's, men took over all the leadership positions. Women found it more difficult to be heard, and lost much of the scope they had in their own societies. It has been argued that in some ways women face greater barriers in mission today than they did in the early years of this century.

If Priscilla be the equal of Aquila . . .

The words about the long stretch of country still to be traversed have a very modern ring to them. Helen's fear that women's interests would be overlooked has proved well founded. The evangelising of children is often left to women, and so is work with other women outside the Church.

Helen assumes that a female viewpoint is different from a male one. Different methods may be needed for reaching men and for reaching women. And one can agree with her without necessarily assuming fundamental differences between all men and all women. But ninety years on, there are more similarities between the world of many women and the world of men than when she wrote. Continued separation means continued marginalisation of women. In any case, most parts of the Church assume that their thinking and writing about evangelism is inclusive of all people.

What would Helen Barrett Montgomery write today? I think she might see that many men are ready to work together with women. But others are not. And she would say now, as she said then, 'Have women no contribution to add to missionary wisdom?' In most missionary societies the voices of women are now heard. But when it comes to evangelism, my perception is that there is still a long way to go. Some denominations have separate 'women's ministries' departments. The danger is that, while they empower women within them, they make little impact overall, just as the women's missionary movement made little lasting impact on mission thinking. I look forward to the day when men and women can work together in such a way that all the voices are heard, and that the particular concerns of men and women are given equal importance.

What do women have to contribute to thinking on evangelism today? I do not want to stereotype women, but some women do have particular experience and approaches which are needed. Women are less likely to see conversion as an isolated, in-dividualistic event, for example. They may be better at working at a personal level, and in cycles, rather than being task-oriented and linear.

The presentation by women at Kanuga was an interesting example of a more participative style. It used a large number of women to introduce different sections and to offer different perspectives. It enabled a number of women to participate, and in such a way that none would have felt too overwhelmed by the experience. Perhaps this is one way ahead for involving women and giving them experience of speaking, though from a practical level it may be more difficult to organise.

She did what she could

One of the reasons we can have confidence that women have much to contribute is because they have made significant contributions in the past, despite the restrictions.

At the time of the evangelisation of Europe, one of the few ways in which women could be involved was through orders of nuns. Lioba (700–779) was descended from an illustrious West Saxon family and educated in a nunnery at Wimborne, where she became known for her intellect and her holiness. She was invited by her cousin Boniface, one of the distinguished missionaries of the Middle Ages, to help with evangelism in Germany. She experienced a feeling of personal calling to this task, and in 748, with five other nuns and six monks, she went to begin her challenging work.

Soon Lioba herself became abbess of a community at Bischofsheim on the Tauber, and there she trained and sent out leaders to establish new religious houses. Such was the esteem in which she was held that her position 'was not merely that of a ruler, but of a teacher and expositor, and she . . . became so learned in the Scriptures and so wise in counsel that bishops often discussed church matters with her'.[15]

Selina, Countess of Huntingdon, has been mentioned earlier. Early Methodist preachers were often hounded by officials, and her influence helped them gain a hearing. She sent for the Wesleys to preach in her chapel and in 1748 she appointed Whitefield as her chaplain.

Then in 1760 she opened a chapel in Brighton, the first of many. It is estimated that 100,000 people heard the gospel in the sixty chapels that she sponsored. Church planting on this scale was seen as a threat to the Anglican Church, and her chapels became dissenting chapels with her name attached, hence the name 'The Countess of Huntingdon's Connexion'. She also founded a college for the training of ministers, and she functioned much like an abbess of the medieval period, virtually as a bishop, visiting chapels to oversee the work and taking charge of the pastoral training and finance. Some of the graduates of her training school went to America to evangelise the American colonies, and the rest preached all over England. Her prayer might find an echo in the hearts of many women – and men: 'May He increase my faith, animate my heart with zeal for His glory, enlarge my sphere, and make me more faithful in the sphere in which I serve.'[16]

Hannah More (1745–1833), jilted at the altar, turned to blaze a trail for women. She earned her fortune by her writing. She wrote plays which were a success on the London stage. She set up a new programme of popular education in schools near her native Bristol. She wrote Cheap Repository Tracts, which aimed to teach religion and morality in homely language, and their success led in 1799 to the formation of the Religious Tract Society, to promote cheap popular religious literature. She believed, like most people of her day, in sexual differentiation, and that men were formed for public life, but she did not believe that women should be seen and not heard. She was convinced that women had a civilising effect, and was not afraid to speak out with her own views. The 'Old Bishop in Petticoats', as one man called her, gave away Bibles, prayer books and Testaments, so that poorer people could read them.

When she and her sister visited the village of Cheddar in 1789, she found 'as much knowledge of Christ as in the interior of Africa', and reflected that while Britain was sending out missionaries 'to our distant colonies, our own villages are perishing for want of instruction'.[17] In 1789 she opened Cheddar School, which began to teach the Scriptures and basic skills to adults and children.

> The grand subject of instruction with me is the Bible itself . . . To infuse a large quantity of Scripture into their minds, with plain practical comments in the way of conversation, is the means which I have found, under Providence, instrumental in forming the principles and directing the hearts of youth. God has promised His *blessing* on His Word.[18]

She focused particularly on the parables in Luke 15 and on the beginning of Genesis to explain the fall, and encouraged the children to learn various other important chapters of the Bible by heart. She wrote a book on prayer for young people, and encouraged mothers to teach their children the Lord's Prayer, explaining each sentence or clause. Within a decade, the weekly church attendance in Cheddar had risen from fifty to seven hundred, and there were similar transformations in other villages.

Hannah had met Robert Raikes and Sarah Trimmer, who had pioneered Sunday Schools, and such schools already existed in a couple of Mendip villages. But Hannah's scheme was for something greater than Sunday Schools. The fact that she is popularly associated with Sunday Schools is perhaps typical of the way in which women's contributions are sometimes minimised by focusing on those of their achievements which are most like 'women's work'.

Mighty forces of the Cross

Even before the mission field opened up to women, they began to take initiatives, to found organisations and to think strategically. In 1800 Mary Webb formed the Boston Female Society for Missionary Purposes, described by her biographer as 'the first women's missionary society in the world'.[19] Missionary support was one of the few areas open to women. All the more remarkable was the fact that Mary Webb was confined to a wheelchair. But for fifty years she was secretary-treasurer of the organisation and generated support for home and foreign missions.

In 1834 David Abeel, a missionary in China, appealed in London and America on behalf of the women in China, 'O bring us some female men'. Inspired by women in Britain, Sarah Doremus wanted to found a female agency, but was initially thwarted by those opposed to single women in missions. Not until 1860 was she able to organise the Women's Union Missionary Society, which she continued to direct until her death in 1877. Many other women's societies followed.

One important initiative was the use of Bible women. National women were already being used by missionaries to reach other women. But in order to make her mission more effective, Adele Fielde (1839–1916) took up the idea and made it a major part of mission strategy for Baptists in China, establishing a training school and developing courses. Helen

Barrett Montgomery describes what followed from her work:

> The Bible woman has become an institution. Her work is indispensable; she multiplies the missionary's influence, goes before to prepare the way, and after to impress the truth. One of the humblest, she is at the same time one of the mightiest forces of the Cross in non-Christian lands. She is first of all an evangelist. From door to door she goes, repeating portions of the Scriptures, or reading the Bible, singing hymns, praying, telling her own personal experience of God's goodness. She may be the only Christian woman in a village. She may teach the little village school, she may nurse the sick in seasons of pestilence, she may gather together a Sunday School, she may teach needlework and reading to the shut-in women of the zenanas.[20]

Adele Fielde trained around five hundred women to evangelise and train their own people. This had far-reaching effects, leading to the use of Bible women in many countries and to an increased appreciation of the capabilities of national believers.

One solution to the general exclusion from mission thinking was for women to develop new concepts for world evangelisation. The ministry which became known as Gospel Recordings arose almost by accident. Joy Ridderhof left her missionary work in Honduras due to poor health. While recuperating in California, she hit on the idea of sending messages back to Honduras on records. This proved so successful that a ministry arose involving using bilingual tribespeople to tape gospel messages in tribal languages which had not yet been reached by Bible translators and linguists. People were able to hear the gospel in their own language for the first time. Now we are using tapes and videos to communicate the gospel to Westerners who have become part of a 'non-book' culture!

An article by another woman led to the founding of what later became the Mission Aviation Fellowship, which now operates in thirty-one countries throughout the world. Elizabeth Greene was a pilot in the US Air Force during World War II. After the war she wrote an article for a Christian magazine presenting the need for missionary aviation. The idea was taken up by a Navy pilot, who invited her to join him and others in putting her idea into action.

Pioneering urban mission

Other women, when still denied access to the mission field or wanting to combine evangelism more easily with their domestic responsibilities, found their 'field' closer to home. An army of women descended on the cities.

The first mass movement to involve women in urban mission was the Sunday School movement, which began in the 1780s. Most of the teachers in Sunday Schools and Ragged Schools were women, both in Britain and America. At first there was opposition to women's involvement, but in the nineteenth century, when increased stress was placed on the civilising influence of women, it was seen as more acceptable and an extension of their domestic duties.

It was this possibility for women to be involved in philanthropic work that enabled Ellen Ranyard (1810–1879) to set up her London Bible and Domestic Female Mission (later the Ranyard Bible Mission). When Ellen was converted, she set out to spread the word by selling cheap Bibles, and when her family had grown up and she moved to London in 1857, she struck on the idea of selling Bibles to the poor.

Mrs Ranyard was partly inspired by the use of 'native agency'. By the middle of the nineteenth century, Bible women were beginning to be used on the mission field. At the same time, women were starting to do visitation in their own cities: in urban parishes there was too much visiting for clergy to do, so women became official 'district visitors', lending tracts and evangelising.[21] The London City Mission had already seen the need to employ women, but did not do so (though other evangelical town missions did employ women as salaried full-time evangelists).[22] This failure left the field wide open to others.

In 1859 Ellen Ranyard published *The Missing Link*, arguing that Bible women were the 'missing link' between the working poor and the gospel. The first women were paid ten shillings a week, and sold Bibles and advised on domestic matters. The mission developed, until by 1867 there were 234 Bible women, and professional nurses were also employed to attend to physical needs. Mrs Ranyard insisted that the women should come from the working class themselves, but they were supervised by middle-class women.[23]

The first task was to persuade women to purchase Bibles. They were then invited to meet with others in the home, for a discussion about various methods of self-improvement. A third stage was for women to accompany the Bible women to a mission room, to be taught more about the Christian faith, and finally to be incorporated into the life of a local congregation.

Thus Mrs Ranyard started not only a women's mission but the first paid social workers in England, and the scheme spread to other English cities.[24]

In the United States, Phoebe Palmer was an evangelist and a leader in the Holiness movement, but she was also a pioneer of social welfare projects. She was involved in establishing the Hedding Church, a city mission work which represented the early beginnings of the later settlement houses. As she grew more involved with the poor on a personal level by visiting homes and prisons, she became aware of their material needs, and as a result founded the Five Points Mission. This was a mission project in New York that housed twenty poor families, and provided schooling and religious training. According to a historian of the period, the beginnings of Protestant institutional work in the slums can be traced to this mission.

Women continue to take initiatives in urban mission. In Peru, Rosario Rivera, a former communist guerrilla, found that church attendance was not enough. She wanted to help the poor, and had soon started a mission to the children of Lima's slums. By 1986, 2,500 children were being reached through her ministry of breakfast and Bible lessons. The idea was for the children to learn the whole Bible in a year. Rivera drew together churches, trained volunteers and organised the operation, and also campaigned to get better basic amenities for the area. Her experience as a guerrilla was turned to good effect: she had learnt to organise and take initiatives, but instead of obeying her guerrilla leaders, she started to obey God![25]

With the growing gap between rich and poor in Britain, there is an urgent need for women again to see the need for such Christian work. Preaching evangelism is often valued more highly than social evangelism, and the latter can easily become social work with no Christian focus. Those who want to be valued learn to be 'up-front' people; if they pursue a 'caring' model they are sometimes made to feel that this is not really being an evangelist. Even in an organisation like the Church Army, where men and women work together as evangelists, I am told that men tend towards up-front work and women the more social work, which is, as a result, undervalued.

But this kind of mission is true incarnation: God getting his hands dirty in the realities of life. Times change and the needs of each generation are different, but perhaps we have come full circle. Women have been to the mission field, and now mission partnership means that fewer pioneers are needed in non-Western countries. Meanwhile Britain has become a mission field. Pioneers are needed here to face difficult situations, to live in the inner cities and outer estates, to work with those whose lives are dominated by alcohol or drugs, and who are trapped in poverty, to tell children who know nothing about God that he loves them.

Women writing books

One final area in which women have proved themselves, yet have often been overlooked, has been in writing on mission and evangelism. Some of the books by women have been mainly on the work of women, such as the one by Helen Barrett Montgomery. There have been a number of books on 'missionary heroines'. In the heyday of the women's missionary movement, many books were written on women in other religions to help missionaries communicate the gospel across cultures, and some of these were of wider importance in the field of cross-cultural mission.

One such book came from the pen of Pandita Ramabai (1858–1922). The daughter of a wandering Hindu guru, who broke with Hindu tradition and allowed his daughters to become Sanskrit scholars, she eventually was drawn to Christ. She founded a school at Poona (now Pune) for child widows, which operated on Christian principles and taught the Bible. Ramabai did not believe in actively evangelising pupils, but that the work of the Holy Spirit would turn them to Christ. Many girls did indeed profess faith in Christ.

Ramabai was critical of missionaries who did not respect the cultures in which they were working, and was convinced that the only way to convey the gospel effectively to India was to avoid making it alien to Indian culture and the Hindu Scriptures. Her book, *The High-Caste Hindu Woman*, emphasised the importance of understanding the culture and lifestyle of these women, and helped to improve understanding of this little-known segment of Hindu society.[26]

B.V. Subbamma was another woman whose missiological work arose out of her own experience. A caste-Hindu, Subbamma was introduced to Christianity while attending a mission school in South India. As she read the Bible she came to faith in Christ. But baptism presented an obstacle: 'I was definitely not prepared to leave my own Kamma people and join some other community. At the same time I longed to be baptized since I understood one had to be baptized if he wished to be a disciple of the Lord.'[27]

Subbamma experienced considerable opposition from her family, but was eventually baptised and joined the Church, which involved identification with Harijan (outcast) Christians. As she began to get involved in women's work in India she began to explore alternative concepts of caste evangelism. How to approach the caste system was an issue which exercised the minds of missiologists; although it was a barrier, Subbamma concluded that it was so embedded in the culture that it could not be ignored. She continued her research at Fuller Theological Seminary and published her conclusions in *New Patterns for Discipling Hindus* (1970): it was not helpful for missionaries to disrupt caste exclusiveness. Her work was a significant contribution to evangelistic strategy for reaching Hindus, and also had wider implications regarding evangelism and culture. Subbamma also served as principal of a Bible training school and as an evangelist.

One of the first women to write for men as well as women was Constance Padwick, who served in the Middle East for forty years. She wrote on Muslim evangelism, publishing articles in mission journals and many books. She also proposed a strategy

of evangelism which involved building bridges of love and understanding. One of her books, *Muslim Devotions*, first published in
1961 and viewed with some scepticism, has recently been re-
published. It is based on her study of the Awrad and Ahzad, Sufi
manuals of prayer, and is seen to be of value today for helping
Christians understand the religious thought of Islam. Some of
Constance Padwick's best missiology may have been overlooked
because it is woven into the pages of her missionary biographies.[28]

Today there are encouraging signs that some writing by
women is following the example of Padwick and writing not
about and for women, but about general issues of evangelism. As
women and men work together it is good to see that women can
contribute more broadly. But one area in which women seem to
have made surprisingly little contribution is books on personal
evangelism. If it is true that women are better at personal faith-
sharing than men, how is it that most of the books on the subject
of faith-sharing are written by men? How is it that most of the
material intended for use in faith-sharing – *Becoming a Christian,
Journey into Life, Why Jesus?* – is written by men?

It is not that women do not write books. There are a good
number of Christian books written by women. But many of them
are on issues which have come to be associated with women:
spirituality, parenting, relationships, children's stories. A notable
exception was Rebecca Manley Pippert's *Out of the Saltshaker*,
published in the USA in 1979 and the following year in Britain.
More recently, Christine Dodd wrote what she described in her
subtitle as 'a workbook for the Decade of Evangelization'; *Called
to Mission* was published in 1991 and reprinted several times. As
its subtitle suggests, it is written primarily for Catholics, by the
Adult Education Adviser for the Roman Catholic diocese of
Hallam. Is there anything exceptional about these two books, or
their authors? Why have not more women written on the subject
of evangelism?

Out of the Saltshaker is subtitled, '*Evangelism as a way of
life*'. It does not have a consciously female perspective, but
Rebecca Manley Pippert's famous comment that 'There was a
part of me that secretly felt evangelism was something you
shouldn't do to your dog, let alone a friend', is a reaction to the
conviction that 'much of our evangelism is ineffective because

we depend too much upon technique and strategy. Evangelism has slipped into the sales department.'[29] The book had an unusual honesty. In the stories she tells, the author makes herself vulnerable. I do not think it is too much to claim that Pippert's book had a significant influence on current approaches to evangelism. There are now many more books which focus on the way in which evangelism flows out of relationship.

Called to Mission begins like this: 'It was Sunday morning and she was sitting in her usual place in St Edwin's church. As she looked around her it suddenly dawned on Elizabeth just how many people had smiled at her that morning; just how many people she knew and just how different they all were.'[30] It is intended to help 'ordinary' Christians who feel unsure about all this mission and evangelisation business. It is designed to help people to tell their stories, to find out for themselves what they have to share, rather than to tell them how to do it. It has questions for reflection and group work. There is no set formula of 'the gospel', but an opportunity to work out what is the good news that you have to share. Again, evangelism is seen to flow out of relationships, and out of one's own story.

This understanding is not unique to women, but it seems to be the way in which much current thinking is going (the *Emmaus* course, for example, with its emphasis on people's *oikos*, their network of relationships). It would be interesting to find out whether women are less likely to use booklets and set prayers than men are; I would suspect that they are.

One of the few books I have found on the subject of women and evangelism is *Gossiping the Gospel: Women Reflect on Evangelism*, which was produced by a group of women in New Zealand. The group was ecumenical, and worked collaboratively; the text was written and circulated for comments, which were then incorporated. It is a method which works well. But the sadness of the book for me was that most of the women contributors had been alienated by the Church, through its neglect of issues important to women, especially justice and other social issues, and its failure to hear women's voices. Thus for some of the writers, 'evangelism' was more about accepting people as they are, recognising the divine in people, empowering women, than about challenging them to follow Christ. But while we may see that as insufficient, we also need to allow those insights to challenge views of evangelism which have concentrated too much on personal piety and not enough on living out Christ's radical values in the world.

Our Time Has Come, a collection of papers from the first Pan-African Christian Women's Assembly held in 1989, includes chapters specifically on evangelism, and the need for women to play their part in fulfilling the Great Commission runs right through the book. Madelaine Kayumba, an evangelist, and wife of a Rwandan bishop, has written a book called *Women in the Bible*.[31] Its aim is to inspire women to use their talents, to help them to discover what the Bible really says about women, and to help them to be involved in decision-making. Her method was to take women of the Bible and see what lessons they have for today's women. That includes seeing Mary Magdalene and Priscilla as among the first apostles to the mission field.

In many cultures, women are realising the power of writing to awaken women to their God-given tasks. As well as women who can write on all aspects of evangelism, we still need more women who can theologise about women and mission. We need women who can write about the Bible and draw out new insights about women. We need books and booklets for evangelism which use inclusive language. We need material which focuses on those issues which most concern women.

Ruth Tucker, who has written many books and articles on women in mission, wonders if her books show more interest in personal problems and family issues than a book written by a man might. Several women have recently begun to consider the question of whether women approach mission any differently from men.[32]

In his book, *Reaching a New Generation: Strategies for Tomorrow's Church*,[33] Alan Roxburgh focuses on community, ecology and spirituality as key values for which people of today are increasingly looking. A yearning for community, a desire to save the earth from ecological destruction and a thirst for an experience of spiritual reality are also things which motivate many women, including those who would call themselves feminists and many who have left the Church. The book is not addressed particularly to the needs of women, but it perhaps shows that issues sometimes seen as 'women's' are more universally desired. If the insights of both men and women are contributed to evangelism strategy, we will have more chance of meeting the challenges of our world.

A fearful symmetry

With all these examples of women who have gone before, why are women not making more contribution to evangelism today? Faced with a changing role, the need is for Christians who can listen to society and adapt evangelistic strategies accordingly. In an increasingly fragmented post-modern world, there will no longer be big answers, perhaps, but a need for many strategies to meet many kinds and conditions of people.

Women, who have pioneered women's work and taken the gospel to the most difficult places in the world, can surely find ways of taking the gospel to 'feminist' women, that great 'unreached people group' of the modern world. But they need to be encouraged. Today's Church seems to find the culture around us more of a threat to be protected from than a mission field to be converted.

And women can do far more. There are many other missionary challenges which might be overcome if women were allowed to make their contribution: challenges about how to reach one kind of people or another, and challenges about mission itself. It seems that much of the Church has lost its nerve when it comes to mission. Women need to be invited on to decision-making committees. Perhaps women can do better than recent initiatives which have involved evangelism 'from a distance' rather than the more costly evangelism which involves incarnation. I cannot imagine any woman advocating mission by means of the impersonal distribution of literature. The gospel needs to be lived out.

Is fulfilment of the Great Commission being hindered because women are not equal co-workers at all levels of decision-making and mission activity? During the era of the women's missionary movement women could not work with men, but women at least had solidarity with each other. Today we have a Church in which women and men work together – in theory anyway. Since two-thirds of the churches' 'manpower' for evangelism is female, and women have not been allowed to exercise their full potential, who knows how much more effectively the task might be done if women were allowed to participate as equals?

In thinking about evangelism, women have often been restricted to women's work, work which is an extension of the family: work with toddlers, reaching mothers of school-age children at the school gate, reaching friends and neighbours. Some women are concerned to reach women of other religions through friendship evangelism. But on the whole we seem to have become very tame, very unadventurous. Cannot original thinking and the pioneering adventurous spirit of women be translated to evangelism in the tough mission fields of today: high-rise flats and inner-city ghettos, affluent suburbs, drug and party cultures, young and lone parents, New Agers?

If the missionary call comes from God, it is often mediated through human beings. Many women were called into mission or evangelism through hearing another woman speak of her experience. If that happens less and less, women may find it more difficult to hear the call of God on their lives. We need to make sure that girls and young women in the Church today hear the stories of women who have gone before, and of women in our own day who are attempting great things for God.

In a few years' time, it may be unnecessary to talk in these gendered terms. The Bible does not assume such compartments, and to attain once again a biblical partnership will be to allow the voices of all to be heard and thus to ensure that all whom God has gifted in this way can hasten the day when the gospel will be preached to every people and every nation.

For reflection/action

1. Who is responsible for evangelism in your church? Who does the teaching and training in evangelism?
2. Look at how your church mission and evangelism committees are made up. Are women involved in decision-making? Do women and men work

together? Observe a meeting and see if women have a fair proportion of 'air time'.

3. Look at your evangelistic literature. Is it women-friendly?

4. Do you ever hear men put women down or make jokes at their expense? If you are a man, do you challenge the comments? If you are a woman, how do you feel? What is likely to happen to a woman who is often put down or made to feel foolish? Arrange to have a discussion where men and women listen to each other's feelings about this.

9

Women: 'Go and tell'

You see things and say 'Why?' But I dream things that never were; and I say, 'Why not?'[1]

In her book, *Split Image*, Anne Atkins quotes a friend of hers.

He had been to a depressing and decadent party, and was burning with compassion for the people he had met. 'The only thing in life worth doing,' he said with genuine feeling, 'is preaching the gospel of Christ.' Then he looked at his little daughter. 'Next time we must have a son,' he said to his wife, 'so that he can do just that.'[2]

Was he right? Is it only sons, and not daughters, of God who can preach the gospel of Christ? I think not.

'The Lord gives the command: great is the company of women who bore the tidings' (Psalm 68:11).[3] Great indeed is the company of women who have appeared in the pages of this book, and there are many, many more. The Bible and the whole of church history bear witness to the contribution of women to the mission of the Church. Take away the work of evangelism done by women and you might ask how Europe would have been evangelised. The great missionary movement of the last two centuries could never have happened without women pioneers, women preachers, women teachers, women strategists . . . women bearing the tidings in every possible way.

But it also seems clear from the stories of women that they

have faced many obstacles in their attempts to play their part in proclaiming the gospel. They have been lectured for being un-biblical, derided for being unfeminine, guilt-tripped for being unmotherly. Yet they have persisted. I have structured this book by dividing it into different areas of life: a woman's Jerusalem – her home; Judea and Samaria – her friends and neighbours, church planting; and the ends of the earth – preaching, teaching and planning for the whole world. But such distinctions soon break down. Those who have tried to confine women's ministry to Jerusalem, or Judea and Samaria, have found that it does not work. Such women either lose confidence in their ability to witness at all, or find that God does not respect such boundaries. A woman who is a disciple of Christ will share the good news with her family and friends. Then she will share it with neigh-bours. Then she starts visiting a few houses, or meeting larger groups, and soon thinks how much easier it would be if she could speak to those people all together. And so 'gossiping the gospel' easily becomes 'preaching'.

Go and make disciples

Women were the first to be told the news of the resurrection of Jesus from the dead. They were then commanded to proclaim it to the men: ' "Don't be alarmed," the angel said. "You are looking for Jesus the Nazarene, who was crucified. He has risen! He is not here . . . But go, tell his disciples and Peter, 'He is going ahead of you into Galilee' " ' (Mark 16:6–7). We are told that the women fled, and said nothing to anyone (verse 8). We may pause to consider why they did not speak, but we cannot deny that they were commanded to do so. And in the longer ending of Mark's Gospel, Mary Magdalene goes and tells the other dis-ciples, and Jesus rebukes the Eleven for their 'lack of faith and their stubborn refusal to believe those who had seen him after he had risen' (Mark 16:14).

In Luke's version of the story the women do tell the disciples, 'but they did not believe the women, because their words seemed to them like nonsense' (Luke 24:11). How often have women been impelled by the call of God within them, to 'go, tell', but have been prevented either by their own sense of inadequacy, as in Mark, or been stopped in their tracks because they are 'only women', as in Luke?

No one seriously thinks that the Great Commission of Matthew 28:18-20 was given only to men. Women are called to fulfil it as much as men are. The whole Church, men and women, are commanded by Jesus to go to all nations, to make disciples, to baptise them and to teach them. Thus in all four Gospel accounts, women are sent out as evangelists.

And when the day of Pentecost came, and the Spirit was poured out, Peter, for all his faults, must have thought women were included, or why did he choose to quote those verses from Joel, that 'your sons and your daughters will prophesy . . . Even on my servants, both men and women, I will pour out my Spirit' (Acts 2:17,18)?

God has called women. God equips women. Women may sometimes seem weak in the world's eyes, but God has a special place for them. According to 1 Corinthians 1:26-9, 'God chose the foolish things of the world to shame the wise; God chose the weak things of the world to shame the strong . . .' Socially and economically, women are still the 'weaker sex' around the world. But sometimes this has been precisely why God has been able to use them. Used to obedience, they have obeyed. Used to gathering together for support, they have empowered one another. Used to struggling to survive, they have struggled to find a voice.

The Lord giveth the word

There is a final reason why the Church needs to promote the full equality of women in the task of evangelism. It is this. The annals of the Church suggest that when God sends revival, women are right at the forefront of it. When revival comes to the Church, there is no time for arguments about which sex should do what. Women have played a major part in many revivals. This book has made reference to the time of Wesley, Finney's revival, the 1859 Evangelical Awakening; and there are others: the Welsh Revival of 1904, the East African Revival, 1927-1937 in China. The prominence of women in leadership seems to be a characteristic of revival history.[4] Revivals provided greater outlets for women than they generally had in the established churches. When the Church is involved in mission, women are doing it. When women are free to evangelise, the Church grows.

Marie Monsen, a Norwegian missionary, went to China in 1901 with the Norwegian China Mission. 'Don't be a Jonah,' a gospel preacher had challenged. She did not dare disobey God's call. Once there, ostensibly to do educational work, she soon realised that much of the church was not really converted. In 1907 she heard of revival in Korea and began to pray for revival. She read about revival. She longed for revival.

In 1927, as she and three other women were praying for the women of China, one 'received a word from the Lord: "The Lord giveth the word: the women that publish the tidings are a great host." (Psalm 68:11 RV) It seemed to sink into our hearts and lift us out of our discouragement.'[5] As political unrest forced women out of their homes, Christian women witnessed to them, and the congregation in her church grew. Courses for Bible women were joined by wives of missionaries, desperate to learn to play their part. Revival broke out, and everywhere Marie went, leading meetings, preaching and teaching, revivals followed: 'Sometimes I personally had to leave before the revival broke out, but we always knew it was coming.'[6] A book on the revival in Shantung told how 3,000 were added to the church in a year, lives were transformed, and they in turn went out to spread the good news. God raised up other women to do the work of an evangelist.

Towards the end of Monsen's story of the 1927–1937 Awakening in north China, we read these words: 'In times of revival it was not unusual for humble-minded men to say to the women God in His grace was using: "I thought God would use me in the work you are doing." One even said with tears: "We men have failed. Now the Lord is showing us what He can do through women." '[7] Would the fuller ministry of women hasten the revival for which we pray?[8]

Discarded because of their sex

But how many such talents have been buried? What a waste this has been to the Church – and a source of much pain to many women. In a lecture given to the Evangelical Missionary Alliance in 1994, Elaine Storkey talked about the responsibility of men:

> Here's a challenge for them: let them imagine what it's like to be a woman, especially women of a few decades ago who were involved in missionary work. How did it feel to serve overseas for many years, come home and never be allowed to use the calling and gifts God had given? Only when we put ourselves in another's shoes do we experience what many women have known: the longing to serve God, even knowing the gifting of God, yet being discarded because of their sex.[9]

Many years ago Catherine Booth suggested how great a loss to the Church has been that caused by misapplication of biblical texts:

> Judging from the blessed results which have almost invariably followed the ministrations of women in the cause of Christ, we fear it will be found, in the great day of account, that a mistaken and unjustifiable application of the passage, 'Let your women keep silence in the Churches,' has resulted in more loss to the Church, evil to the world, and dishonour to God, than any of the errors we have already referred to.[10]

There is no doubt that at times in the history of the Church, women have been prevented from exercising the gift of evangelism fully, and that is one reason why we have not seen more women evangelists.

So there are a number of things which account for the relative lack of women in evangelism. Some Christians have come to the conclusion from the biblical evidence that the Bible forbids it. So, they would argue, women have not been evangelists because they have been obedient to Scripture. But it is possible to interpret the biblical evidence very differently, and many would account for the lack of women in the same way as Catherine Booth does, as due to a misuse of Scripture. We could also mention social and cultural features; today, as in New Testament times, a variety of factors account for the varying attitudes towards women's roles. And so, social and cultural factors have also encouraged or hindered the full participation of women in evangelism. But if women have been held back merely for cultural reasons, it is time to let the Bible challenge the culture of our world, rather than drag behind it.

Roll away the stone

It is not too late to wake up to the truth of those words of Catherine Booth, even 140 years on. Fredrik Franson suggested that women are like the last group of workers to be hired, in Jesus' parable of the workers in the vineyard in Matthew 20:1–16. 'Why have you been standing here all day long doing nothing?' the landowner asked. 'Because no one has hired us,' they answered (verses 6–7). Now the time is late, and women are needed to join in.

A recent article on the connection between women and missions suggests that the disappearance of the women's missionary movement and the under-use of women in mission have been tragedies, but women may be the key to reaching many of the unreached people of our world, the 1.2 billion people who have not yet heard the gospel. If, as it seems, in some people groups women are most responsive to the gospel, women may be those best equipped to reach them. Thus, Bryant Myers suggests, 'we need to give preference to recruiting, training and supporting far more women if we are to reach the unreached'.[11]

And what is true of overseas mission is true of home mission. Now that world mission is about partnership, the distinctions between home and overseas mission break down. Women may be well equipped to reach into many communities, women may plant new forms of church, women may come up with new ideas, women may teach evangelism more effectively.

There are many signs of life, and of promise for the future. There are now many opportunities for training in evangelism available, including correspondence courses which have a practical component. Parachurch organisations such as Operation

Mobilisation, Youth For Christ and Oasis give young women and men evangelism training and short-term opportunities. Growing numbers of women work alongside men in open-air evangelism, in universities and colleges, in mission teams. The ordination of women to the priesthood in the Anglican Church is opening up new opportunities for women.

We are also seeing a shift in our understanding of how we do evangelism. The 'preacher' model may be less relevant to the needs of our time. There are some opportunities in the media for evangelism, which women may find more comfortable – and who knows what will open up through the Internet? The current focus in the Anglican Church on becoming 'missionary congregations' may help to draw attention to evangelistic gifts in the whole Church rather than to those with an up-front ministry, and thus be more valuing of women's abilities; and Robert Warren's own advocacy of women's ministry should ensure that women are not left out of the thinking.

In an article on women in evangelism written in 1986, Kathy Keay suggested what individuals and churches could do for things to change: identify women with the gift of evangelist; see women as preachers, not those preached *at*; deal with sexist attitudes; use women alongside men in mission teams; appoint more church-based evangelists, including women; transform women's groups into effective bases for evangelism; appoint more women to lead parachurch groups and teach evangelism.[12] Some progress has been made in the last ten years, but that is still an essential agenda.

When someone asked D.L. Moody what a woman can do to serve Christ, he replied, 'What could they not do?'[13] Phoebe Palmer wrote in 1859, 'The church in many ways is a sort of potter's field where the gifts of women, as so many strangers, are buried. How long, O Lord, how long before man shall roll away the stone that we may see a resurrection?'[14]

The Church needs to use all its resources – men and women – to reach the variety of men and women from all backgrounds and cultures who do not yet know Christ. May God speed the day when hosts of women as well as men are lifting up their voices (Isaiah 40:9) and proclaiming, 'Here is your God!'

APPENDIX

The 'difficult' passages: does the Bible support women's public ministry?

> Many thoughtful men have been led to examine the Word of God anew, to learn if it really be so that the Scriptures silence the testimony which the Spirit so signally blesses.
> (A. J. Gordon, 'The Ministry of Women', 1894)

The passage in 1 Timothy 2:11-15 has been described as 'the single most effective weapon to keep women from active and equal participation in the church'. On that much there is general agreement. To those who believe that women have been wrongly excluded from certain ministries, it has been a barrier because of poor interpretation. To those who believe that women have been rightly excluded, it continues to be the key passage where Paul makes the case most clearly. Although 1 Corinthians 14:34-5 has some bearing on the participation of women, it is the 1 Timothy passage on which the case for restrictions on the ministry of women stands or falls.[1] While some would argue that these passages apply only to authoritative teaching or leadership in the Church, in practice, because evangelism has so often involved preaching, women's evangelism has also been restricted.

There is a huge collection of scholarly literature on these passages, and the arguments continue to rage. Those not familiar with theological debate need at least to be aware that prominent church scholars and leaders are divided on the interpretation of these verses. Sometimes what is said to be the 'clear teaching of

Scripture' is a simplistic reading of an English translation. What we read in our Bibles is a translation from Greek, and there are a few places in the New Testament where it is difficult to be sure that any particular translation is right, let alone work out what it means and how to apply it to our situation today.

In the Church today, Christians take a variety of approaches. Many, relying on one strand of scholarly opinion, see Paul's words as applying to a particular context, which has now changed. They see them outweighed by other Scriptures, and by examples of women in ministry in the early Church and ever since. But a fierce debate continues. One scholar recently suggested a truce.[2] But that is impossible if both sides of the debate want to work out what God is saying to us through Paul's writing. The answer we come to will affect the lives and ministry of one half of God's workforce.

So it is important to come to some kind of conclusion. This appendix is an attempt to clarify the issues and to review the debate, before showing how my own conclusions bear on the argument of the rest of the book.

The early Church

Some people speak or write as if the debate about Scripture and the role of women is a modern one. But it has gone on right through the history of the Church. It is useful to see the kind of arguments which have been used throughout the ages. Some have already been referred to, in chapter 3.

The church fathers tended to go further than we might today in applying Scripture to restrict the ministry of women. Origen, for example, used 1 Corinthians 14:34 against a heretical sect, Montanism, which allowed women to be prophetesses, and cited 1 Timothy 2:12 in support of this also. He saw women as being banned from public and official teaching, when women would take authority over men. 'Men should not sit and listen to a woman ... even if she says admirable things, or even saintly things, that is of little consequence, since they come from the mouth of a woman.'[3] He does, however, argue that according to Romans 16:1-2 which mentions Phoebe, 'this text teaches with the authority of the Apostle that even women are instituted deacons in the church'.[4]

Chrysostom referred back to the fall. Woman 'asserted her authority once and asserted it badly'. Eve 'taught the man once, upset everything, and made him liable to disobedience. Therefore God subjected her, since she used her rule, or rather, her equality of honor, badly.' Thus women should not teach authoritatively. But he allowed them to give non-official teaching and encouraged them to study theology. They will have salvation (1 Tim. 2:15) 'through having children'.[5]

We have no record of what women thought of these interpretations. Down the centuries of church history, most theology has been done by men. But we do have some responses of women from earlier than might be expected. One of the earliest examples of women countering from Scripture their exclusion from ministry was the pamphlet by Margaret Fell, *Women's Speaking Justified, Proved and Allowed of by the Scriptures*, published in 1666. One of her main arguments was from Acts 2, where Peter quotes from Joel that 'your sons and daughters shall be prophets'.[6] She is one of many women and men who have noted the numerous places in Scripture which seem to support the equality in ministry of men and women, as opposed to the single one which seems to deny it.

The debate begins

The first record of any real debate, where we can see what was said and argued on both sides, comes from the time of Wesley. Wesley cited both 1 Corinthians 14 and 1 Timothy 2 in defending Methodism in 1748, partly to distance the new church from Quakerism, which denied that Scripture barred the ministry of women.[7] But in the freedom of the new religious movement, women began to share their experience of God and to preach. Wesley saw such women as exceptions.[8] His position was inconsistent: a rigid interpretation of Paul, but admitting the possibility of exceptions.[9]

As women began to hear God's call, to the mission field or to preaching at home, the debate continued. By the end of the nineteenth century there were a variety of responses to Paul's apparent restrictions. Elizabeth Cady Stanton, for example, in *The Women's Bible* (1895), gives a number of reasons for not taking 1 Timothy 2:11ff. at face value. Some of them are naive, others are more weighty. She argued that Paul did not understand women, that seeing what women have achieved in the nineteenth century makes nonsense of his words, that teaching is one of the 'most necessary qualifications of motherhood' (and so Paul's words are nonsense), that Paul was prejudiced against women, that his words are inconsistent with Galatians 3:28, that they are affected by the view of woman as the origin of sin, and she suggests that Paul's views are at variance with those of Jesus.

Katharine Bushnell, writing with a knowledge of Greek and Hebrew in *God's Word to Women* (1923), gives a more careful interpretation. God had called her to be a missionary preacher, and she told God that if he would prove to her that Paul was not against women preaching, she would obey.

Regarding 1 Corinthians 14 she anticipates more recent theologians. When Paul says, 'it is not permitted unto them to speak . . . as also saith the law' (v. 34), which law does he mean? She discusses how some interpretations of chapter 14 conflict with chapter 11, and considers the cultural context. She believes that the fact that women in Asia Minor had more freedom than their Jewish counterparts was a problem. She argues that Paul was not uttering his own words: 'We believe this is the language of the Judaizers at Corinth, which has been reported to Paul, and which Paul quotes to answer back in the words: "What! came the Word of God out from you? or came it unto you only?" – with what follows to the end of the chapter.'[10]

She suggests that the importance of Paul's words in 1 Timothy 2 have been exaggerated, since Paul is merely stating his practice and giving Timothy advice. The verses have then been given more force by male prejudice against women. Paul, she argues, is reading the signs of the times, the threat to Christians by the Romans. The opportunities for women in Christianity were so different from those in Judaism that this created a major point of animosity, and a danger for the Church. She cites a number of other expositors, and challenges the current translation of verse 12 which read, 'But I suffer not a woman to teach, nor to usurp authority over the man'; the words 'usurp' and 'the' do not appear in the Greek. She claims that Paul is merely trying to prevent women being martyred. She paraphrases: 'I should not allow a woman to teach or control a man. They are attacking our reputation for common decency, and we must meet it by separating the women from the men, and having them keep very quiet.'[11]

As the numbers of women on the mission field and in home ministry increased, male theologians began to write in greater numbers, on both sides of the debate. Chapter 3 mentions the article by A. J. Gordon, published 1894, 'The Ministry of Women'. He argued that according to 1 Timothy 2 and 1 Corinthians 11, women were not excluded from praying. 1 Corinthians 14:34–5 probably referred to a particular circumstance, and should be interpreted in its context. He noted that the translation of *diakonos* as servant when referring to Phoebe is misleading when the same word is applied to Paul and Apollos, and other male leaders of the Church.

The year 1941 saw the publication of the book by John Rice which addressed what the evangelist thought were infractions of biblical practice, on the mission field as well as at home. His view was challenged a few years later by P. B. Fitzwater, an esteemed professor of systematic theology at Moody Bible Institute, who distinguished between teaching with authority and other ministries. He believed that women could preach, for example, though he thought that women preachers would always be the exception rather than the rule because of their situations as wives and mothers. He argued that in 1 Corinthians 14 Paul is 'simply reproving abuses', not giving a command of absolute silence.[12]

The interpretation of Charles Ryrie, however, writing in the late 1950s, has had greater impact. He wrote, 'We conclude ... that the early church did not make a practice of permitting women to speak in their public meetings.'[13] According to 1 Corinthians 11 women may have prayed and prophesied, but Ryrie thought this rare, and probably limited to the Corinthian congregation. Thus any kind of speaking in public worship was an exception. Ryrie's views had a wide influence on other interpreters.

Modern interpretation

The debate has continued. But the issue has become more focused in recent years for several reasons. Women, previously not involved in theological study, have begun to re-examine the key passages and issues; we have a greater knowledge of the social background and context of Scripture, and of its relevance to interpreting Scripture; and we understand more about interpretation: how to understand a text and relate it to our situation today (hermeneutics); we no longer see taking single verses out of context, for example, as an acceptable way of reading Scripture.

But still evangelical interpreters come to opposite conclusions about the same passage! This may seem amazing, but that is what happens. What makes the difference between one conclusion and another is the various tools or approaches that an interpreter uses to come to his or her conclusions.

One way of ensuring that a correct conclusion is reached might be to agree a set of principles of interpretation. Various attempts have been made at this in recent years, which have been helpful. Before I continue by discussing recent viewpoints I will suggest some principles on which most evangelical interpreters would agree – the 'rules', if you like. However, as you will see, these still allow people to arrive at very different interpretations!

Hermeneutical principles

1. The Bible is the Word of God, and thus one expects to find consistency. One passage of Scripture should not be interpreted in such a way as to contradict other passages, or the broad sweep of Scripture.
2. Priority must be given to clear and unambiguous passages over difficult and obscure ones. But the latter must not be ignored.
3. Narrative and propositional statements must be interpreted in the light of each other. The type of writing must be considered – letters, for example.

4. Interpretation must take account of the background and cultural context.

5. Interpreters need to be aware of their own presuppositions and how these may influence their interpretation.

6. Any interpretation should build on previous work, but tradition is not sacrosanct. Any current interpretation may be challenged in the light of new understandings of language, culture or other relevant evidence.

7. Application based on any interpretation has to consider how a biblical situation relates to a situation today, and whether a command or practice applied only to its original context or is of permanent and unvarying application.

8. Application also needs to consider whether (in this case) the ministry of women is a doctrine of first order importance, or whether it is one where churches interpret the Bible differently and therefore vary in practice (as in church order, baptism, politics, etc.).

It is clear from these that we need to keep in mind the broad sweep of Scripture as we look at particular passages. Relevant parts have been discussed in several chapters of this book. You will recall that starting from Genesis, moving through the Gospels, to Paul in Acts and on to Galatians 3:28, we see that men and women were created equal for partnership, and in the New Testament are called, commissioned and equipped for evangelism. So let us now turn to current thinking on the specific passages.

1 Corinthians 14:34-5

This passage is less important for our purposes, but has often been quoted or cited in this debate, so I will deal with it briefly.

A roughly word-for-word translation from the Greek is as follows:

As in all the churches of the saints let the women be silent in the churches; for it is not permitted to them to speak, but let them be subject, as also the law says. But if they wish to learn/know anything, let them question their husbands at home; for it is a shame/shameful for a woman to speak in church.

This passage, taken at face value, appears to contradict 1 Corinthians 11:5, which deals with what women should be wearing on their heads when they pray or prophesy in public. So, following our first principle above, there must be more to 1 Corinthians 14 than this. Most modern interpreters consider the context of worship, and conclude that the 'silence' is not absolute. A particular kind of silence must be meant.

A variety of interpretations have been offered. One is that neither 1 Corinthians 14:34–5 nor 1 Timothy are by Paul, and therefore the views on women in them can be ignored or treated differently. But for most evangelicals this is no answer. The passage is in God's Word and must be there for a reason. The following are mentioned by Craig Keener in his book *Paul, Women and Wives:*[14]

1. These two verses are a later addition to the passage. But the evidence for this is weak.
2. It might be a quotation from Paul's enemies, which is refuted – as Bushnell suggested. This is unlikely.
3. Worship was segregated, so for women to call out to their husbands was noisy and disruptive. But there is no evidence that men and women were segregated.
4. It is about the abuse of gifts of the Spirit such as prophecy or tongues, and that is what Paul is prohibiting. But, unlike 1 Corinthians 11, the context is not about these issues. The Greek word used for 'speak', *laleo*, is the ordinary word for speaking. If speaking in tongues were meant, some other word would be used.
5. It is about judging prophecies, which is the subject of the immediately preceding verses. Keener argues that this is unlikely. However, this is the conclusion drawn more recently by Edward Donnelly.[15] He

supports this argument by reference to 1 Timothy 2 and the idea of 'a usurping of authority' (which of course assumes a particular understanding of that passage); and by the reference to the 'law' which he takes to be the 'creation order' of Genesis 2 and 3 (which involves another set of assumptions by no means generally accepted, as chapter 6 makes clear). Donnelly concludes that since most churches do not have prophecies brought, the matter of women judging prophecies is irrelevant, but 'the principle of submission is taught, with the implication that such submission extends to refraining from authoritative speaking'.[16] However, it is more commonly argued that this passage has nothing to do with authoritative speaking. Verse 35 suggests that the problem has more to do with asking questions than with judging or weighing prophecy.

6. Some interpreters have argued that the 'speaking' is teaching, and that this is what is forbidden. George Knight, like Donnelly, interprets this verse in the light of 1 Timothy 2 and says that 1 Corinthians therefore forbids women to teach men.[17] However, as already stated, the concern of verse 35 is with asking questions. A more convincing interpretation, in my view, and on which there is considerable recent consensus, is that:

7. The speaking is about asking questions in the service. Women were interrupting the teaching with questions. When the background and cultural context are taken into account, according to the principles above, it is clear that women were less well trained in the Scriptures, and therefore would have understood less of what was being taught. Paul is encouraging them to learn (as in 1 Tim. 2:11), but not so as to cause disruption in worship. The concluding verse 40: 'everything should be done in a fitting and orderly way', shows that the passage is about order in worship. In order to 'catch up' with their Christian education, they are instructed to ask their husbands

at home. Keener suggests that Paul is giving short-range and long-range solutions to this problem: to stop interrupting the worship, and to gain the knowledge they had been lacking. Kenneth Bailey suggests the following paraphrase:

> Women, please keep silent in worship and listen to the female and male prophets. Don't interrupt them with questions, and don't talk/chat in church. If you can't understand what is being said, ask your husbands at home. They understand more Greek than you do and will be able to explain things to you.[18]

The verses therefore have nothing to do with whether a woman should teach or speak in the church today. This is the interpretation which I accept as doing most justice to the text in the context of the whole of Scripture and in accordance with principles of good interpretation.

1 Timothy 2:11-15

The NIV, fairly representative of modern translations, reads:

> A woman should learn in quietness and full submission. I do not permit a woman to teach or to have authority over a man; she must be silent. For Adam was formed first, then Eve. And Adam was not the one deceived; it was the woman who was deceived and became a sinner. But women will be saved through childbearing – if they continue in faith, love and holiness with propriety.

This is the only passage in the New Testament which is unambiguously about the issue of women teaching, and appears to be an explicit prohibition. Beyond that, almost anything I say about it is open to debate! But I shall attempt to set out some recent views and my own conclusions. This verse, as I have already noted, has been used to bar women from aspects of evangelistic ministry. But even if one accepts that Paul forbids the *leadership* of women, and even that is not agreed, is that necessarily relevant to the ministry of *evangelism*?

Debate about this passage is going on at several different levels. One strand concerns whether Paul's prohibition is intended to be a universal one or whether it is only relevant in the context of the letter. Is it to be interpreted as a permanent restriction or a temporary one? If the former, why are Paul's rules about head-coverings in 1 Corinthians 11 considered no longer literally applicable, while the prohibition in 1 Timothy 2, which deals with a similar situation in Ephesus, is held to be universally binding? If, however, it is only a temporary prohibition in a particular cultural context, then there are no biblical restrictions on the ministry of women.

But if we consider that Paul meant it to be a permanent universal restriction, the next question is to decide how this restriction should be applied, in accordance with the last two hermeneutical principles above. Paul is barring women from something, but what exactly is it? Ordination? The position of elder or pastor-teacher? The role of ruling elder? How do these contemporary notions of leadership relate to the situation Paul was addressing? If women are excluded from authoritative teaching, does it make a difference that Paul and the other apostles were effectively making doctrine, which became an authoritative text, whereas today a preacher bases his or her words on that same authoritative text?

Another level of debate is about how to understand particular words. The word *authentein* (v. 12) for example, translated here as 'have authority': does it mean to have authority, to domineer, take or usurp authority, or to be responsible for something? The word is not the usual one for authority, and its precise meaning is unclear. There are numerous other difficulties, such that the least one can say is that it is not, as some have claimed, a clear passage.[19] In a recent book, R.T. France writes, 'We have to admit that we know too little about the circumstances of the letter, and that there are too many obscure or ambiguous features to the argument, to allow any exegesis to claim to have uttered the last word.'[20]

One would then invoke principle 2 above, which is to interpret it in the light of other passages which are clearer. But that is easier said than done. There are no other passages which forbid women teaching or leading. A supposed ban on the teaching and leadership of women hangs on the interpretation of these few difficult verses.

In the light of the first principle of interpretation, one obvious way forward is to consider the rest of the evidence about women in the New Testament – and the Old Testament. As has been shown, there are a number of references in Acts and the letters of Paul to women who may have been teachers or leaders in the Church. Then one needs to note the immediate context. Part of this passage which is clear is verse 11. Paul uses the imperative: 'a woman should learn', or 'let a woman learn' – as she has not done before.

As is suggested by my discussion elsewhere in the book of some of the other passages about women, I think the weight of evidence for women leading and teaching is greater than that against it, and I would argue for women being fully able to respond to God's call to leadership and teaching roles. But that conclusion is not accepted by some. Let me set out some possible interpretations of the passage, and then explore them. They are not exhaustive, but will cover the most important points which need to be considered.

1. It prohibits women usurping the authority of men. 'Paul forbids not the exercise of authority, but. domineering bossiness.'[21]
2. It is a prohibition of women teaching which applies only to Ephesus.
3. It is a prohibition of women teaching which appeals to creation order and therefore has universal validity.
4. It is a prohibition of women teaching a particular heresy.
5. It is a mixture of universal and permanent principle, with its local and cultural expression.

Domineering bossiness

This interpretation depends on a particular understanding of *authentein.* This is a rare Greek word, and this is the only occurrence of it in the New Testament. Interpreters cannot therefore compare it with other NT uses, but only with other uses outside the NT.

The major alternatives are 'have authority' and 'domineer'. In favour of the latter translation is the fact that the word is not the one which Paul might have been expected to use to mean normal 'authority'. It is suggested that in some of its uses there is a pejorative tone to it, which accounted for the KJV translation 'usurp authority'. The associated noun in one Greek text was used to refer to a murderer. Kenneth Bailey, writing with knowledge of Middle Eastern culture and languages, suggests that it has overtones of these, and early translations into Arabic or Syriac all imply domineering or bullying.[22]

So one assumes that some women in the church in Ephesus, a society more open to women's involvement than the Jewish or Greek one, and converted from a pagan religion in which they had some leadership role, were acting in a way which was inappropriate. One might paraphrase the verse: 'I do not allow these ignorant women to batter the men. They are to stop shouting and calm down.'[23] Domineering is inappropriate for women and men. But here the women are at fault. So Paul is addressing a local situation, not making a universal rule.

This understanding of *authentein* has been challenged on the basis of other uses of the word which do not have these pejorative overtones. Due to lack of evidence, the debate is unlikely to be resolved.

Trouble with women in Ephesus

Several other arguments have been put forward which also suggest that Paul's words refer to a local problem rather than making a universal principle. These include:

1. The need to guard against Christianity coming into disrepute by women taking authority in the church when they would not usually have done so in the household.

2. The fact that Paul is concerned about false teaching, and much of it is being spread by women in the congregation. Women were not so well educated as men, so would have been easier prey for the false teachers mentioned in the letters to Timothy.

3. Women are not to teach until they have learned sufficiently. The verse about teaching follows one about learning. When women have learned, it is implied, they will be able to resist false teaching, and pass on true teaching accurately.

4. The wording may suggest instruction which is specific rather than universal. The use of 'I am not allowing' may suggest a personal preference, and the present tense is less forceful than the command which precedes it, 'let a woman learn', which may be read as universal.

5. Paul does not assume that Timothy already knows this rule, which one might have expected if it was a universal one. He does not remind Timothy of it, as he sometimes reminds his recipients of things they already know.

These interpretations deal with verses 11 and 12. But verses 13–15, which are closely related, must also be considered. There are two arguments from Genesis. The second, in particular, in verse 14, is very confusing, since it appears to contradict Paul's writings elsewhere. Usually it is Adam who was deceived, Adam who is held to be the first to sin. It is possible that Paul intends in this context to imply that Eve was like the women of Ephesus – inadequately educated – and that is why she was deceived. He is drawing an analogy, rather than stating a doctrine. Verse 15 is also difficult to interpret. I will return to it later.

Even if Paul's words do amount to a ban on teaching by women at Ephesus, how much further do they apply? Do they just apply to a problem in Ephesus? Or do they involve a general principle which applies more widely – bearing in mind that other similar rules are not applied today?

No *women in the pastoral office*

Commentators who take the passage as a universal ban on particular ministries for women usually assume that it is simple to understand. 'I do not permit a woman to teach or to have authority over a man; she must be silent.' We are simply to take those words at face value. Among the most recent proponents of this argument are the contributors to books edited by Brian Edwards *et al.*[24] They put forward a number of reasons, which I will discuss briefly in turn:

1. First, there is the weight of tradition. 'For over nineteen hundred years most Christians have understood that Paul is prohibiting women from teaching publicly or holding ruling office in the church.'[25] But principle 4 above reminds us that tradition may be questioned in the light of new evidence. Furthermore, the historical perspective of this book reveals that this apparent prohibition of Paul has been challenged more often than many people realise.

2. Paul does not qualify his prohibition. There is nothing to tell us it is not a universal prohibition. There is no reference in the text to women's lack of education or societal disapproval. The prohibition on teaching is emphasised by the word order: in Greek 'to teach' is brought to the beginning of the verse, followed by 'woman'.[26] There is a clear antithesis in verses 11 and 12: women are to learn, but not to teach. But such simple, clear meanings come from English translation. The Greek is complex, and one cannot draw conclusions from such things as word order. Just as there is nothing to tell us it is not a universal prohibition, there is nothing to tell us it is.

3. The word *authentein* simply means 'to have authority'. Its position near the word 'in quietness' argues for 'having authority' rather than 'usurping authority'. The word, *didaskein*, used for 'teach' is that used for public and official teaching, which is

authoritative. Thus both words are about an authoritative ministry, that of preaching or elder-ship.[27] I have already dealt with this word, and the fact that conclusions about its meaning are almost impossible. *Didaskein* does not necessarily mean public authoritative teaching.

4. The passage is a natural outworking of the notion of creation order. The Old Testament, Jesus and Paul show a distinct pattern of biblical manhood and womanhood. Men and women were created to have different and complementary roles. In Genesis 2 God gave the man authority and the role of 'head', and the woman the role of 'helper'. In the Old Testament women could not be religious teachers or priests. Jesus appointed only male apostles. Patriarchy is God-given. I have dealt with most of these arguments in chapter 6: patriarchy is not necessarily God-given, and the idea of gender difference and roles in Scripture is false. There are other ways of accounting for Jesus' choice of twelve male disciples.

5. The outworking of creation order is made clear in the reasoning of verses 13–14, where Paul refers back to Genesis 3. Paul makes his argument rest on principles derived from the Old Testament. Adam was formed first, then Eve (v. 13): there is a priority in creation, a hierarchy established by God (Gen. 2:7). Eve usurped her God-given role (v. 14), and was deceived. Adam should have asserted his headship. 'The role reversal at the fall is a further argument, according to Paul, that the final responsibility and authority legitimately rest with the man. Thus Paul in 1 Timothy 2:8–15 draws from the Old Testament narratives abiding principles for male-female relationships and applies them to his contemporary context.'[28] This also accounts for verse 15: women ' "will be saved through childbearing" – that is, through developing true womanliness in whatever spheres are available to them'.[29] These arguments I have also discussed in chapter 6. Genesis

2 and 3 are read quite differently by most commentators. The argument that the fall came about because Eve usurped her God-given role in the male – female hierarchy is mainly a recent one, and circular, adduced to bolster this interpretation of 1 Timothy 2. Paul himself in Romans places the blame on Adam.

6. The working, 'I do not permit', is authoritative. Paul is using his divinely-given authority. It sounds categorical.[30] This is a subjective argument. I have mentioned above the argument that the use of 'I' may imply personal preference.

7. Galatians 3:28 is not a paradigm passage in favour of equality, but about women as well as men being included in the divine promise of salvation made to Abraham (Gal. 3:16). The verse does not necessarily imply a change in human relationships. There are no examples of women in the New Testament teaching authoritatively or having leadership authority. All the examples commonly cited are of women exercising other forms of ministry. In response to this, I have discussed Galatians 3:28 in chapter 3. Priscilla taught an apostle; Phoebe, Junia and others appear to have been apostles or other kinds of leader in the early churches. Furthermore, it could be argued that authoritative teaching relies on the authority of the Scripture expounded, not the authority of the speaker, and that stress on the 'authority' of leaders is out of place when Jesus taught his followers to be servants.

Different commentators have slight variations in what is not permitted by Paul, but the prohibition here is usually seen to include authoritative teaching, the teaching of men, and leadership: the office of 'ruling elder' or 'pastor-teacher'. Mothers can teach their children (see 2 Tim. 1:5; 3:15), and women can teach in the home (Acts 18:26) and teach other women (see Titus 2:3–4). However, the case for such a prohibition is far from made with the above arguments.

But even supposing that Paul did intend a ban on women's teaching and having authority over a man, there are further questions about how this is to be applied today. If it is a principle from creation order, then it is meant to apply to the whole of society rather than just the Church. The author of one essay advances the argument that a woman may only influence a man in a non-personal way; for example, a woman may design the traffic pattern of a city's streets, but she will not direct the all-male traffic warden team![31] The paucity of practical examples in the book edited by Edwards suggests that even if the argument were right in theory, in practice it is completely unworkable.

There are also contradictions in Edwards' book. The chapter on women in church history cites many women evangelists. It is even suggested that women can be evangelists (but not hold pastoral office).[32] Another author, however, argues that God 'sent men not women to act as heralds of the good news of the kingdom'.[33]

Furthermore, the task of evangelism is wide-ranging. Women can be evangelists, but cannot preach or lead. So what can they do? Can they give a testimony? Can they read a sermon written by someone else? Can they teach their children? At what age does a woman's son become a man whom she cannot teach? If she talks to neighbours and teaches them informally in her home, at what stage does a such a group become a church in which she can no longer teach or lead?

If there is such a complete universal prohibition of particular roles for women in society and the Church, it is totally unworkable. In which case, since I cannot believe that God would have given us unworkable rules, perhaps, after all, it is not quite so complete . . .

I suffer not a woman

The fourth line of interpretation is a variation on the second, but takes rather a different approach. Research on the background to the church in Ephesus by Catherine Kroeger resulted in a series of papers, followed by a book published in 1992.[34] The book's thesis is this: what has traditionally been understood as an absolute and universal scriptural injunction undergoes transformation when seen against the background of Ephesian paganism, becoming instead a quite specific restriction imposed in order to curb the spread of certain heretical teachings.

The city of Ephesus is described as 'a bastion of feminine supremacy in religion'. There was a form of gnosticism in existence which misrepresented the Jewish Scriptures, including the story of Adam and Eve. Women appear to have been responsible for disseminating much of the false teaching.

The Kroegers' translation of 1 Timothy 2:12 is as follows: 'I do not permit woman to teach nor to represent herself as originator of man but she is to be in conformity [with the Scriptures] [or that she keeps it a secret]. For Adam was created first, then Eve.'[35]

It is impossible to go into much detail; the authors' argument takes up a whole book! They argue that 'to teach' should not be understood in absolute terms, but with the implicit content of wrong doctrine. 'I do not allow' is taken to refer to a limited situation rather than a general one. The translation of *authentein* is key to the argument of the book. Various options are reviewed and the one the Kroegers take is 'one who is an author of an action, is responsible'. The phrase normally translated 'to be in silence' is translated 'to be in conformity'.

The rationale for this prohibition of women's teaching is found in gnostic reinterpretation of the story of Eve, which accounts for verses 13–15. According to gnostic mythology Eve pre-existed Adam and was responsible for bringing him life. Hence the need in verse 13 to assert that Adam was created first. Gnosticism also held that Eve was wiser than Adam and instructed Adam. Hence verse 14. 'Women are forbidden to teach that female activity brought man into existence because, according to the Scriptures, Adam was created first. Eve, for all her desire to bring enlightenment, did not bring gnosis [knowledge] but transgression.'[36]

Verse 15 must be understood against this false teaching, which included the idea that women should become as much like men as possible. Rather than referring to the Christ, or to protection in childbirth, or to woman's observing her proper role of motherhood, Paul is arguing against the gnostic view that matter and bodies (and hence childbearing) were unspiritual. 'Woman can be saved while she still possesses that distinctive which most decisively sets her apart from man ... Salvation is available to the female as well as the male, and she need not surrender her gender'.[37]

This interpretation has gained numbers of supporters as well as some critics. It takes account of verses 13–14 without resorting to the dubious interpretation of creation order. It includes a very satisfactory understanding of verse 15, and avoids replacing justification by faith with justification by childbirth! But it has been claimed that the Kroegers' translation of verse 12 is idiosyncratic and does not hold up, their translation of *authentein* is questionable, the evidence in the book of women holding leadership positions in Ephesian religion is flawed, and the evidence for gnosticism so early is not well founded.[38]

Essential revelation and cultural expression

John Stott is one of those who has responded to the Kroegers' argument. He affirms it as remarkable and painstakingly researched, but also feels it is too ingenious. In a recent discussion of these verses, he elaborates his approach made earlier in *Issues Facing Christians Today*. 'God always spoke his word in particular historical and cultural settings,'[39] and this causes problems for interpretation. The Bible is a mixture of principles which are universal and culture which is changeable. Stott stresses the need, when dealing with the cultural element in Scripture, to avoid the two extremes of rigid literalism which enthrones the cultural form, and cultural relativism which may minimise eternal truth. With typical graciousness he puts forward a mediating position, a 'principle of cultural transposition' in order 'to discern in Scripture between God's essential revelation (which is changeless) and its cultural expression (which is changeable)'.[40]

In applying this to 1 Timothy 2:11–15, Stott suggests that the double antithesis in verses 11 and 12 ('a woman should learn in quietness and full submission', and she is not 'to teach or to have authority over a man') may be seen as a mixture of essential revelation (the submission-authority antithesis) and first-century cultural expression (the silence-teaching antithesis).

Thus, he argues, it is unbiblical to impose restrictions on women's teaching. Women can teach, and they do not have to be silent. These were temporary local outworkings of a general principle. In any case, he notes, women teach under the authority of Scripture, not on their own authority, and the leadership which follows Christ's example is about service, not authority. However, he thinks that attempts to 'soften' the teaching of verses 11 and 12 by suggesting they are Paul's personal opinion, or are about 'domineering' are unsatisfactory. There is, he argues, an abiding principle of female submission to male authority.

On verse 15, Stott suggests that 'through childbearing' should be read as 'through the birth of a child' – referring to Christ. He concludes his discussion by suggesting that further theological reflection is needed on such issues as complementarity and the roles of men and women.

The distinction Stott makes between culture and principle is, he admits, not evident from the text itself, but he cites verses 8, 9 and 10 as examples of similar distinctions. Some people may find this too arbitrary, and confusing in its application; and it is by no means clear that one should separate 'in full submission' from its apparent reference to the way in which a woman should learn. But this approach will undoubtedly serve to continue the debate in a way which takes the cultural context of Scripture seriously, while wanting to safeguard biblical truth, and which affirms women in their desire to use their God-given abilities in his service.

And so the debate goes on.

In conclusion

On balance I have come down on the side of the view that the prohibition on teaching and taking authority is a temporary, culturally conditioned one, like the requirement for veils, for example. The abiding principle from this passage is the disqualification from teaching of anyone who is not well enough taught to be able to distinguish truth from error.

The passage in 1 Corinthians 14:33–5 seems to have nothing to do with teaching or preaching. On 1 Timothy 2:11–15 I find the Kroegers' argument quite persuasive, along with other similar ones. I believe that to take the prohibition as limited to the context is in harmony with the practice of Paul, his teaching elsewhere, including Galatians 3:28, and the attitude of Jesus towards women. I await further studies with interest.

This book is written on the basis that Paul did not mean to restrict the ministry of women, whether by forbidding them to preach, to teach, or to exercise a ministry of leadership. The Bible, therefore, nowhere places limits on what women may or may not do, in evangelism or any other ministry.

For reflection/action

1. If you believe that 1 Timothy 2 places permanent restrictions on the ministry of women, how is this applied consistently in your church today? How do you reconcile these restrictions with the clear commission of Jesus to preach the gospel?

2. 'Phoebe could not be a minister because she was a woman. Junia couldn't be a woman because she was an apostle. The Elect Lady must be a church because she couldn't be a lady. Prisca couldn't be a woman because she instructed Apollos.' Is tradition always right? What might make us question our assumptions about our interpretation of Scripture?

Notes

Chapter 1   Women and evangelism

1. Phyllis Thompson, *Each to Her Post* (Hodder/OMF, 1982), p. 97.
2. See Ruth Tucker and Walter Liefeld, *Daughters of the Church: Women and Ministry from New Testament Times to the Present* (Zondervan, 1987), p. 269. Her ministry was compared to that of D. L. Moody.
3. See D. Hawker, *Kanchi Doctor* (Scripture Union, 1984).
4. See Flora Larsson, *My Best Men are Women* (Hodder and Stoughton, 1974), ch. 2.
5. Olive Anderson, 'Women Preachers in Mid-Victorian Britain: Some Reflections on Feminism, Popular Religion and Social Change', *The Historical Journal*, Vol. XII, no. 3 (1969), p. 471.
6. Miriam Adeney, 'Esther Across Cultures: Indigenous Leadership Roles for Women', *Missiology*, Vol. XV, no. 3, (July 1987), p. 326.
7. John Finney, *Finding Faith Today* (Bible Society, 1992), p. 38.
8. Beulah Wood, 'The Tribe of Martha and Priscilla', *Evangelical Review of Theology*, Vol. 18 no. 2 (April 1994), p. 153.
9. See Teresa Okure, 'The Significance Today of Jesus' Commission to Mary Magdalene', *International Review of*

Mission, Vol. XXXI, no. 322 (April 1992). She argues that in John's writing, one enters into the mission of Jesus not so much by being commissioned as by opening oneself to it: mission is witnessing to him, confessing of him and abiding in him (p. 178).

10. There are various ways of clarifying the difference between mission and evangelism: mission to those in the Third World, evangelism to those in the West; mission as evangelism plus social concern; mission as being wider than evangelism, while evangelism is the heart of mission. The first of these is now redundant. The second reflects a debate about social concern which is now largely past. The third I do not find particularly helpful, since if evangelism is the heart of mission, it is hard to see what then mission is which is not evangelism. I would see evangelism as the activity of the Church in making Christ known by word and deed, with the intention of giving people the opportunity of responding to the good news and living under the Lordship of Christ in the community of his people, the Church. This will often include social action as part of living out God's love for all people, but it will always be more than that.

11. Miriam Adeney, 'Women of Fire', *Crux*, Vol. XIX, No. 3 (Sept. 1983), p. 28.

12. Quoted in Rick Yohn, *Discover Your Spiritual Gift and Use It* (Tyndale House, 1974), pp. 80–1.

13. Quoted in Lavinia Byrne, *The Hidden Tradition* (SPCK, 1991), pp. 142–3.

14. Ruth Tucker, *Women in the Maze* (IVP, 1992), p. 254.

Chapter 2   Women preachers: deterred but determined

1. Fanny Woodman, quoted in Sean Gill, *Women and the Church of England: From the Eighteenth Century to the Present* (SPCK, 1994), p. 183.

2. Quoted in Deborah Valenze, 'Cottage Religion and the Politics of Survival', in Jane Rendall (ed.), *Equal or Different* (Basil Blackwell, 1987), p. 48.

3. ibid., p. 48.

4. ibid., p. 50.
5. Some recent research questions the value of mass evangelism. John Finney, in *Finding Faith Today* (1992), concludes that evangelistic events alone account for less than 5 per cent of adult decisions in church membership (see ch. 4). But for many they are still an important part of a process.
6. G. B. Hill (ed.), *Boswell's Life of Johnson* (Clarendon Press, 1934), Vol. 1, p. 463.
7. Paul Chilcote, *She Offered Them Christ: The Legacy of Women Preachers in Early Methodism* (Abingdon Press, 1993), p. 12; Alister McGrath, *Bridge-building* (IVP, 1992), p. 217.
8. Chilcote, *She Offered Them Christ*, p. 13.
9. ibid., p. 31.
10. ibid., p. 117.
11. Quoted in Tucker and Liefeld, *Daughters of the Church*, p. 263.
12. Quoted in Kari Malcolm, *Women at the Crossroads* (IVP, 1982), p. 125.
13. John Rice, *Bobbed Hair, Bossy Wives, and Women Preachers* (Sword of the Lord, 1941), p. 59.
14. This is suggested, for example, by Alison White, in 'Bearers of an Idle Tale', *Anvil*, Vol. 13, no. 1 (1996), pp. 24, 26.
15. ibid., p. 23.
16. ibid., p. 31.
17. Quoted in Ann Loades, *Searching for Lost Coins* (SPCK, 1987), p. 68.
18. Quoted in Chilcote, *She Offered Them Christ*, p. 49.
19. Deborah Valenze, *Prophetic Sons and Daughters: Female Preaching and Popular Religion in Industrial England* (Princeton University Press, 1985), ch. 9; D. Colin Dews, 'Ann Carr and the Female Revivalists of Leeds', in Gail Malmgren (ed.), *Religion in the Lives of English Women* (Croom Helm, 1986), pp. 76, 79.
20. Quoted in Tucker and Liefeld, *Daughters of the Church*, p. 265.
21. Quoted in Tucker and Liefeld, *Daughters of the Church*, p. 260.
22. Quoted in Virginia Rounding, 'The Sins of the Fathers',

Church Times (9 Aug. 1996), p. 11.

23. Quoted in Tucker and Liefeld, *Daughters of the Church*, p. 261.

24. Quoted in Miriam Adeney, 'Women of Fire', *Crux* (Sept. 1983), p. 25.

25. ibid., p. 29.

26. Miriam Adeney, 'Esther Across Cultures: Indigenous Leadership Roles for Women', *Missiology*, Vol. XV, No. 3 (July 1987), p. 324.

27. Mary Slessor, towards the end of her life, quoted in Richard Symonds, *Far Above Rubies: The Women Uncommemorated by the Church of England* (Gracewing, 1993), p. 223.

28. Audrey Shilling, 'Decline of the Single Woman', *Church Times* (21 Oct. 1994).

29. Peter Williams, 'The Missing Link: The Recruitment of Women Missionaries in some English Evangelical Missionary Societies in the Nineteenth Century', in F. Bowie, D. Kirkwood and S. Ardener (eds), *Women and Missions: Past and Present* (Berg, 1993), p. 51.

30. Mildred Cable and Francesca French, *Something Happened* (Hodder and Stoughton, 1934), p. 142.

31. Norman Grubb, quoted in Ruth Tucker, 'How Faith Mission Pioneers Understood Women's Roles', *Priscilla Papers*, Vol. 10, no. 2 (Spring 1996), p. 4.

32. Elaine Lawless, 'Rescripting their Lives and Narratives: Spiritual Life Stories of Pentecostal Women Preachers', *Journal of Feminist Studies in Religion*, Vol. 7, no. 1 (Spring 1991), p. 69.

33. Quoted in Deborah Kirkwood, 'Protestant Missionary Women: Wives and Spinsters', in F. Bowie, D. Kirkwood and S. Ardener (eds), *Women and Missions*, p. 27.

34. Quoted in Peter Williams, 'The Missing Link: The Recruitment of Women Missionaries in some English Evangelical Missionary Societies in the Nineteenth Century' in *Women and Missions*, p. 63.

35. Quoted in Lavinia Byrne, *The Hidden Journey* (SPCK, 1993), p 32.

36. Quoted in Tucker and Liefeld, *Daughters of the Church*, p. 308.

Chapter 3   Women preachers: commissioned and called

1. 'The Female Preachers' Plea', by 'a Bible Christian Woman' (wife of W. O'Bryan), and published in the *Primitive Methodist Magazine*, 1821, quoted in Valenze, 'Cottage Religion and the Politics of Survival', in *Equal or Different*, pp. 48–9.

2. Anderson, 'Women Preachers in Mid-Victorian Britain', p. 478.

3. See Nancy Hardesty, *Women Called to Witness: Evangelical Feminism in the 19th Century* (Abingdon Press, 1984), pp. 162–4.

4. Phoebe Palmer, *The Promise of the Father* (Henry V. Degen, 1859), p. 6.

5. Frances Willard, *Woman in the Pulpit* (Linthrop Co., 1888), p. 34.

6. See Williams, 'The Missing Link', p. 52.

7. ibid., p. 53.

8. Ralph Kee, 'Revelation, Proclamation and Women's Responsibility: A Systematic Theology in Two or Three Pages', *Priscilla Papers*, Vol. 16, no. 4 (Fall 1992), p. 11.

9. See Ben Witherington III, 'Rite and Rights for Women – Galatians 3:28', *New Testament Studies*, Vol. 27, no. 5 (Oct. 1981), p. 543, and footnotes for examples on both sides of the debate to that date.

10. See ibid., p. 594 and footnote 2 for examples; a more recent one is Brian Edwards, 'Leadership in the Bible', in Edwards (ed.) *Men, Women and Authority* (Day One Publications, 1996), p. 55, the source of this quotation.

11. F. F. Bruce, *The Epistle to the Galatians* (New International Greek Testament Commentary) (Paternoster Press, 1982), p. 187.

12. ibid., p. 190.

13. ibid., p. 190.

14. Quoted in Roger Green, 'Catherine Booth: Model Minister', *The War Cry* (26 October 1996), p. 5.

15. Tucker, *Women in the Maze*, p. 209.

16. A. J. Gordon, 'The Ministry of Women' (1894), p. 6.

17. Quoted in Amy Oden (ed.), *In Her Words: Women's Writings*

in the History of Christian Thought, (SPCK, 1995), p. 280.

18. Thompson, *Each to Her Post*, p. 82.

19. Alan Burgess, *The Small Woman* (Evans, 1957), p. 16.

20. See Chilcote, *She Offered Them Christ*, p. 43.

21. Quoted ibid., p. 62.

22. ibid., p. 64.

23. ibid., p. 64.

24. In a letter written on 14 February 1761, quoted ibid., p. 65.

25. Quoted ibid., p. 101.

26. Quoted in Chilcote, *She Offered Them Christ*, p. 113.

27. ibid., p. 115.

28. ibid., p. 115.

29. D. MacHaffie, *Readings in Herstory* (Fortress Press, 1992), p. 147.

30. ibid., pp. 152–3.

31. Quoted in Tucker and Liefeld, *Daughters of the Church*, p. 273.

32. ibid., p. 274.

33. Anderson, 'Women Preachers in Mid-Victorian Britain', pp. 470–1.

34. Quoted in Tucker and Liefeld, *Daughters of the Church*, p. 390.

35. W. G. Godbey, *Woman Preacher* (Pentecostal Publishing Co., 1891), pp. 12–13.

36. Corrie ten Boom, *Tramp for the Lord* (Hodder and Stoughton, 1974), p. 42.

37. ibid., p. 46.

38. Jill Briscoe, *Christianity Today* Forum, 'Ministering Women', *CT* (April 1996), p. 17.

39. Kate Davies, 'My Best Men are Women', *Alpha*, June 1996, p. 7.

40. In 1993, 16 out of 71; in 1994, 17 out of 76; in 1995, 22 out of 72; in 1996, 16 out of 62.

41. Quoted in Malcolm, *Women at the Crossroads*, p. 126.

42. Gavin Reid, 'The Decay of Evangelists?' *Anvil*, Vol. 13, no. 1, p. 49.

43. Adeney, 'Esther Across Cultures', p. 331.

44. ibid., p. 326.

45. See Larsson, 'My Best Men are Women', p. 64.

46. Jocelyn Murray, 'Gender attitudes and the contribution of women to evangelism and ministry in the nineteenth century', in J. Wolffe (ed.), *Evangelical Faith and Public Zeal: Evangelicals and Society in Britain 1780–1880* (SPCK, 1995), p. 107.

47. Larsson, 'My Best Men are Women', p. 16.

48. ibid., p. 64.

49. A. E. Reffold, *A Noble Army of Women: the Story of Marie Carlile and the Church Army Sisters* (Church Army, 1947), p. 14.

50. Joan Hudspeth, 'Women in ministry with special reference to Marie Carlile and the work of the Church Army Sisters' (unpublished thesis) p. 53.

51. Quoted in Valenze, *Prophetic Sons and Daughters*, p. 149.

52. ibid., p. 109.

53. Chris Wright and Chris Sugden (eds), *One Gospel – Many Clothes: Anglicans and the Decade of Evangelism* (EFAC/Regnum Books, 1990), p. 184.

54. Gavin Reid, 'The Decay of Evangelists?' *Anvil*, Vol. 13, no. 1, pp. 54–6.

Chapter 4   Women and personal evangelism

1. Finney, *Finding Faith Today*, p. 43. Evangelistic events were a supporting factor for another 13 per cent of people, but friends were a supporting factor for another 39 per cent of men and 40 per cent of women.

2. David Sanderson, *The Work and Office of an Evangelist* (Grove Books, 1995) p. 18.

3. Quoted in Sharon James, 'Roles without Relegation', in Brian Edwards (ed.), *Men, Women and Authority* (Day One Publications, 1996), p. 234.

4. Quoted in ibid., p. 234.

5. See David Bosch, *Transforming Mission: Paradigm Shifts in Theology of Mission* (Orbis Books, 1991), pp. 8, 49–50.

6. Quoted in Tucker and Liefeld, *Daughters of the Church*, p. 102.

7. ibid., p. 114.

8. Caroline Marshall, 'Catherine of Sienna', *Christian History*, Vol. X, no. 2 (Issue 30), pp. 8–11.

9. Quoted in Malcolm, *Women at the Crossroads*, p. 111.

10. Quoted in Tucker and Liefeld, *Daughters of the Church*, p. 214.

11. Os Guinness, *The Gravedigger File* (Hodder and Stoughton, 1983), p. 48.

12. Origen calls her an 'apostle', and says, 'Here a woman preaches Christ to the Samaritans.' John Chrysostom compares her work of evangelism favourably with that of the Twelve.

13. Ruth Calver, 'Involvement for the Full-time Housewife', in Kathy Keay (ed.), *Women to Women* (MARC, 1988), p. 59.

14. Margaret Burton, *Women Workers of the Orient* (Central Committee on the United Study of Foreign Mission, 1918), p. 224.

15. Ruth Tucker, 'African women's movement finds massive response', *Evangelical Missions Quarterly*, Vol. 22, no. 3 (July 1985), p. 283.

16. ibid., pp. 284–90.

17. Jackie Bowler, 'Free to be Me', *Redemption*, (Sept. 1994), p. 27.

18. Kari Malcolm, 'Why we need women evangelists around the world', *Priscilla Papers*, Vol. 3, no. 2, p. 8.

19. Quoting John R. Mott; quoted in Ruth Tucker, 'Female Missionary Strategists: A Historical and Contemporary Perspective', *Missiology*, Vol. XV, no. 1 (Jan. 1987), p. 82.

20. Adeney, 'Esther Across Cultures', pp. 328–9.

21. Wendy Hill, 'Working With Unwed Teen Mothers: An Interview', *Urban Mission*, November 1989, pp. 33–4.

22. Kathy Keay, 'Christianity and Feminism: Must We Choose?' in Keay (ed.), *Women to Women*, p. 98.

23. Grove Books, 1994.

24. See Barbara Temple, *Exclusive Language: A Hindrance to Evangelism Among Women* (Grove Books, 1988).

25. Quoted in Tucker and Liefeld, *Daughters of the Church*, p. 338.

26. *This is the Laity* (Catholic Truth Society, 1989), pp. 20, 21.

27. Daisy Washburn Osborn, 'Women in Evangelism', in

Catherine Clark Kroeger, Mary Evans and Elaine Storkey (eds) *Women's Study New Testament* (Marshall Pickering, 1995), pp. 457, 458.

Chapter 5   Women and their families

1. E. Hennecke, *New Testament Apocrypha*, II, ed. R. McL. Wilson (Lutterworth Press, 1965), p. 279.
2. Quoted in Bonnie Anderson and Judith Zinsser, *A History of Their Own: Women in Europe from Prehistory to the Present*, Vol. 1, pp. 72–3.
3. Bede, *Ecclesiastical History of the English People* (Penguin, 1990), p. 124.
4. See Valenze, *Prophetic Sons and Daughters*, Introduction and ch. 12.
5. Quoted in Malcolm, *Women at the Crossroads*, p. 122.
6. ibid., pp. 199–200.
7. ibid., pp. 200, 201.
8. Finney, *Finding Faith Today*, p. 38.
9. ibid., p. 39.
10. John Finney, *Stories of Faith* (Bible Society, 1995), p. 26.
11. Marion Stroud, *Loving God But Still Loving You* (Alpha Publications, 1995), pp. 26, 27.
12. ibid., p. 35.
13. Quoted in John Stott, *Guard the Gospel: The Message of 2 Timothy* (IVP, 1973), p. 27.
14. Judy Mbugua (ed.), *Our Time Has Come: African Women Address the Issues of Today* (Baker Book House/Paternoster Press, 1994), ch. 20.
15. Quoted in Tucker and Liefeld, *Daughters of the Church*, p. 299.
16. ibid., p 123.
17. Marshall Broomhall, *Hudson Taylor: The Man who Believed God* (China Inland Mission, 1929), p. 24.
18. Quoted in Jill Evans, *Beloved and Chosen: Women of Faith* (Canterbury Press, 1993), p. 203.
19. Luther on Marriage (1522), quoted in MacHaffie (ed.) *Readings in Herstory*, p. 71.

20. Ingrid Trobisch, 'Family Life', in Mbugwa (ed.), *Our Time Has Come*, p. 41.
21. Polycarp, *Letter to the Philippians*, 4.
22. Quoted in Tucker and Liefeld, *Daughters of the Church*, p. 247.
23. Quoted in Rebecca Lamar Harmon, *Susanna, Mother of the Wesleys* (Hodder and Stoughton, 1968), p. 57.
24. Quoted in Chilcote, *She Offered Them Christ*, p. 19.
25. Quoted in Tucker and Liefeld, *Daughters of the Church*, pp. 237–8.
26. ibid., p. 267.
27. Quoted in Adeney, 'Women of Fire', *Crux*, Vol. XIX, no. 3, p. 30.

Chapter 6   Women and gender difference

1. Kathy Keay, 'Independent Women', *Third Way* (March 1991), p. 25.
2. Anne Atkins, *Split Image: Male and Female after God's Likeness* (Hodder and Stoughton, 1987), p. 13.
3. A. J. Kostenberger, T. R. Schreiner and H. Scott Baldwin (eds), *Women in the Church: A Fresh Analysis of 1 Timothy 2: 9–15* (Baker Book House, 1995).
4. Gilbert Bilezikian, *Beyond Sex Roles: What the Bible Says About a Woman's Place in Church and Family* (Baker Book House, 1985), p. 208.
5. Quoted in Ann Loades, *Searching for Lost Coins: Explorations in Christianity and Feminism* (SPCK, 1987), p. 68.
6. Quoted in Evans, *Beloved and Chosen*, p. 128.
7. ibid., p. 149.
8. Susan Alice Watkins, Marisa Rueda and Marta Rodriguez, *Feminism for Beginners* (Icon Books, 1992), p. 17.
9. Quoted in Byrne, *The Hidden Tradition*, p. 139.
10. ibid., p. 24.
11. Watkins, Rueda and Rodriguez, p. 61.
12. John Piper, 'A Vision of Biblical Complementarity: Manhood and Womanhood Defined According to the Bible', in John Piper and Wayne Grudem (eds), *Recovering Biblical Man-*

hood and Womanhood: A Response to Evangelical Feminism
(Crossway Books, 1991), pp. 35, 36.

13. Raymond Ortlund, 'Male-Female Equality and Male Head-ship', in ibid., p. 98.

14. ibid., p. 101.

15. ibid., p. 107.

16. See Richard Hess, 'The Role of the Woman and the Man in Genesis 3', *Themelios*, Vol. 18, no. 3 (April 1993), pp. 15–19. Hess notes that God never names the *man*, and that it is logical and necessary that the man names the woman. He concludes that the passage gives no explicit justification for male domination.

17. For example, Psalm 121:1–2 and discussion in Carol Myers, *Discovering Eve: Ancient Israelite Women in Context* (Oxford University Press, 1988), p. 85; also Exod. 18:4, Deut. 33:26, Ps. 33:20).

18. See R. K. McGregor Knight, 'A Response to the Danvers Statement' (unpublished paper, 1989, for a conference of Christians for Biblical Equality), which refutes all the claims concerning so-called biblical manhood and woman-hood.

19. Ortlund (in *Recovering Biblical Manhood and Womanhood*, p. 106) argues that male headship is built into the pre-fall order of creation. But this is disputed by many, who see in Genesis 3:16b an indication that male domination is part of the result of the fall – which is ultimately reversed in Christ. Richard Hess takes this view (pp. 17–18). Adam's sin was that he acted on what his wife said, when he should have known better, since God had spoken directly to him on the matter.

20. C. Powell, 'A Stalemate of Genders? Some Hermeneutical Reflections', *Themelios*, Vol. 17, no. 3 (April/May 1992), p. 15, notes that 'if on creational grounds a woman's role is to be around the man and have children, presumably all men are to be gardeners!' Powell notes that much biblical inter-pretation of Genesis 2 and 3 has been influenced by early theologians who thought that woman was essentially inferior to man or, as Aquinas thought, a misbegotten male.

21. James Borland, 'Women in the Life and Teachings of Jesus',

in Piper and Grudem (eds), *Recovering Biblical Manhood and Womanhood*, p. 113.

22. ibid., p. 122.

23. Sheila Stephen, 'Women are Different!', in Edwards (ed.), *Men, Women and Authority*, p. 210.

24. Gregg Johnson, 'The Biological Basis for Gender-Specific Behavior', in Piper and Grudem (eds), *Recovering Biblical Manhood and Womanhood*, p. 282.

25. ibid., p. 293.

26. Mary Stewart van Leeuwen, *Gender and Grace: Women and Men in a Changing World* (IVP, 1990), p. 63.

27. Lynda Birke, *Nature and Culture: Biology and the Development of Sex Differences* (Open University Press, 1983), pp. 38–40.

28. ibid., p. 63.

29. van Leeuwen, *Gender and Grace*, p. 67.

30. Anne Moir and David Jessel, *Brainsex: The Real Difference Between Men and Women* (Mandarin, 1991), p. 8.

31. ibid., p. 77.

32. Elizabeth Morelli, 'The Question of Woman's Experience of God', in Alvin Kimel (ed.), *Speaking the Christian God: The Holy Trinity and the Challenge of Feminism* (Gracewing, 1992), pp. 222–36.

33. ibid, p. 236.

34. ibid., p.236; Mary Evans points out the same warning in her book *Woman in the Bible* (Paternoster Press, 1983), p. 105: 'The more the distinction between the sexes is stressed, the greater the tendency to assume that men relate to God in a different way from women.'

35. See van Leeuwen, *Gender and Grace*, ch 7, for details.

36. Piper, 'A Vision of Biblical Complementarity', in Piper and Grudem (eds), *Recovering Biblical Manhood and Womanhood*, p. 46.

37. Anne Borrowdale, *A Woman's Work: Changing Christian Attitudes* (SPCK, 1989), pp. 13, 15, 22.

38. Deborah Tannen, *You Just Don't Understand: Women and Men in Conversation* (Virago Press, 1992).

39. Myers, 'Recognizing the Connection', *Priscilla Papers*, Vol. 9, no. 3 (Summer 1995), p. 8.

40. Carol Gilligan, *In a Different Voice: Psychological Theory and Women's Development* (Harvard University Press, 1982).

41. Elaine Storkey, 'So What's the Difference?', *Third Way* (December 1985), p. 27.

42. Moir and Jessel, *Brainsex*, p. 165.

43. Storkey, 'So What's the Difference?', p. 27.

Chapter 7   Women and church planting

1. Mildred Cable and Francesca French, *Something Happened* (Hodder and Stoughton, 1934), p. 153.

2. Jim Montgomery, *DAWN 2000: 7 Million Churches To Go*, (Highland Books, 1990), p. 53.

3. Martin Robinson and Stuart Christine, *Planting Tomorrow's Churches Today*, (Monarch, 1992), p. 212.

4. Bob Hopkins, personal correspondence, July 1996.

5. Martin Robinson, 'New Churches for a New Challenge', *Church Growth Digest*, Vol. 15, no. 4 (Summer 1994), p. 13.

6. However, it has been suggested that some of the success stories of church planting obscure the fact that most of the new worshippers are not converts, but come by transfer. See Geoffrey Walker, 'A Critical Examination of the Church Growth Movement with Particular Reference to the Anglican Parish of Chester-Le-Street, Co. Durham' (MA dissertation, 1993, published by Christian Research). Walker questions the claim that church planting is necessarily a more effective means of church growth than growing existing churches (p. 28).

7. John Drane, *Paul* (Lion, 1976), p. 60.

8. C. L. Chaney, *Church Planting at the End of the Twentieth Century* (Tyndale House, 1991), p. 40.

9. Lamar Wadsworth, 'Who was the "chosen lady" of II John?' *Priscilla Papers*, Vol. 10, no. 3 (Summer 1996), pp. 1–5, gives seven reasons for taking this position rather than the metaphorical view.

10. Quoted in Mary Grey, 'She is a Great Man: Missiology from a Christian Feminist Perspective', *International Review of*

Missions, Vol. LXXXI, no. 322 (April 1992), p. 207.

11. ibid., p. 302.

12. ibid., p. 303.

13. Ruth Tucker, *Guardians of the Great Commission* (Zondervan, 1988), p. 42.

14. Cable and French, *Something Happened*, p. 244.

15. Robinson and Christine, *Planting Tomorrow's Churches Today*, p. 41.

16. Quoted in Tucker and Liefeld, *Daughters of the Church*, p. 309.

17. D. Hawker, *Kanchi Doctor* (Scripture Union, 1984), p. 13.

18. David Littlewood, 'Dancing in the aisles with Hockley's dynamic duo!' *Joy*, (March 1996), p. 36.

19. Tucker, *Women in the Maze*, p. 9.

20. See, for example, the chapter by Ann Wooderson, 'Pioneering on a Council Estate', in B. Hopkins (ed.), *Planting New Churches* (Eagle, 1991), and a tape by Patricia Wick from the Anglican Church Planting Conference.

21. F. B. Hoyt, ' "When a Field was Found too Difficult for a Man, a Woman Should be Sent": Adele M. Fielde in Asia 1865–1890', *The Historian*, 44 (May 1982), pp. 314–34.

22. Monica Hill, 'Some Practical Experiences in Different Areas', in Monica Hill (ed.), *How to Plant Churches* (MARC Europe, 1984), p. 69.

23. Peter Nodding, *Local Church Planting*, (Marshalls, 1994), p. 34.

24. Council Debate: 'Church Planting Concerns and Challenges', *Church Growth Digest*, Year 15, Issue 2 (Winter 1993/94), p. 11. Other 'snippets' from a discussion on the role of women in church planting included: 'Where men are leading, you build a *network* church; where women are leading, you build a *neighbourhood* church. Many women bring friends to church; then the women bring men.'

25. Nancy Reed, 'Women's Bible Studies: Key to Church Growth', *Evangelical Missions Quarterly*, Vol. 31, no. 1 (Jan. 1995), pp. 72–6.

26. Robinson, 'New Churches For a New Challenge', p. 13.

27. Ann Wooderson, 'Pioneering on a Council Estate', in Hopkins (ed.), *Planting New Churches*, pp. 37–48.

28. Charlie Cleverly, *Church Planting: Our Future Hope* (Scripture Union, 1991), p. 75.

Chapter 8   Women as thinkers and decision makers

1. Conference of Missionary Societies' 'Report on the conditions of women's work', quoted in Minna Gollock, 'The Share of Women in the Administration of Mission' *International Review of Mission*, Vol. 1, no. 4 (Oct. 1912), p. 681.
2. John Finney, *Finding Faith Today*, pp. 23–4.
3. Anne Graham Lotz, 'A Sister Speaks', *Christianity Today* Forum on 'Ministering Women', CT, 8 April 1996, p. 17.
4. J. H. Oldham, *Florence Allshorn and the Story of St. Julian's* (SCM, 1951), p. 60.
5. Elaine Storkey, *What's Right With Feminism* (SPCK, 1985).
6. Also see the report, *A Fearful Symmetry: The Complementariness of Men and Women in Ministry* (SPCK, 1992).
7. Aruna Gnanadason, 'Women in the Ecumenical Movement', *International Review of Mission*, Vol. XXXI, no. 322 (April 1992), p. 238.
8. A. Nichols (ed.), *The Whole Gospel for the Whole World* (Lausanne Committee, 1989), p. 67.
9. Minna Gollock, 'The Share of Women in the Administration of Missions', *International Review of Missions*, Vol. 1, no. 4 (October 1912), p. 677.
10. ibid., p. 687.
11. Byrne, *The Hidden Journey*, p. 138.
12. Quoted in Tucker, 'Female Missionary Strategists', p. 79.
13. Quoted in Tucker and Liefeld, *Daughters of the Church*, p. 312.
14. MacHaffie (ed.) *Readings in Herstory*, p. 137.
15. Quoted in Tucker and Liefeld, *Daughters of the Church*, p. 136.
16. Quoted in Malcolm, *Women at the Crossroads*, p. 115.
17. Jeremy and Margaret Collingwood, *Hannah More*, (Lion, 1990), p. 80.
18. ibid., p. 93.
19. Albert Vail, *Mary Webb and the Mother Society* (American

Baptist Publication Society, 1914), p. ii.

20. Byrne, *The Hidden Journey*, p. 68.

21. See Donald Lewis, *Lighten Their Darkness: The Evangelical Mission to Working-Class London, 1828–1860* (Greenwood Press, 1986), p. 40 ff.

22. See Donald Lewis, 'Lights in Dark Places: Women Evangelists in Early Victorian Britain, 1838–1857', in W. J. Sheils and D. Wood (eds), *Studies in Church History*, 27 (1990) pp. 415–27.

23. ibid., p. 422.

24. F. K. Prochaska, *Women and Philanthropy in 19th Century England* (Clarendon Press, 1980), p. 127.

25. John Maust, 'Rosario Rivera: Reaching Lima's Children', *Missiology*, Vol. XV, no. 3 (July 1987), pp. 339–46.

26. See Richard Symonds, *Far Above Rubies: The Women Uncommemorated by the Church of England* (Gracewing, 1993), ch. 2.

27. Quoted in Tucker, 'Female Missionary Strategists', p. 85.

28. Ruth Tucker, 'Women in the Missions Classroom', *Evangelical Missions Quarterly*, Vol. 22, no. 4 (Oct. 1986), pp. 458–61.

29. Rebecca Manley Pippert, *Out of the Saltshaker: Evangelism as a Way of Life* (IVP, 1980), p. 13.

30. Christine Dodd, *Called to Mission: A Workbook for the Decade of Evangelization* (Geoffrey Chapman, 1991), p. 1.

31. This book was described in a fairly recent but undated supplement to *Mid Africa Ministry* magazine.

32. See articles by Mercy Amba Oduyoye and Mary Grey, *International Review of Mission*, Vol. LXXXI, no. 322 (April 1992).

33. Alan J. Roxburgh, *Reaching a New Generation: Strategies for Tomorrow's Church* (IVP, 1993)

Chapter 9   Women: 'Go and tell'

1. George Bernard Shaw, *Back to Methusaleh*.

2. Atkins, *Split Image*, p. 52.

3. NRSV variant reading. This verse has been understood by

many to refer to women. The Hebrew word for 'those who bore the tidings' is feminine (and its Greek equivalent is the word to evangelise). Isaiah 40:9 has been understood similarly. It can be translated as, 'O woman that brings good tidings to Zion, get you up to a high mountain; O woman who brings good tidings to Jerusalem, lift up your voice with strength.' Here the herald (the one addressed) may be assumed to be female because of the feminine participles and imperatives in the Hebrew. Alec Motyer suggests the reference is to an unnamed female herald, modelled on Miriam (Exod. 15:20). Women were commonly regarded as the ones who did the most to spread abroad the message of victory. Alternatively, the cities are taken to be feminine ('O Zion . . . O Jerusalem . . .'), but in vv. 1-2 the message is *to* Jerusalem. Commentators are puzzled by this verse, and the Hebrew allows for either possibility.

4. Mimi Haddad, 'Women and Revival Work: Acts 2:17-21 – Revival's Magna Charta', *Priscilla Papers*, Vol. 8, no. 3, (Summer 1994), p. 10.

5. Marie Monsen, *The Awakening: Revival in China 1927–1937* (China Inland Mission, 1961), p. 35.

6. ibid., p. 68.

7. ibid., p. 111.

8. This question was asked around a hundred years ago by an Anglican laywoman, Constance Coleman, quoted in Byrne (ed.), *The Hidden Tradition*, p. 28.

9. Michele Guinness, *Made for Each Other: Reflections on the Opposite Sex* (Triangle, 1996), pp. 174–5.

10. Quoted in Tucker and Liefeld, *Daughters of the Church*, p. 14.

11. Bryant Myers, 'Recognizing the Connection: Women and Missions', *Priscilla Papers*, Vol. 9, no. 3 (Summer 1995), p. 9.

12. Kathy Keay, 'Women in Evangelism', *Christian Woman* (Aug. 1986), pp. 45–6.

13. Cited in Patricia Gundry, *Woman Be Free!* (Zondervan, 1977), p. 104.

14. Palmer, *The Promise of the Father*, p. 341.

Appendix   The 'difficult passages'

1. Bruce Barron, 'Putting Women in Their Place: 1 Timothy 2 and Evangelical Views of Women in Church Leadership', *Journal of the Evangelical Theological Society*, Vol. 33, no. 4 (Dec. 1990), p. 452.

2. ibid. p. 459.

3. Quoted in Tucker and Liefeld, *Daughters of the Church*, p. 106.

4. ibid, p. 107.

5. ibid., p. 125.

6. ibid., p. 231.

7. Chilcote, *She Offered Them Christ*, pp. 32, 80.

8. ibid., pp. 44, 59.

9. ibid., pp. 70, 86.

10. Katherine C. Bushnell, *God's Word to Women* (undated reprint of undated edition, but known to have been published privately in 1923), para. 208 (the book has no page numbers).

11. ibid., para. 326.

12. Tucker and Liefeld, *Daughters of the Church*, p. 405.

13. ibid., p. 405.

14. Craig Keener, *Paul, Women and Wives: Marriage and Women's Ministry in the Letters of Paul* (Hendrickson Publishers, 1992).

15. Edward Donnelly, 'Should Women Preach?' in Brian Edwards (ed.), *Men, Women and Authority* (Day One Publications, 1996).

16. ibid., p. 118.

17. See Keener, *Paul, Women and Wives*, p. 80, for a summary of Knight's view and Keener's refutation of it.

18. Kenneth Bailey, 'Women in the New Testament: A Middle Eastern Cultural View', *Anvil*, Vol. 11, no. 1 (1994), p. 17.

19. Donnelly, 'Should Women Preach?' p. 118: 'Nothing could be clearer. The words are simple, the grammar straightforward, the meaning obvious.'

20. R. T. France, *Women in the Church's Ministry: A Test-Case for Biblical Hermeneutics* (Paternoster Press, 1995), pp. 69–70.

21. Steve Motyer, 'An Eternal Problem: Women and Silence',

Church of England Newspaper (19 Feb. 1993).

22. Bailey, 'Women in the New Testament', p. 21; also see Keener, pp. 108–9.

23. ibid., p. 21.

24. For Edwards see full reference above; others are Piper and Grudem, and Harper (full references in notes to ch. 6); and A. J. Kostenberger, T. R. Schreiner and H. Scott Baldwin (eds), *Women in the Church: A Fresh Analysis of 1 Timothy 2:9–15* (Baker Book House, 1995). In addition to books mentioned elsewhere in the notes, those who take an opposite view include David Scholer, 'I Timothy 2:9–15 and the Place of Women in the Church's Ministry', in A. Mickelsen (ed.), *Women, Authority and the Bible* (IVP, 1986); Ben Witherington III, *Women in the Earliest Churches* (Cambridge University Press, 1988); Aida Besançon Spencer, *Beyond the Curse* (Hendrickson, 1985); Andrew Kirk, 'Theology from a Feminist Perspective', in Kathy Keay (ed.), *Men, Women and God* (Marshall Pickering, 1987).

25. Edwards (ed.), *Men, Women and Authority*, p. 118

26. ibid., p. 121.

27. ibid., p. 124.

28. A. J. Kostenberger, 'Gender Passages in the NT: Hermeneutical Fallacies Critiqued', *Westminster Theological Journal*, Vol. 56, no. 2 (Autumn 1994), p. 269.

29. Edwards (ed.), *Men, Women and Authority*, p. 129.

30. Ibid., p. 122; Kostenberger, 'Gender Passages', p. 269.

31. John Piper, 'A Vision of Biblical Complementarity: Manhood and Womanhood Defined According to the Bible', in Piper and Grudem (ed.), *Recovering Biblical Manhood and Womanhood*, p. 51 and quoted in Edwards (ed.), *Men, Women and Authority*, p. 219.

32. Edwards (ed.), p. 43.

33. ibid., p. 65.

34. Richard Clark Kroeger and Catherine Clark Kroeger, *I Suffer Not a Woman: Rethinking 1 Timothy 2:11–15 in Light of Ancient Evidence* (Baker Book House, 1992).

35. ibid., p. 103.

36. ibid., p. 113.

37. ibid., p. 176–7.

38. See Kostenberger, 'Gender passages'; and S. M. Baugh, 'The Apostle among the Amazons', *Westminster Theological Journal*, Vol. 56 (1994), pp. 153–171, a review article of the Kroegers' book.

39. John Stott, *The Message of 1 Timothy and Titus* (IVP, 1996), p. 74.

40. ibid., p. 78.